Religion in Fortress Europe

Also Available from Bloomsbury:

Islam and the Governing of Muslims in France, Frank Peter
Religious Diversity in Europe, Edited by Riho Altnurme, Elena Arigita, and
Patrick Pasture
Young Muslims and Christians in a Secular Europe, Daan Beekers

Religion in Fortress Europe

Perspectives on Belief, Citizenship, and Identity in a Time of Polarized Politics

Edited by
Morteza Hashemi and Christopher R. Cotter

BLOOMSBURY ACADEMIC
LONDON • NEW YORK • OXFORD • NEW DELHI • SYDNEY

BLOOMSBURY ACADEMIC
Bloomsbury Publishing Plc
50 Bedford Square, London, WC1B 3DP, UK
1385 Broadway, New York, NY 10018, USA
29 Earlsfort Terrace, Dublin 2, Ireland

BLOOMSBURY, BLOOMSBURY ACADEMIC and the Diana logo are trademarks of
Bloomsbury Publishing Plc

First published in Great Britain 2023
This paperback edition published 2024

Copyright © Morteza Hashemi, Christopher R. Cotter and contributors, 2023

Morteza Hashemi and Christopher R. Cotter have asserted their rights under the Copyright,
Designs and Patents Act, 1988, to be identified as Editors of this work.

For legal purposes the Acknowledgements on p. x constitute an extension of this
copyright page.

Cover image: Saint Peter's Square, Vatican City. Photo by Morteza Hashemi

A catalogue record for this book is available from the British Library.

Library of Congress Control Number: 2022942226

ISBN: HB: 978-1-3503-4110-4
PB: 978-1-3503-4114-2
ePDF: 978-1-3503-4111-1
eBook: 978-1-3503-4112-8

Typeset by Deanta Global Publishing Services, Chennai, India

To find out more about our authors and books visit www.bloomsbury.com and sign up for
our newsletters

Contents

Illustrations

Figures

Tables

Contributors

Tuomas Äystö is a postdoctoral researcher in the Study of Religion at the University of Helsinki. He is currently working on the LEGITREL project (2020–4), led by Titus Hjelm and funded by the Academy of Finland, which analyses Finnish religion and politics. His work has been published in journals such as *Numen, Temenos*, the *Journal of Religion in Europe* and *Culture and Religion*.

Daan Beekers works on religious diversity, religious commitment and heritage in the Netherlands. He obtained his PhD in anthropology from the Vrije Universiteit in Amsterdam. He is the author of *Young Muslims and Christians in a Secular Europe: Pursuing Religious Commitment in the Netherlands*. Currently, Daan is a researcher at the Netherlands Institute for Social Research.

Martin Bürgin studied history, study of religions and political science. He was a fellow at the Leo Baeck Institute in London, co-founded the GRC Peer Group for Religion and Politics at the University of Zürich and is now senior researcher at the Chair for Ecclesiastical History at the University of Bern.

Christopher R. Cotter is Staff Tutor (Lecturer) in Sociology and Religious Studies at the Open University, UK. He is co-founder of the Religious Studies Project, co-editor of *After World Religions: Reconstructing Religious Studies* (2016) and author of *The Critical Study of Non-Religion: Discourse, Identification and Locality* (2020).

Grace Davie is Professor Emeritus of Sociology at the University of Exeter, UK. She is the author of *Religion in Britain: A Persistent Paradox* (2015) and co-editor of *Religion and Welfare in Europe: Gendered and Minority Perspectives* (2017).

Morteza Hashemi is Assistant Professor of sociology at the University of Nottingham. Prior to that, he was a lecturer in sociology and politics at the University of Bristol and a Leverhulme Early Career Fellow at the University of Edinburgh. He is the author of *Theism and Atheism in a Post-Secular Age* (2017), and his main research interests are social theory, sociology of science and technology, medical sociology, sociology of religion, ethnicity, identity and migration.

John Holmwood is Emeritus Professor of Sociology at the University of Nottingham. He is the author (with Gurminder K. Bhambra) of *Colonialism and Modern Social Theory* (2021). He was expert witness for the defence in professional misconduct cases brought against teachers accused of Islamization of schools in the Birmingham Trojan Horse Affair. He is the author (with Therese O'Toole) of *Countering Extremism in British Schools? The Truth about The Birmingham Trojan Horse Affair* (Policy Press, 2018). He is co-chair (with Layla Aitlhadj) of the *People's Review of Prevent*, a civil society–based review of the UK government's counter-extremism strategy, Prevent, which delivered its report in February 2021.

Martina Loth is currently Research Assistant at the University of Innsbruck's Institute for Psychosocial Intervention and Communication Research. Prior to that, she was a doctoral candidate in the Center for Religion and Modernity (CRM) at the University of Münster in Münster, Germany. Her doctoral thesis compares religious identity developments of Alevi and Sunni youth in the Ruhr area in Germany.

Nasar Meer is Professor of Sociology in the School of Social and Political Sciences and Director of RACE.ED at the University of Edinburgh. He was a commissioner on the Royal Society of Edinburgh's (2020–1) Post-Covid-19 Futures Inquiry and a member of the Scottish Government's Covid-19 and Ethnicity Expert Reference Group and the British Council's Outreach Programme. Furthermore, Meer is currently co-editor-in-chief of *Identities: Global Studies in Culture and Power* and co-editor of *21st Century Standpoints* (BSA and Policy Press) and the Palgrave Politics of Identity and Citizenship Series (PPICS).

Hazel O'Brien is a sociologist of religion and a lecturer at South East Technological University, Ireland. She is interested in the relationship between religious, ethnic and national identities. Her research with Mormons in Ireland identifies how tradition operates in both maintaining and disrupting understandings of religious, ethnic and national identities in times of rapid change. She is also the co-editor of *The Study of Religions in Ireland: Past, Present, and Future* with Brendan McNamara.

Mike Slaven is Senior Lecturer in International Politics at the University of Lincoln and author of *Securing Borders, Securing Power: The Rise and Decline of Arizona's Border Politics* (2022).

Acknowledgements

We would like to extend our gratitude to Leverhulme Trust, which funded our Early Career Fellowships at the University of Edinburgh between 2017 and 2020. Our fellowships provided the context for our meeting, as well as the intellectual (and financial) foundation for this volume. In the same vein, we would like to thank our mentors Professor Janet Carsten at the Department of Social Anthropology and Dr Steven Sutcliffe at the School of Divinity. We thank everyone at Bloomsbury and all our contributors, especially Grace Davie for her generous support and thoughtful Afterword. We would like to thank Tariq Modood, Gurminder K. Bhambra, Thomas Osborne, Emilija Zabiliute, Naomi Appleton, Magda Mogilnicka, Stephen Norrie, Jacob Copeman, Kaveri Qureshi, Ayaz Qureshi, Stephen Kemp, Rebecca Marsland, Lotte Buch Segal, Ann-Christin Zuntz, Philipp Hetmancyzk and Sariya Cheruvallil-Contractor. We would also like to thank everyone who has helped us make it through the Covid-19 pandemic thus far – your friendship has meant the world. Finally, Chris would like to thank Sarah-Lou, Ruaridh and Saoirse for the happy home they have provided and for coping admirably with him working from home since March 2020. Morteza also would like to thank his parents and siblings for their love, kindness and support.

Part I

Introduction

Introduction

Religion in Fortress Europe

Morteza Hashemi and Christopher R. Cotter

Europe at the beginning of the 2020s is rather different from the one emerging from the ashes of the two world wars. Reactionary politics, Brexit, populism, military tension with Russia, anti-migration and anti-multiculturalist rhetoric abound – each with their opponents – and combine to produce an image of Fortress Europe, as borders harden in opposition to the 'others' perceived in 'our' midst. Religion-related histories are frequently drawn upon in these debates, from all sides, with Christianity frequently being constructed as inextricably linked to European identities, and Islam as the radical and problematic outsider. This book presents a timely and critical exploration of the entanglement of discourses on (anti-)multiculturalism, (anti-)migration and national identity with discourses of religion and religious rituals. What is the role of religion or its rejection in maintaining or challenging discourses on national identity and citizenship? What are the roles that religion plays on all sides – from Islamophobia of the radical right to the Christian alliances on both sides of the Atlantic, to the Islamic beliefs and practices of European citizens as well as migrant communities? Are there any alliances shaping between belief and unbelief on either side of the battle for the future of Europe? These questions and more motivate the chapters in this timely interdisciplinary collection, with contributions focusing on diverse contexts throughout Europe involving a broad range of religious identifications and actors.

From the point of view of the social sciences, there is a tendency to ignore the plurality of experiences of European religious communities. This might have something to do with our tendency to ignore the fact that religious communities are not homogeneous groups of like-minded people. It might be because Western Europe has been exceptionally (Davie 2002) and consistently considered to be a secularized part of the world (Berger 1999), with many of the social sciences' earliest pioneers occupying positions of secularity and/or scepticism (Bullivant and Lee 2012). In this context, while European intellectuals and scholars have the privilege of a discursive hegemony in social sciences, the much-criticized classical secularization thesis is still operating in the background of mainstream European academia. In other words, although we do not see modernism and decline of religion as correlated trends, still we tend to underestimate the role of religion in public life, with even the academic study of religion itself being dubbed a 'secularist' enterprise by some (Fitzgerald 2000; Ambasciano 2018; cf. Cotter 2020, 25). There has been a systematic blindness to the plurality of religious experiences of communities and their different ways of organizing their social life in Europe. The editors of this volume believe that one of the missing pieces is a collection of case studies about the everyday experiences of religious communities in Europe. This volume tries to play such a role. It consists of chapters on the experiences, attitudes, fears, challenges, hopes, contributions, encounters and, generally, social life of religious communities in Europe and the official policies that directly affect their lives. It aims to show such multiplicity, the agency of religious communities and the vibrancy of their life-experiences.

It is evident that when we are focusing on religion in Europe, the role of Islam and European Muslims plays a major part. Since the beginning of the 2000s until an unforeseen future, Islam in Europe and even what has been dubbed 'European Islam' will play a central role in the academic study of religion (Van den Bos 2012; Nielsen 2002). The number of refugees from Muslim countries was on the rise, and, unlike the Ukrainian refugees at the time of writing, their identity and religion have been at the centre of public discussions in Europe. This justifies the higher number of chapters in this volume that focus on Islam in Europe. Both Islam in Europe and 'European Islam' are themes that are related to migration and movement. They refer to the experiences of migration of Muslims from the subcontinent, the Middle East and North Africa since the end of the colonial era and particularly the end of the Second World War. Such relocation and subsequent demographic transformations are the historical contexts of the constitution of multicultural and multifaith Europe.

The idea of Fortress Europe as a reaction to those events is another aspect of the background of this discussion. Fortress Europe, as Mike Slaven shrewdly observes, is neither a recent phenomenon nor has any clear borders (see his chapter in this volume). It is an imagined geography of identity that needs to be fortified. Yet it is not obvious how and why. That being said:

At no time in history have so many people attempted to cross international borders without authorization, and at no time have so many governments gone to such lengths to try to stop them. All this raises crucial questions about human rights and global inequality, about security, migration and the obligations of governments to refugees and non-citizens in a century that is likely to be dominated by new global mobility. To some extent, therefore, the confrontation between Europe and its unwanted intruders is specific to Europe; but it is also a reflection of a much wider phenomenon. (Carr 2012, 7)

The policies that have shaped the concept of Europe are eternally fluid and mostly reactions to an imagined threat. This volume also sheds light on the interactions of religion and religious communities with such political phenomena as appear in policies of governments and specific controversies.

The second chapter of this volume sets the scene for the rest of the contributions by reviewing the development of the concept of 'Fortress Europe' since the 1990s. Following a chronological review of the history of the concept, Mike Slaven puts forward a typology of the perspectives on Fortress Europe: the conservative, the liberal and the academically critical or politically radical. The main body of this book appears in the form of seven case studies from across Europe. The first two of these studies by John Holmwood and Morteza Hashemi are focused on the UK. Accordingly, in the third chapter, Holmwood examines three cases associated with schooling in the city of Birmingham. Those three cases are the 'Trojan Horse Affair' of an alleged plot to Islamicize British schools and the subsequent moral panic in 2014, the case of gender segregation at Al-Hijrah school in 2017 and finally the parents' protest about LGBT+ teaching at Parkfield and Anderton Park schools in 2019. All these cases are representative of a similar theme that Holmwood recognizes: the emerging role of the Equality Act 2010 as part of what he calls 'muscular liberalism' against minorities. Chapter 4, by Morteza Hashemi, focuses on Scottish Shia Muslim health activists and their contribution in the Scottish National Blood Transfusion Service (SNBTS). These activists have organized the Imam Hussain Blood Donation Campaign, which is named after a religious figure and theologically supported by making allegories between the sacrifices of that figure and modern blood donation. Hashemi argues that these Shia activists are reclaiming their own problematized bodily identity through health activism and blood donation to fellow European citizens.

The next five chapters in Part III are case studies from across the continent. Chapter 5, by Martina Loth, is dedicated to the identity struggles of young Alevis in Germany. Alevis constitute a minority among the majority Sunni migrants from Turkey. Loth reviews some quantitative data about this persecuted minority in the host country and their sense of belonging and religiosity. The chapter also explores cases of redefinition of Alevism through an in-depth examination of four individual cases. Daan Beekers, in Chapter 6, explains what he calls an 'identitarian Christianity' and its antagonism with other confessional religions (including Islam and even other branches of Christianity) in the Netherlands. In particular, Beekers focuses on two current debates surrounding populist politics and the repurposing of church buildings. In both debates, one finds the mobilization and embrace of Christian heritage. In Chapter 7, Martin Bürgin investigates media controversies in Switzerland about the case of Muslim students who refused to shake hands with their female teacher. The reaction of some of the politicians to this controversy is at the centre of Bürgin's chapter when he recognizes that these political figures revived, restored and reinterpreted historical images of nineteenth-century culture wars to put forward legal reforms.

Chapter 8 is written by Hazel O'Brien, and she observes a revival of anti-minority rhetoric in Ireland in recent years. The emergence of a pseudo-right-wing political rhetoric is perplexing as Ireland never developed a strong far-right populist party in the way that one can see in other European countries. O'Brien outlines these new developments in Irish domestic politics and questions the incorporation of religious and ethnic diversity into the dominant Irish identity in the age of the rise of Fortress Europe. Chapter 9 by Tuomas Äystö explores a discourse behind the anti-Muslim and anti-migration political rhetoric of two Finnish political parties. This surrounds the revival of a historical image of Finland as a nation of Christians which serves as a nationalist narrative to oppose pluralist positions in culture, religion, family, gender and sexuality.

After these case studies, the final part (Part IV) of the book on comparative perspectives presents two theoretical insights from Nasar Meer and Grace Davie. Chapter 10 is a reconstructed and updated version of an article by Meer. In this timely chapter, Meer puts forward the concept of 'Muslim consciousness' and the common misrecognition of its features. The Muslim identities in Europe, this chapter argues, are routinely imagined and re-imagined in ways that cannot be reduced to a binary category. Instead, along with the main theme of this book, Meer suggests that we should focus on the specifics of the contexts in which they are experiencing adversities. Finally, in the Afterword, Grace Davie shares her thoughts on the themes that connect the chapters of this volume.

As is only natural with volumes of this nature, there are omissions in the contents that follow, with fewer nations receiving specific attention in the form of case studies than not. However, we hope that the range of case studies presented – from Germany, Ireland, Finland, Switzerland, the Netherlands and the UK – combined with the more sweeping chapters at the open and close of the volume, is both suitably broad-ranging *and* usefully specific. Christianity and Islam, as the historically dominant and currently most contested traditions, respectively, are given a lot more airtime than other traditions for, we think, understandable reasons. However, someone browsing the contents list might also find themselves asking where the religiously 'unaffiliated' are.

A recent Pew Research Center report (2015) positioned the religiously 'unaffiliated' as the world's third-largest 'Major Religious Group', at 16.4 per cent of the global population (with Christians the largest at 31.4 per cent and Muslims the second largest at 23.2 per cent), and across (Western) Europe, statistics tell an even more 'unaffiliated' story. Rates of 'atheism' in the Netherlands, Denmark, Sweden and Norway are somewhere between 27 per cent and 35 per cent (Lee 2013, 590). Forty per cent of French, 29 per cent of Estonians and 27 per cent of Germans claim to believe neither in a god nor any sort of 'spirit' nor 'life force' (Zuckerman, Galen and Pasquale 2016, 5). And data from recent British Social Attitudes and European Social Surveys show that the proportion of those in Great Britain self-describing as having 'no religion' rose from 31 per cent in 1983 to 49 per cent in 2015 (Bullivant 2017, 8). In the face of these statistics, our concern in this volume was to engage primarily with those constituencies that (still) associate with 'traditionally' religious categories and institutions, rather than with the large subsections of European populations who do not, and who arguably share little in common as a coherent group beyond specific acts of (non-)identification (Hashemi 2016; Cotter 2020). However, the norms of the European context/s within which these associations and identifications are enacted daily, and where religion and non-religion are lived, performed and contested, are a persistent theme in the chapters that follow. It is our hope that this volume will complicate the religion/secular dichotomy by shedding some much-needed light on the machinations of religion-related groups within the continent and exposing some of the contours of the not-so-secular hegemony against which they are forced by the vicissitudes of history to act.

Part II

Setting the scene

Fortress Europe

Developments of a concept since the 1990s

Mike Slaven

Introduction

Europe, on the globe, appears as a protuberance upon Asia, and one would have to forgive any schoolchild for not knowing precisely where it begins or ends. Even the task of identifying Europe's largest city and country is not straightforward. The former would be a historic capital of Christendom which is today majority-Muslim, except that a third of its people live across a strait which at its widest roughly equates to the Oresund at its narrowest. Europe's largest country, which both in population and area dwarfs the others by any count, finds itself mostly in North Asia. If we turn from geographical to political-economic Europe, we find that the Eurozone encompasses territory on mainland Africa and South America and an island country wholly in Asia. One can cross on foot between the Kingdom of the Netherlands and the French Republic – an impossibility on European soil itself – by travelling to an island in the Caribbean Sea named for Saint Martin of Tours, 3,500 miles from Galician Finisterre.

What does it mean to fortify such a thing? The purpose of this chapter is to examine how scholarship has tracked social developments since about 1990 to leave us with certain analytical vantage points for understanding what it means to make a 'fortress' of Europe in the early twenty-first century. Any fortification task is complicated and conditioned by the muddled, polysemous character of the Europe whose nations or peoples are to be secured – a lack of clarity which is, of course, portrayed in the current European scene with varying inflections of angst. Europe is at once discrete enough to produce boundless discussion yet inextricably interwoven, by its colonial projects and capitalist expansions, with all other parts of the world against which it may seek to fortify itself. The vagueness of the meaning or core of Europe threatens to create an object for securing with no clear boundaries – a situation which raises further alarm that this reaction itself may threaten 'European values'. The concept of fortifying Europe is at once rooted in territory, while also increasingly unmoored from geographical frontiers, reaching inside European societies. Contestation rages about the purported essence of these societies and how their orders are to be secured, where racial hierarchies increasingly are formally foresworn but effectively justified in terms of religious and cultural difference (Barker 1981; Semati 2010).

In this European scene, a false nostalgia for a world of firmer boundaries is increasingly mobilized in politics (Kinnvall 2018). As it has grown more tangible in recent decades to discuss a political Europe, we can see new forms of European unity reflecting a particular stage of European self-identity rooted in the experience not just of war (as universally recognized) but also of colonialism and empire (Kinnvall 2016). If European integration represents a Kantian project (Kant 1795), then it reflects the Kantian problem of the Other, who, understood by Europeans not to be an agent in the progress of (Europeanized) mankind, therefore must be sentenced to literal or ontological death (Behnke 2008; Gani 2017). We hear much today of migration as one of the 'crises' threatening the European Union (EU) – a continuation of ongoing fretting that Europe's encounters with people who have origins in the Global South will imperil European unity and thus, in some way, the progress or promise of Europe itself (Bhambra 2017, 2016; Wodak and Boukala 2015).

We have seen in response the emergence of many new political and social practices for fortifying Europe. How has scholarship tracked, interpreted and evaluated these developments? Fortress Europe is interpreted at the intersection of larger social developments in European integration, European security and European immigration policy. This chapter then outlines how these developments have been analysed through the scholarly concepts of (EUropeanized) immigration policy failure, securitization and bordering. It concludes by synthesizing three normative accounts of Fortress Europe: the conservative, liberal and radical views.

Fortress Europe in the post-Cold War zeitgeist

We begin, as analyses of these topics often do, with the end of the Cold War. This event occasioned shifts in three major conceptual strands that are interwoven in readings of 'Fortress Europe': European integration, European security and European immigration policy.

European integration

Already in the mid-1980s, a 'new spirit inspiring the construction of the European Community' (EC) began to emerge among its Western European members, and as part of this, the development of common policies towards workers from outside the EC countries seemed distinctly on the agenda (Callovi 1992, 357). The Single European Act in 1986 promised the completion of the EC's internal market by 1992, reducing barriers to the movement of goods and services. The free movement of people (i.e. workers) had seemed a key corollary, at the least, to this market's functioning since the Treaty of Rome in 1957. In 1985, impasse among the EC membership about the abolition of permanent border checkpoints resulted in the Schengen Agreement among France, West Germany and the Benelux Countries, to be implemented over the coming decade.

In this context where Western European countries were already planning to accelerate (economic) integration, the sudden end of the Cold War expanded the horizons. The completion of the single market began to seem a relatively unambitious goal in a global scene where economic competition was increasingly predicted to overtake traditional security competition (discussed subsequently); the grander goal of Economic and Monetary Union (EMU) was visibly on the table as the 1990s dawned (Bergsten 1990, 97). Scholarly use of the term 'Fortress Europe' was at this time dominated by this vision of emergent competition among transnational trading blocs and was discussed in terms of goods and services more so than people (Ebenroth 1990; Sperling 1992). Here, Fortress Europe was protectionist in the classic economic sense, a dark lining to the liberalizing promise of integration within Europe itself.

Amid the liberal zeitgeist of this time, an image of the Fortress Europe concept emerged as 'a construction without inner walls, yet with solid fences against the outer world' (Brochmann 1991, 185; see also Agnelli 1988). As noted, the development of this open area of internal free trade was always considered to have implications for the movement of people. Scholarship, therefore, was by no means ignoring what this account of 'Fortress Europe' implied for migration (B. Hansen 1993). In the functionalist liberal view, European integration would logically yield a need for 'common policy' towards those from outside the EU, since 'the open internal frontiers in the Common Market may imply that anyone entering a member country from outside the Community will have free access to all the other member states' (Brochmann 1991, 185), posing an array of potential social and political problems.

The Maastricht Treaty that emerged in 1992 put a more ambitious post-Cold War inflection on the longer European integration project (Ludlow 2013) – advancing the EMU as an answer to post-Cold War globalization (Jabko 1999, 476) and naming the European Union itself. Stepping beyond 'businessman's Europe', it introduced a notion of EU citizenship – but one which entrenched an image of exclusion within European societies themselves, as it distinguished a European citizenry (however vague) from millions of permanent residents excluded from national citizenship, for instance, Germany's ethnic Turks (Welsh 1993). The expansion of European integration from a purely economic focus to enhanced political and social meanings was therefore already introducing to the 'Fortress Europe' notion complexities which are pronounced today: a metaphor of dominating external walls seemed to encompass and accentuate internal division.

European security

The European security scene of the Cold War needs little rehearsing. What is important to note, however, is the extent to which European security had, for most of the twentieth century, been preoccupied in some way by divisions within Europe and among Europeans, rather than threats bearing upon Europe from 'outside'. During the First World War, the blood-drenching European soil was more explicitly interpreted as a crisis of white civilization that left global white supremacy exposed (Du Bois 1917). In the Second World War and afterwards, the ascendancy of realist international relations (IR) centred the imperative of a supposedly universalized ideal of statesmanlike reason (Freyberg-Inan 2004, 34); while cautioning against assumptions of any state's moral superiority, this view effectively naturalized existing global distributions of power. The entrenched Eurocentrism of major IR perspectives of and during the Cold War is revealed in the era's label itself: war raged hot in decolonizing battles waged by European states abroad in places like Algeria and Mozambique, in proxy superpower wars in places including Indochina and Angola, and in conflicts where Washington and Moscow were not in fact the key players (Berger 2008). However, conflict was mostly cold in a Europe divided by conflicting superpower spheres of influence. There was not war but threat: Europe could be once again turned in battle against itself, mushroom clouds foaming over its cities or tanks flattening the grasslands of the North German Plain.

The end of the Cold War eased Western Europe's intense security dependency on the United States and seemed to raise economic relationships to the forefront, further recentring Europe in Western European politics. The idea that security issues would 'decline sharply' and economic issues would ascend (Bergsten 1990, 96) became Orthodoxy. The absence of security concern would mean a reorientation of international competition towards the economic and a realignment of Europe away from the United States and towards its own integrated trading bloc that would compete in economic terms as rivals with those who had been, in security terms, allies or enemies. IR scholars predicting security's return largely envisioned realist state-security competition (Goldgeier and McFaul 1992; Waltz 1993). Yet the dominant (neo)realist perspective (and, less so, its main neoliberal rival) had lost considerable credibility, lacking any explanation for how ideas-driven shifts in the domestic politics of Eastern European states could have ended global bipolarity (Kratochwil 1993).

By the time the twentieth-century preoccupation with the possibility of war among divided European nations had eased, Europe had lost its global pre-eminence. Clearly, Cold War geopolitical dynamics had, up to this point, held in place certain views of what security encompassed or entailed. Later it would become clear that this view mistook the largely traditional state-security concerns of the Cold War period in Europe for exhausting what 'security' could mean in political discourse. As state-security concern declined in the Global North, analysts would increasingly notice security meanings infiltrating other areas of social life. The lifting of superpower dependence was met by the erasure of East-West schisms, most immediately in Germany, which quickly encountered new challenges from the East, including increased migration (Bulmer and Paterson 1996, 17). In this new configuration, what threatened Europe? Security analysts were beginning to worry that European national identities would be reasserted against integration and therefore peace, and took note that the menace of resurgent nationalism was intertwined with anti-immigration politics and the contestation of identity within Europe as 'societal security' (Wæver et al. 1993). The peace and unity of Europe, then, were still at stake, but in a different way.

European immigration policy

The fall of the Iron Curtain meant in one sense a dissolution of literal intra-European barriers. But at the time the Cold War was ending, the migration and citizenship policies of Western European countries were already in the process of becoming newly salient politically. Stresses experienced by control systems due to these movements from the East were becoming intertwined with movements from the South, into one larger perceived control problem. In countries like Germany, despite very large volumes of people coming from the East, challenges from the South were immediately identified as presenting much greater longer-term issues (Faist 1994a).

The racist character of European immigration policy in the post-Second World War period had been clearly identified at the time, especially in some countries like the UK and France which experienced substantial immigration from countries they had colonized (R. Hansen 2000; Solomos 1993, 63–5). The literature on European migration control entering the 1990s nonetheless was quite ambivalent about highlighting this: the 'closure' of Western European migration post-1973 was often interpreted as a restriction of labour migration following from the end of the post-Second World War 'economic miracle', though subtextually, this had seemed to be 'primary crafted in reaction to noneconomic factors' (B. Hansen 1993, 231). Indeed, these moves sought to restrict the immigration of already-settled immigrants' family members, who had been deemed 'unwanted' (Joppke 1998), as Western European political leaders declared the experience of immigration (especially by non-Europeans) post-Second World War as a unique event, not to be repeated (Ellermann 2015). While in some regards this 'closure' had not really occurred (Geddes 2001, 35) – substantial family immigration still occurred during this period – this was nonetheless perceived as a stable paradigm.

From the late 1980s, some Western European countries' immigration control systems were under growing stress from increased asylum claims from the Global South. Thus, by the time the Cold War ended – introducing new possibilities and challenges to the East, and broaching what further integration would mean for movements of people – an 'onset of mass asylum seeking' (Guiraudon and Joppke 2001, 2) had already emerged for many Western European countries, part of a 'new migration world' that challenged their control. South–North dynamics that were previously considered to have been slowed to politically sufficient levels during the 1970s re-intensified. Worries about control capacity in the new post-Cold War context were soon exacerbated by war in the former Yugoslavia, which seemed to fulfil Western European fears of inevitable new waves of refuge-seeking Easterners (van Selm-Thorburn 1998, 3). This all amounted to a rapid break from the previous paradigm and an immersion into a new period of perceived challenges, which produced enduring new problem conceptions – especially around the difficulties of control – along with new Europeanized dimensions, growing from the ongoing integration trend (Geddes 2018).

The early 1990s saw social backlash against many of these new dynamics. Even in the liberalizing post-Cold War scene, politicians saw an autochthonous desire for restriction as self-evident, not simply attributable to economic concerns. Rather, hostility to immigrants was seen to be 'especially strong if the fear of economic competition is combined with ethnic prejudice' (Welsh 1993, 30). 'The discourse that one hears about Europe's (in)ability to absorb and integrate foreign populations thus reads in part as the expression of the indigenous population's fears about its own future in the new Europe' (Ireland 1991, 477). Critical scholarship saw how this new politics was revolving not around protectionism per se but around the – especially Southern – Other: 'the opening doors to the East is followed by closing doors to the South' (Morokvasic 1991, 71). To the extent that 'Fortress Europe' was developing, people were feeling it unequally according to their race, ethnicity and gender (Kofman and Sales 1992).

In sum, we see in this early period an initial, more liberal image of Fortress Europe – one of freedom on the inside, but high walls all round – coming under challenge by a critical view which started to see Fortress Europe as less tied to territory. Today, it is easy to identify the contradictions of these two images: one, the clearing away of internal frontiers surrounding labour, trade and investment, enabled by an external wall; and the other, an opening to the East that accompanied closure to people from the Global South.

More generally, we can see developing in the post-Cold War Europe three concurrent and intertwining trends. First, there was a sense that European immigration control systems were coming under increasing stress and needed to exert more forceful steering of 'unwanted' immigration dynamics if they were to meet political demands. Second, European integration was progressing faster than ever before towards its telos of rational cooperation as a way towards lasting peace, meaning a growing European role for addressing shared 'problems', including the challenges of the movement of people. And, third, nationalism in Europe – seen clearly by many as a (dormant) menace – was becoming intertwined with a new identity politics roiling within European societies themselves, with migrants cast as a fifth column or a foil.

Understanding developments in Fortress Europe

From these starting points it is possible to discern three intellectual frames – which, it must be said, often dialogue and overlap – that provide vantage points on the development of 'Fortress Europe': the concept of (EUropean) immigration policy failure (largely from political science), the securitization of migration (with roots in IR) and bordering (more or less, a sociological view).

(EUropean) immigration policy failure

The emergence of prominent new forms of ('unwanted') migration as 'wicked problems' for European states coincided with the zeitgeist of burgeoning European integration. This combination has had important effects on (a) the ways in which immigration policy has been deemed to continue to 'fail' and (b) the extent to which this purported failure itself has become 'EUropeanized'.

From the politics of immigration perspective, Europe's liberal states were dealing more and more with accepting large amounts of immigration that were politically 'unwanted' but unworkable to effectively exclude (Freeman 1994). Was this mainly because of domestic–political constraints having to do with national rights regimes and employer interest groups (Joppke 1998; Freeman 1994), or did liberal supranational governance (Sassen 1996) – as embodied, for instance, in the EU – play the key role in this tension? If European integration was widening and deepening precisely to tackle jointly transnational issues which demanded transnational solutions, then the challenges of this 'new migration world' were, in some way, prime candidates for EU competence. On the other hand, migration touched upon sovereignty in basic and potentially politically explosive ways. EU states approached the Europeanization of migration policy with deep ambivalence, and very unevenly – advancing broadly shared political goals of hollowing out asylum rights, but little else as it regarded non-EU citizens.

While, for migrants, 'Fortress Europe' had originally seemed to mean common policy towards non-EU citizens in general, it was in fact asylum seeking, especially from the Global South, which came to dominate discussions about common EU policies towards non-EU citizens. Quickly it became apparent that 'EU states [were] particularly interested in improving the control of refugee flows before the evolving union eliminates internal barriers to freedom of movement' (Barutciski 1994, 32). This did not at all mean a transfer of policymaking primacy upwards to the EU level: individual European states increasingly sought to externalize border control through, for instance, carriers liability (Cruz 1995); to harden their own asylum determination systems in a form of crisis response (Alink, Boin, and T'Hart 2001); and to attempt to reduce asylum through welfare-state interventions (discussed subsequently). Overall, states' interventions had no very clear effect on reducing the volume of asylum seeking (Hatton 2004, 17).

In this situation, from the second half of the 1990s, scholars were taking increasing note that national asylum and immigration policymakers were attempting to develop European forums in order to enact more effective exclusionary policy (Henson and Malhan 1995; Lavenex 2006; Guiraudon 2000; cf. Shearmur 2021). This was usually seen as an attempt to escape the rights regimes and liberalism embedded within European states. The development of the Dublin Regulations and law-enforcement tools like the Eurodac fingerprint database exemplified this trend. While the image of a comprehensive European governance of non-EU immigration was suggested by the Treaty of Amsterdam in 1997 and the following summit in Tampere in 1999, this did not emerge; even more narrowly on asylum, pooling of sovereignty towards asylum seekers developed lopsidedly, 'as regards their rejection' (Guild 2006, 636). The rational liberal ideal of European governance as an arena for collective resolution of transnational problems, in some way advancing humane 'European values' – perhaps through sharing responsibility for offering refuge in peaceful and prosperous Europe – increasingly collided with the reality that European forums were developing as sites for advancing the exclusionary goals of member-state administrations (Boswell 2000).

This dynamic created a sense of uncertainty about whether there was a 'Fortress Europe' to speak of. Europe may have had largely in common the resistance of certain forms of 'unwanted' Southern immigration, but this was not driven by the European level or even mainly enacted there (Geddes 2001; Shearmur 2021). Regardless, the sensation that movements of people were becoming increasingly central to EUropean politics would endure. When it came time for Eastern European candidate countries to begin to accede to the EU, despite the continually growing sense that immigration ought to be an area of broadened EU competence, it nonetheless remained the case that if there was a 'Fortress Europe', this was something mostly to be executed by the member states (Phuong 2003).

The period since 2004 has seen deep intensification of the association between immigration controversies – often rendered as febrile popular dissatisfaction with failed immigration control – and Euroscepticism. Labour and family immigration from the ex-communist accession countries became intertwined with anxiety about 'unwanted' migration from the Global South to which European integration had allegedly left everyone in some way vulnerable. Populist radical-right parties were seen to mobilize and capitalize upon the segment of European electorates most concerned about this (Mudde 2004). The strengthening relationship between an insistence on more effective immigration control, intolerance of non-Christian religions and Euroscepticism was apparent across Europe (de Vreese and Boomgaarden 2005; Hobolt et al. 2011) but became most explicit in the UK following its decision to allow unfettered labour migration from the 2004 accession states (Evans and Mellon 2019; Dennison and Geddes 2018). With intra-EU migration newly salient, the juggernaut of EU expansion encountered a roadblock in Turkey's accession candidacy, which united advocates of Christian and secular Europe in unease (Hurd 2006).

EUropean responses to further increases in asylum seeking via the Mediterranean in the 2010s dispelled most doubt about whether a 'Fortress Europe' was being attempted. Post-Arab Spring instability in Libya and Syria early in the decade loosened routes into Europe and triggered efforts to harden and externalize the EU's borders (Bialasiewicz 2012). The summer of migration in 2015 – the so-called migration crisis – was the signal event in these developments. Different European countries differently blamed European integration: Southern European countries of arrival were overwhelmed by Dublin Regulation duties, transit countries saw themselves as victims of Schengen and northern destination countries' calls to EU partners to share the 'burden' met with refusal (Thielemann 2018). The perceived failure to control immigration at Europe's frontiers, where the EU seemed in some way inadequate, accelerated the Europeanization of the external EU border (Niemann and Speyer 2018), for instance, in the continued growth of Frontex, and the EU-Turkey deal. Belying this crisis of EU control, however, is the reality that member states never ceded the level of sovereignty in immigration which public political discourse has taken as fact. The methods by which states policed their borders during 'crises of Schengen' did not involve truly new practices, but rather were long-standing policing methods, merely intensified (Casella Colombeau 2020). The rapid welcoming of refugees from Ukraine in 2022, including in Eastern European countries – forced to emigrate by a war which both resurrected state-security fears of a Cold War vintage and was spurred by international conflicts over European integration – underlined just how discretionary and political, and unrelated to European states' social 'capacity', attempts to exclude asylum seekers from the Global South have been.

These developments, all in all, leave us with a first main perspective: one of enduring immigration policy failure. This sees the continued experience of politically 'unwanted' migration amid escalating restriction efforts as the enduring 'normal' condition of liberal states, magnified since the 1980s. Scholars approach this common point from two main angles. The first is that EUropean states continue to fail at meeting stated control objectives. Inasmuch as these objectives are unattainable, this suggests a failure of political leadership, leaving immigration policy hostage to inflamed public opinion thus entrenched failure. The second, starting from the effects of policy implementation, is that the EU and its member states are failing migrants and failing themselves by not living up to humane, sometimes explicitly 'European', values (van Selm 2016). The Fortress Europe that has been attempted represents a failure to deal rationally and cooperatively with immigration issues, rooted in the narrow range of ways national politicians have been willing to cooperate, while eroding the human rights at the supposed centre of European progress.

Securitization

As mentioned, the end of the Cold War occasioned some major shifts within IR. Its heretofore dominant, economistic 'neo-neo' theories had largely treated politics *within* nations as outside the analytic focus of a discipline about politics *among* nations. But after social movements within states and transnationally among their peoples had caused a major shift in the geopolitical order, it became clear to a broadening array of scholars that taking the state as the unquestioned dominant unit of IR analysis was no longer tenable. The discipline grappled with how ideas could shape international order largely through the rise of constructivism as a new disciplinary paradigm.

An interest in ideas' effects on international order had to a certain extent long been of interest to IR liberals and was especially central to critical IR. Constructivism lent ideas more of a constitutive role in shaping identities which guided state action than IR liberalism did while seeking to be more discernible to 'mainstream' IR scholars and more anchored in state behaviour than critical analyses of knowledges and discourses were (Adler 1997). Constructivists provided perspectives on how developments in societies 'below' the state could shape state action and how transnational social connections among these sub-state actors could diffuse similar norms and notions of order across different societies and their states (Finnemore and Sikkink 1998). With their interest in civil society and notions of appropriate conduct in international politics, constructivists have been seen as carrying the banner of some liberal values, even if they diverge substantially from liberal IR theory (Steele 2007).

Security has largely been a province of IR, and constructivism was translated into security analysis mostly through the development of securitization theory (Wæver 1995; Buzan, Wæver, and de Wilde 1998). In a way, securitization theory did for threat what other constructivist scholarship did for norms. Through a certain domestic–political process, any issue, in principle, could become treated in a certain 'securitized' way, defined by existential threat and requiring exceptional measures. Importantly, in this view, the state need not be what is threatened. This turned the focus of security analysis away from states' presumed suspicion of each other (rationally growing from international anarchy) and towards an understanding of what issues were constructed socially as threats; similar societies may undergo similar (or linked) processes of threat definition that securitize the same sorts of phenomena (Wæver 2000). Decentring the state, there was now such a thing as 'societal security' to which different nations may see coinciding threats.

From the start, securitization scholars have seemed to agree that securitization (a) is mostly a bad thing and (b) is particularly ripe to occur where immigration is concerned. Elites were liable to try to securitize issues for short-sighted political gain (Wæver 1995), when all in all, it was better for issues to be governed in a 'normal' rather than securitized way. Securitization threatened to revivify the kind of nationalism that had previously savaged Europe; anti-immigration politics was becoming the flashpoint of that danger (Wæver et al. 1993). Things became characteristically more complicated as critical scholars became involved in securitization discussions. If immigrants were increasingly problematically identified as a security problem (Huysmans 1995), this alleged threat was in some way insoluble: the securitization of migration unleashed not a politics of emergency but a governmentality of unease (Bigo 2002) or an indelible politics of insecurity (Huysmans 2006), where social relations of insecurity needed to be sown for purposes of political legitimacy in the contemporary European scene. And if constructivist securitization scholars craved less securitization and more 'normal' politics, inasmuch as 'normal' meant a liberal politics-as-usual, was that really so great for the marginalized anyway (Aradau 2004)?

The already ascendant securitization concept struck a chord with the major security reorientations of the post-9/11 period (including the later bombings in Madrid and London), widely perceived as offering an opportunity for European authorities to securitize migration (Boswell 2007, 589). It provided a viewpoint on how different societies may identify common threats to their security, with or without supranational entities to guide a response. As the threat was identified with people of origins in the Global South – and many such people were already living in European societies due to postcolonial migration and later asylum seeking – distinctions between internal and external security blurred (Pastore 2001). Various aspects of threat regarding migration, borders and Others blended into a diffuse security problematique (Huysmans 2006, 2014). The intensification of security practices around immigration provided growing material for examining the varied ways that security was articulated or contested in politics, beyond the original securitization theory. At the EU level, responses often did not conform to securitization theory's model of emergency treatment but rather to logics of escalating risk at Europe's frontiers (Neal 2009). Within European societies, however, prominent political discourse often did reflect existential stakes (for social identity, if not the state) and exhortations of emergency treatment, often specifically surrounding Islam (Kaya 2009; Fox and Akbaba 2015).

In the 'Fortress Europe' which has developed surrounding Mediterranean crossings, especially in the wake of summer 2015, critical security scholars have noted the convergence of several logics. In one way, the denial of safe passage to Europe – in progress since border externalizations in the 1980s – manifests a necropolitics (Basaran 2015) indifferent to the survival of black or brown bodies (De Genova 2018). In another, the practices and discourses of EUropean border-guarding, under the Frontex banner, have merged the imperatives of border security (the external walls of 'Fortress Europe') with life-saving (of those imperilled by Europe's original denial of safe passage), which purportedly reflects humanitarian ('European') values (Pallister-Wilkins 2015; Perkowski 2018).

Despite divisions among security scholars, this all reveals a second vantage point on 'Fortress Europe', through securitization. Different European societies may undergo similar or linked threat-construction processes which identify the imperilling of something deemed central to society or identity; security practices (fortification) in response may occur inside or outside of a supranational structure. The securitization of migration is about internal difference as much as external frontiers. Scholars seem to agree this is in some way negative, but constructivist and critical security scholars differ on the worth of the 'normal' politics at stake in the original theory. In one reading, while there are of course grave implications for immigrants, one gets the sense that the real tragedy is the triggering of a retrogression of European politics away from liberal-pluralist ideals. In another reading, those liberal-pluralist ideals merge with and justify the repressive practices of Fortress Europe, as European politicians fear the consequences of an uncontrolled encounter with the Southern, especially Muslim, Other. Emergency in Europe is increasingly the norm (White 2015; Neal 2012). In any event, securitization per se is unlikely to offer any real social solution.

Bordering

If in the early 1990s, 'Fortress Europe' implied a high wall on the outside and freedom within, by the early 2000s inner 'social marginalization' had clearly also become a central thing to analyse in considerations of the fortress (Geddes 2001, 34). In part this was evident because throughout the 1990s, European states had increasingly used welfare interventions to try to control immigration (Slaven, Casella Colombeau and Badenhoop 2021). Changes to welfare states amid continued immigration prompted substantial reflection on the nature of European social citizenship (Ferrera 2005). Beyond the main immigration-politics literature – principally in sociology, but also in human geography and some more critical politics contributions – a view emerged which has looked beyond territorial boundaries towards a broader repertoire of practices that enact European borders both territorially and also in deterritorialized ways. The state of neoliberal globalization and burgeoning European integration had in a key respect made borders 'no longer localizable', disjointed from previous visions of sovereignty (Balibar 2002, 91) and increasingly centred across social life (Brambilla 2015).

In this view, what is at stake in the building of Fortress Europe is not just access to European territory or European safety from (Islamic) terrorism, though this is still at stake (Vaughan-Williams 2008). Even more fundamental are questions of membership and belonging in European societies – which immediately become questions about who is entitled to share in European nation states and their resources. Contributions drawing from systems theory identified how questions about membership and belonging bind together social systems that otherwise operate on very different premises – such as welfare, the labour market and immigration – drawing in more of society to migration control while creating friction and 'fog' (Bommes and Sciortino 2011). If states could not keep out the unwanted territorially, then other social systems became sites for enacting symbolic dedication to their exclusion (Faist 1994b) or to try to make their lives in Europe unworkable (Sales 2002).

Here, Fortress Europe is envisioned not just as a curtain wall but rather more like a castle, with its batteries and barbicans but also gated keeps. European welfare states constitute one 'donjon' within Fortress Europe, where the valued possessions of Europeans, allegedly threatened by immigration, are hoarded behind further barriers (Engbersen and Broeders 2011). To a certain extent, this 'bordering' has been conducted by and oriented towards states, pursuing the official ends of effectuating territorial exclusion through punitiveness or deterrence (Squire 2009; Bommes and Geddes 2000; Slaven 2021). This underlines the extent to which immigration control functions have been 'outsourced' to further social sectors as part of the state pursuit of control over, in particular, 'illegal' migration (Düvell 2006), a key categorization whereby racism in Europe is operationalized (de Noronha 2019).

Sociological approaches, however, have opened up views on how these kinds of practices have not just policy implications but much broader social effects. This is a key observation within the conceptualization of (everyday) 'bordering' (Yuval-Davis, Wemyss, and Cassidy 2019), which does not see territorial exclusion as the sole goal of bordering practices within European societies but rather reads them as larger technologies of social order. Requiring citizens to work as guards at the gates of welfare, health care and finance reifies division and gives everyone in society – not just immigrants or their descendants – roles in an interminable pageant of (un)deservingness and (un)belonging. Beyond any enhancement of immigration policing functions, this creates societies of suspicion. Much bordering does relate to state policy objectives (Yuval-Davis, Wemyss, and Cassidy 2018), but in this reading, bordering also represents a strategy of political management, compensating for the neoliberal European state's withdrawal from matters of economic fairness (Yuval-Davis, Wemyss, and Cassidy 2019, 14–18). A post-sovereign age has necessitated new images of (non)cititzenship, a gap filled with bordering.

All of this lends us a third and final account of Fortress Europe, focused on the larger sociological aspects of this bordering. Here, Fortress Europe is not just about governing who is allowed to stay in Europe or warding off what threatens Europe or Europeanness. Fortress Europe responds to uncertainty regarding the purpose of the state in the post-Cold War neoliberal Europe and is about what European citizenship means as social membership. The construction of Fortress Europe is about, and occurs within, the interior as much as the exterior. It pursues policy ends, but also pursues the entrenchment of social division for purposes of maintaining social legitimacy for state practices. In this Fortress Europe, there are fewer and fewer villagers who are innocent bystanders to this anxiety-inducing scene, as increasingly we are all cast as suspected invaders or upstanding guards.

Conclusion: Fortress Europe in conservative, liberal and radical readings

What does all of this say about what it means to fortify early twenty-first-century Europe? What re-emerges is the polysemous and unstable nature of the Europe which is fortifying: its contested core values, its shifting authorities, its 'new migration worlds' challenging sovereign control, its muddling of external and internal security, its stressed sinews of membership. Consequently, there is certainly a decreasing sense among scholars that Fortress Europe is tied in some functional way to the lifting of barriers within Europe itself. It is also relatively clear that Fortress Europe is not a general construction towards the outside world. Rather, it is people with origins in the Global South whose presence and claims are understood as threats. In some way, this fortress is clearly European if not always EUropean – growing out of a certain unity of Europe in how its societies assess their place in the world and what may threaten them, if not always from European integration, per se.

Where are the borders of Europe, and (how) ought they to be defended? The earlier parts of this chapter tracked different scholarly readings of Fortress Europe, but the idea of 'Fortress Europe' has always occurred at their intersection and has been less contested along disciplinary lines than normative (political) ones. So, this chapter concludes by synthesizing three broad perspectives on Fortress Europe: the conservative, the liberal and the (academically) critical or (politically) radical.

The conservative view sees European societies – similarly situated in the world, their 'genuine' memberships comparably defined and with relatively more in common (including their enemies) than what divides them – engaging in coinciding processes of defining threats which reach largely concurrent conclusions. Whether Europe is fundamentally Christian, post-Christian or secular (critics might say these all regardless mean 'white'), the threat is most immediately Islam (or, more mildly, some Muslims, who nonetheless always seem to imply the menace of all) and secondarily an increasing diversity that has confused European societies, their morality and their coherence. More basically, however, the threat is a lack of control against these forces and others which may emerge, which may strip Europeans of what belongs to them. Radicals are mainly to blame for the former, and liberals mainly for the latter. Thus, European security is not to be found in a European integration process which may or may not be beneficial in other regards but whose inveterate permissiveness and liberalism make it incapable of this kind of protection. This conservative perspective on Fortress Europe is, of course, championed much more frequently in popular political debate than in the academy. Among academics, its relatively small band of scholarly defenders are much more discussed than they are admired. Subscribing to such views depends on legitimizing concepts of self-interest among native European 'somewheres' (Holmwood 2020), which most scholars have little trouble understanding as 'intellectual justification for racism' (Meer 2019, 502).

Somewhat more complex is the liberal view of Fortress Europe – one fraught with anxiety and ambivalence. Walls and barriers would seem antithetical to the liberal vision. Yet, as the earliest liberal musings on a 'Fortress Europe' reflect, this view in some way necessitates those walls, since the zone of internal freedom is always vulnerable to those outside who cannot or will not play by the same rules. The liberal reading contains a great amount of genuine concern for immigrants, often discussed in terms of humanitarianism and especially human rights, paramount values which the conservative view disparages. But these are frequently articulated through a discussion of 'European' (always, somehow, concurrently universal) values – in this account, secular ones – which are at stake in dealing with the outsiders who arrive at and within Europe. In addressing this situation, manifesting European values is paramount. But do these outsiders – who are, after all, not Europeans – really subscribe to those same values? While certainly much of importance is at stake for the rights and well-being of the migrant, there is always a gnawing worry that this encounter with the Other will cause Europe to be (in the word's original sense) *brutalized* – that is, transformed into a brute, in a regression from the image of enlightened and progressive Europe. Division and nationalism may kindle, thwarting the European destiny that has delivered a seventy-five-year miracle of prosperity and peace. For that reason, this encounter must be carefully managed. Radical objections are naïve. The mechanisms of Fortress Europe are, in this account, often denied as such – after all, such a fortress would contradict European progress – but, rather, are measures to address a challenge.

The radical view – articulated in academia within critical scholarship – certainly targets the chauvinism of the conservative view and the violence it legitimizes. But it also inveighs against the exclusions – and even the violence – justified within the liberal view. The radical account rejects the conservative view of European superiority as well as the liberal European self-image of ever-unfolding progress, both understood as fictions which legitimize and indeed require exclusionary exercises of power. Consequences of European violence surround us in ways which have been easy for most in Europe to deny and which deeply complicate the very notion of what and who belongs to Europe. In this view, peace and freedom in Europe cannot be built on the chauvinist identity politics of conservatives, nor on liberal pieties of universal values which are always said to be most of all manifested in particular (i.e. European) communities. The path forward towards justice is not European integration as we have known it but more transformative concepts of solidarity – ones which acknowledge the state of today's world as a consequence of European exercises of domination and which break from how both the conservative and liberal views have centred competing visions of the idealized European as the paramount subject of politics. In this view, Fortress Europe in all its forms must be torn down as part of a society rebuilt. Any understanding of the boundaries of Europe is ultimately a vision of Europe itself.

Part III

Case studies

Multicultural anxieties in England

Schooling liberalism and the problem of religious expression

John Holmwood

Racist and xenophobic hostility towards ethnic and religious minorities is on the rise. The primary focus of this hostility in Europe and North America is Muslim minority communities, but it can equally be directed at minorities expressing Orthodox Jewish, Sikh, Hindu and Pentecostal Christian faith commitments (or, indeed, those expressing Roman Catholic and Protestant beliefs, even where these are part of the local 'tradition'). Nor is it a feature only of far-right political discourse. Across Europe, 'multiculturalism' has been decried by politicians in the mainstream, both right and left, for encouraging the self-segregation of minority communities and their separation from mainstream values of local political cultures.[1]

The concerns arise, in part, because of the divergent religious sensibilities of white-majority and ethnic minority populations. There is a decline not only in church attendance but also in religious identification among the former, whether Anglican or Roman Catholic, while the latter show high levels of participation and identification with a variety of minority faiths. Among Christians, any increase in religious observation is associated either with Evangelical churches or with new migrant communities of Roman Catholics from Eastern Europe (see Commission on Religion and Belief in British Public Life 2015).

This development has elicited concern on the part of liberals, including academics. A dominant understanding of modernity involved the 'secularisation thesis' of the declining significance of religion and its retreat from public life (Bruce 2011). While some continue to maintain the relevance of secularization as a broad trend, that is little consolation in the face of the fact that population movement – migration – has meant that, empirically, any supposed underlying trend towards secularization is occurring alongside its opposite. Liberals confront a resurgence of religion, just when they thought it was in decline. Moreover, the white-majority population is older than those of ethnic minorities, so there is an increasing proportion of school children who are from minority religious backgrounds. The dynamics of residential segregation, together with policies promoting parental choice of schools for their children, have also made ethnic and religious segregation in schools more acute, with white parents moving their children from schools with even a small proportion of ethnic minority children. Religion in schools, then, has emerged as a focal point of concern.

This has a somewhat paradoxical character. Historically, schooling in England was initially provided by religious bodies, first the Anglican Church and then the Roman Catholic Church (after the re-establishment of their dioceses in the 1850s). The independent schools favoured by the upper-middle and middle classes – the 'public schools' such as Eton, Winchester or Harrow – are also religious foundations and frequently single sex. Publicly funded education developed as a supplement to that provided by religious organizations, whose schools were partially incorporated into a state system of publicly funded education, such that around a third of all such schools are 'faith schools', or 'schools of a religious character' as they are more properly described.

However, it would be wrong to describe all other schools as 'secular'. Since the 1944 Education Act, and re-affirmed in the 1988 Education Act, all publicly funded schools must teach religious education and have a daily act of collective worship. Each must be done ('wholly or mainly') from a Christian perspective (albeit non-denominational), reflecting the fact that, as the 1988 Act put it, the 'religious traditions of Great Britain are in the main Christian whilst taking account of the teaching and practices of the other principle religions represented in Great Britain'. Put very simply, all publicly funded schools in England are required to have a Christian religious ethos, whether or not they are designated as faith schools (of course, there are some, albeit very few, non-Christian faith schools – primarily Jewish). The 1944 Act made these arrangements the responsibility of local education authorities and their local Standing Advisory Council on Religious Education (SACRE), who were also responsible for granting 'determinations'. These allowed non-Christian worship where the religious make-up of the pupils made alternative arrangements more appropriate. The schools that I will discuss later in this chapter had had approval for Islamic collective worship since the 1990s.

The demographics described earlier have de-stabilized these arrangements. This has occurred together with government hostility to local authorities leading to the development of 'academy' and 'free' schools outside local educational authority responsibility and answerable only to the secretary of state for education (around 75 per cent of secondary schools in England are now academies, and the Department for Education has recently announced that all schools should be incorporated within multi-academy trusts by 2030). This is something that I will develop later, but academy schools are also no longer under the jurisdiction of a local SACRE. On the one hand, an increasingly secular white-majority population had allowed collective worship in schools to atrophy, with no pressure from parents to maintain it (the minority of parents for whom it is an issue have access to Christian faith schools). On the other hand, in schools with a high proportion of pupils from minority religious backgrounds – in the schools I will discuss in this chapter, the proportion of Muslim heritage pupils was in excess of 95 per cent – the purpose of applying for a 'determination' was precisely in order to practise the legal requirement of collective worship. As we shall see, it will be *their compliance with this requirement* that comes to be seen as involving a failure to respect 'British values' of democracy, religious tolerance and the rule of law.

In short, I shall suggest that the demographic situation is one that is fertile ground for liberal anxieties, anxieties that are easily aligned with populist and xenophobic movements. The possibility of such an alignment has been subject to earlier sociological reflection, largely forgotten, which I will set out in the next section before I return to the case studies that I will address in the main body of the chapter.

Religion and liberalism

In a recent article, Adam Seligman and David Montgomery (2020) pose an acute dilemma, one which they suggest defines our age: How do we recognize the importance of *community* (especially, religious community) in a liberal polity? In what follows, I shall agree with them that the language of human rights is not the solution to the 'contemporary challenge of constructing civil society' (2020, np), not least because liberals have increasingly constructed religion as hostile to rights.

In the first instance, this might appear to be counter-intuitive. Human rights are usually understood as favouring respect for difference and, thus, for multiculturalism within a liberal framework. This was the position of the Runnymede Trust's influential *Commission on the Future of Multi-Ethnic*

Britain under Bhikhu Parekh (2000). It argued that national identity should be understood as inclusive of ethnic minorities and should express their right to co-determine the political community to which they belonged, within the constraints of procedural norms of commitment to the rule of law, democracy and religious tolerance. The report sought to represent Britain as a 'community of communities'. However, it met with great hostility from the right-wing press and conservative politicians over what was seen to be an association of the tag 'British' as code for racism (McLaughlin and Neal 2004). In the words of the front page story in the *Daily Telegraph*, echoed again after the recent Black Lives Matter protests, it was seen as an attempt to 'rewrite our history' (Johnston 2000).

It is the specifically liberal critique of this idea of multiculturalism that is my concern here. Amartya Sen (2006), for example, has argued that British multiculturalism had diverted from a path towards integration and has, instead, become a form of *plural mono-culturalism*. This was because it has involved an underlying communitarian philosophy that raised group membership over individual choice. The former, according to Sen, 'concentrates on the promotion of diversity as a value in itself. The other focuses on the freedom of reasoning and decision-making, and celebrates cultural diversity to the extent that it is as freely chosen as possible by the persons involved' (2006, 150). It is a fine distinction and one that frequently depends on the eye of the beholder, but we can note that, in the case of schooling, it carries the strong implication that while liberal values may be taught to children, since they are assumed to inculcate the capacities necessary for free choice, religion is understood as potentially a form of indoctrination prior to a child having the capacity to choose.

Of course, the UN Declaration on Human Rights does enshrine religious freedoms in articles 18 and 26. In the UK, the idea of protected rights was extended in the Equality Act 2010 from race and ethnicity, gender and disability, to include age, gender re-assignment, marriage or civil partnership, pregnancy and maternity, sexual orientation, and religion and belief. As might be anticipated, it is the inclusion of religion and belief that causes the most difficulty, although there are collateral problems associated with gender and gender re-assignment (as the current dispute between gender-critical feminists and transactivists indicates, to which I shall return). Essentially, as we have seen, standard interpretations of liberal rights associate them with individual 'choices', rather than with group membership. So, from this perspective, racial and ethnic discrimination are properly to be understood in terms of discrimination against individuals on the basis of an ascription of characteristics falsely attributed to a group.

The difficulty with religious belief is that it involves something secular liberals wish to be able to characterize as false, while arguing that individuals should not be discriminated against on that basis. But religion is also associated with ('backward') values that potentially conflict with the very values intrinsic to the idea of rights. Thus, the gay rights activist Peter Tatchell argues for a 'progressive multi-culturalism' and against the inclusion of religion where 'a perverse interpretation of multiculturalism has resulted in race and religion ruling the roost in a tainted hierarchy of oppression. In the name of "unity" against Islamophobia and racism, much of the left tolerates misogyny and homophobia in minority communities' (2009, np). There is little evidence of what he claims, and, in this way, an 'authoritarian' and secular liberalism comes into public alignment with right-wing arguments about the 'nation' – white and Christian – where it is expressed as a form of 'femo-nationalism' (Farris 2017) or 'homo-nationalism' (Puar 2007).

This alignment has been made easier by the way in which mainstream Christianity in the United States and Europe has moved in the direction of secular individualism, as described powerfully by Robert Bellah (2002). The dominant self-understanding of liberalism is that it derives from the idea that in God's eyes all are equal, as that has been filtered through a liberal sensibility of individual conscience. For Bellah, even Catholicism has adopted the register of Protestantism. As we have seen, Sen describes multiculturalism as a form of identity politics, but, for Bellah, this is seriously misleading. According to him, 'identity' is integral to the very development of the liberal understanding that Sen endorses. Let me return to Seligman and Montgomery to explain. According to them, religion should be understood in terms of 'membership' (or *being*) rather than 'identity', and we can parse Bellah's argument as saying that Protestantism and American culture have come into alignment just in so far as the former has become a matter of 'identity'. This is something other sociologists of religion have also proposed, with the associational aspects of religion expression – practices undertaken in common and affirming membership – declining as 'believing' replaces 'belonging' (Davie 1994).

But for Seligman and Montgomery, as for Bellah, and, indeed, minority religious communities themselves, this shift is troubling – religion and membership remain integral as *communities of belonging*, not of *choice*. Religious communities practising their faith necessarily gather together to conduct rituals, pray, celebrate feast days and organize charitable activities. They do so separately from others who do not share their faith. This expression of difference is not a form of self-segregation but a way of expressing belonging and a common life together. There is no aspect of it that implies any deficit with regard to a commitment to the rule of law, democracy and religious tolerance.[2] Indeed, they might also seek to ensure that their children can participate fully in the public life that those norms facilitate, for example, by acting to improve schools and enhance employment opportunities or by safeguarding children from, say, the risks of drugs and knife crime. The careful reader will rightly think that I am describing the Muslim community schools that I will later discuss (but it could just as easily be that I am describing the historical impetus to the rise of public education through the activities of various religious organizations and charities).

But, if, in many Western countries, religion has re-aligned and declined (for majority populations), this has also helped to undermine a wider sense of 'belonging' and the common good, leaving a vacuum at the heart of their social and political life. Bellah's approach draws on Tocqueville, who placed religion at the centre of his account of modern democracy (in America), albeit, largely unremarked in the secondary literature. Thus, he outlined how the spirit of equality animated the (white) population of America, and it is this that he believed was the ground for democratic institutions. However, he also argued that religious belief was necessary. Religion is positive for democracy, Tocqueville argued, by providing a source of meaning beyond self-interest to which a society of equals might otherwise be prone, and it also protects from popular enthusiasms (see Avramenko 2012). 'Despotism', Tocqueville wrote,

> may be able to do without faith, but freedom cannot. Religion is much more
> needed in the republic ... [that French proponents of liberty] ... advocate than
> in the monarchy they attack, and in democratic republics most of all. How could
> society escape destruction if, when political ties are relaxed, moral ties are not
> tightened? And what can be done with a people master of itself if it is not subject
> to God? (2000, 294)

As Bellah outlines, the decline of religion is associated with identity politics, where multiculturalism functions to endorse individual expressions of difference: as he puts it, 'we are all different; we are all unique. Respect that' (2002, np). For him, this is not a true plurality but is itself 'monocultural', with the very idea of a common life together at risk. Bellah writes from a Christian perspective, but he argues that it is necessary to learn from the example of other religious traditions:

> We need the non-Protestant traditions, and the most thoughtful and self-
> critical sector of the Protestant tradition, to remind us that we are citizens of
> a deeply flawed city of man and that we badly need to recover an idea of the
> common good toward which we can aspire in the face of the disintegrative

tendencies not of cultural pluralism but of radical individualism. Breaking
the hold of the monoculture is, in my opinion, our greatest and most urgent
challenge. (2002, np)

What Bellah calls the 'monoculture of radical individualism' is precisely what
liberalism bequeaths to the modern political community. It cannot provide
belonging, and so it leaves a vacuum, one that is readily filled by populism and
xenophobic mobilizations of 'the people', what Tocqueville would regard as
forms of despotism to which democracies are prone. I am far from suggesting
that religion is the only source of associational belonging. The point is that the
free reign given to markets in the provision of services and public goods has
meant a hollowing out of a range of associational arrangements, as described
by Putnam, for example, in his *Bowling Alone* (2000). Paradoxically, given this
wider decline of other associational activity, religious organizations become
more visible, especially those serving minority communities.

Multiculturalism as participation – the three cases

I now want to change tack to consider the current anxieties around
multiculturalism in the context of Britain as a postcolonial polity. At the height of
Empire, Britain exercised political domination over around 400 million people.
One thing can be agreed, Empire was necessarily multicultural. It reorganized
the geography of the nation by extending subjecthood to everyone within the
Empire on an equivalent basis. Populations migrated from Britain to its colonies,
and others came to Britain as subjects, not as aliens. In that sense, Empire made
the nation multicultural, and the evolution of democracy made its subjects
into citizens with claims as equals. Here we might contrast, as does Bhambra
(2019), those who move to other lands to impose a new order – colonialists –
and those who move within the space of Empire to seek a better life and to live
within the order they find. The 'threat' the latter pose, it would seem, is only a
threat to identity and to privilege, constituted simply by their willingness to live
differently (within their separate communities of belonging) as equals.

Our current dilemma, then, is not so much one constituted by multiculturalism
as by the requirement on the part of the white majority (within what has come to
be deemed 'the nation') of giving up, what Danielle Allen (2004) has called, the
'habits of domination' with which they were previously associated and replacing
them with new habits of equality. The past of Empire cannot be expunged from a

nation's history in understanding who it is, and the past requires a reckoning of what Empire did to the nation. Decolonization is not only an external process of giving up sovereignty, it is an internal process of reconstruction. In these terms, then, I suggest that the issues that I address here should be thought of in terms not of an opposition between rights-based claims and communities of belonging but rather of a failure to overcome (racialized) hierarchies of domination in recognition of the equal rights of others, including their right to constitute a community of belonging within the national polity.

Allen's discussion of the 'unlearning' of habits of domination is developed in the context of the civil rights struggle in the United States, specifically school desegregation in Little Rock, Arkansas (which comes to be enshrined in the Supreme Court's 1954 ruling known as *Brown v Board of Education*). The moment – epitomized in the well-known photo of student Elizabeth Eckford's calm presence in the face of a baying mob – is one of a seismic shift in the habits of unequal citizenship, where practices based upon the domination of one group and the acquiescence of another begin to break down as a formerly excluded group affirms its presence as constituent members of the public. The reaction of the dominant group is a response to the challenge to its privileges.[3]

The 'Birmingham Trojan Horse affair'

The current opposition to multiculturalism in England has a similar character, which I will discuss through the experience of a British Muslim community in Alum Rock, Birmingham, and allegations of a takeover of schools by supposed Islamists that emerged in early 2014 – the 'Trojan Horse affair'.[4] An alleged 'plot' was promoted by right-wing media and think tanks, such as Policy Exchange, leading to peremptory and authoritarian government action against teachers and governors. Although presented in terms of illegitimate behaviour by some members of a 'self-segregated' community of belonging acting contrary to 'British values', I shall argue that it should instead be understood as a demand for participation on equal terms. Significantly, however, the Equality Act 2010 came to be used against the community and not in their support.

Park View was a small secondary school in Alum Rock with around 600 pupils mainly of Muslim heritage – 98.9 per cent by the time of the affair. It was also an area of severe economic disadvantage with 74 per cent of pupils in receipt of free school meals, compared with a Birmingham average of 28.9 per cent and a national average of 15.2 per cent (Holmwood and O'Toole 2018). It had been identified as one of the worst-performing schools in the country in the 1990s and was the focus of an ugly and condescending BBC Panorama television programme titled *Underclass in Purdah* (McLoughlin 1998). In 1996, a new chair of governors, Tahir Alam, previously a pupil at the school, was appointed and began a programme of improvement together with a newly appointed head teacher, Lindsey Clarke. By 2006 it was one of the most improved schools in the country, and by 2012 it was judged by Ofsted inspectors to be 'outstanding' and in the top 14 per cent of all schools in the country. The inspectors described it as a 'truly inclusive school in which there is no evidence of discrimination and students, sometimes with major disabilities, are welcomed as members of the school community'.[5] Under the government's programme for academy schools, successful schools are encouraged to leave local education authority control and become academies and to form a trust to incorporate other, failing, schools and introduce their successful practices to improve them. Under the auspices of the Department for Education, the school incorporated two other schools, with plans for other schools to follow. All were Muslim-majority schools.

In March 2014 a leaked letter purporting to outline a plot to 'Islamicize' schools, with Tahir Alam at its centre, filled the media headlines. Emergency inspections of twenty-one schools were called, along with special investigations for the City Council and the Department for Education, the latter conducted by the former head of counterterrorism at the Metropolitan Police. Allegations of extremism, the undermining of British values and undue religious influence were made. Governors (including Tahir Alam) and teachers were dismissed, and proceedings for professional misconduct begun. The latter cases dragged on until May 2017 and collapsed as a consequence of serious impropriety on the part of government lawyers and their failure to disclose evidence. In the meantime, academic performance at the schools slumped and has not yet recovered. The participation of Muslims as governors, teachers and senior leaders in education in Birmingham was also significantly reduced, notwithstanding that the BAME school population is 66.6 per cent compared with 28.9 per cent nationally.

One of the claims made in official reports against the school was that it had an Islamic religious ethos, despite being a 'secular' state school, as the Clarke Report (2014) described it. As we have seen, all publicly funded schools are required to have religious education and daily acts of religious worship of a Christian character. Park View had had a determination for Islamic worship since 1996 and had submitted its 'assembly plans' for scrutiny to the appropriate body, the local SACRE. Moreover, the Islamic 'ethos' of the school had been noted by Ofsted inspectors and had been positively endorsed as contributing to its success.

What I have just set out could as easily be seen as a model of *multicultural integration*. The Islamic ethos of the school elicited trust on the part of parents – it provided the school with what Seligman and Montgomery (2020) call 'moral credit'. The school endorsed the backgrounds and traditions of the pupils as both Muslim and British and, by allowing the 'whole child' to be in school, elicited identification with aspirations for academic success. Parents *may* have been conservative on gender issues – many parents are, and not only Muslim parents – but all girls were given opportunities to succeed; indeed, in an overall academic performance well above the national average, girls outperformed boys. The subsequent very significant decline in academic performance at the 'Trojan horse' schools involved a serious loss of opportunities for boys and girls alike.

Al-Hijrah school and 'unlawful' gender segregation

The question that arises is why the Equalities and Human Rights Commission (EHRC) took no interest in the affair.[6] One reason is that the government had responded to the Trojan Horse affair by introducing a requirement on all schools to teach 'fundamental British values' and to do so as part of a revised Prevent strategy to counter non-violent extremism (the Clarke Report had initially indicated that teachers and governors were extremist, but no such charges were brought forward in the misconduct cases, which instead addressed 'undue religious influence' – see Holmwood and O'Toole 2018). As the policy evolved, the Equality Act 2010, itself, became the definition of 'British values'. The 2017 Conservative election manifesto invoked action against racism (which had led to the formation in 1997 of the Commission for Racial Equality, the forerunner of the EHRC) as a model for action against extremism. It stated that extremism, 'especially Islamist extremism, strips some British people, especially women, of the freedoms they should enjoy, undermines the cohesion of our society and can fuel violence. To defeat extremism, we need to learn from how civil society and the state took on racism in the twentieth century' (2017, 54). The EHRC declared on its website that one of its priorities would be to ensure 'the education system promotes good relations with others and respect for equality and human rights' in implicit acceptance of the government's narrative.[7]

This bears upon another case, that of Al-Hijrah school in Birmingham. Founded in 1988, it was a co-educational Islamic faith-designated school for pupils aged four to sixteen. The school separated pupils in all lessons, breaks and movement around the school from year 5 (i.e. from ages nine to ten), in effect operating as two separate schools for boys and girls albeit on the same site. Although the school had been improving academically, in 2016 a special Ofsted inspection focused on its practices of segregation, declaring them to be unlawful under the Equality Act 2010. This was notwithstanding that these practices were openly advertised to parents and were fully visible to the authorities, including Ofsted in previous inspections. Moreover, the school claimed that while it provided separate education for boys and girls, it was equal.

The school sought a judicial review of the 2016 Ofsted Report, arguing 'bias' and that Ofsted had not demonstrated that the separate education of boys and girls had been to the detriment of either group. The school authorities were granted permission for review in November 2016 on the second of the grounds. Ofsted, in turn, appealed against this decision. Ofsted (or, more properly, HM chief inspector of education, children's service and skills) was joined by the secretary of state for education, as first 'intervener', the EHRC as second 'intervener' and Southall Black Sisters and Inspire (a Muslim women's rights organization concerned with combatting extremism) as third 'interveners'. The latter were allowed to present written evidence but not make direct representations to the court. In effect, they represented the position of 'progressive multiculturalism', as discussed earlier.

Judgement was made in October 2017 (*Ofsted v Al Hijrah*, 2017), with the ruling that there was indeed a detriment, in principle, and that the gender segregation was unlawful under the Equality Act 2010. The Court of Appeal did not find that there was a *collective* harm. However, it did rule that individual girls and boys were deprived of the possibility of interacting with members of the opposite sex despite it being at a co-educational school. They therefore suffered some detriment and were discriminated against. Lady Justice Gloster dissented from the idea that there was no need to address the issue of the collective harm, as had been argued by the third interveners, and provided a minority judgement.

Ofsted's inspection report in 2016 stated that Al-Hijrah's gender segregation policies 'does not accord with fundamental British values and amounts to unlawful discrimination' and, further, that it 'does not give due regard to the need to foster good relations between the genders, and means that girls and boys do not have equal opportunities to develop confident relationships with boys and vice versa. This is contrary to fundamental British values and the Equality Act 2010.' In its inspection report and in its appeal, Ofsted (and other interveners) also drew a parallel between racial segregation in South Africa and in the United States. In particular, reference was made to the judgement in *Brown v Board of Education*. This case, as we have seen, led to the formal desegregation of schools in the United States, and its citation implies that the lessons that can be drawn from it are unequivocal.

However, despite being a milestone case, there is a considerable difference of opinion about its consequences. Charles M. Payne (2004) suggests that it is a milestone in search of a signifier. De jure desegregation did not give rise to de facto desegregation, and, in many respects, the education of African American children was worse after *Brown v Board of Education* than it was before (as has been the case for the 'Trojan Horse' schools). Moreover, the judgement focused on the 'psychic harm' done to African American children by segregation rather than on the equal freedom of parents to choose a school for their children's education. It was this supposed psychic harm that the judgement sought to ameliorate, not the harms of racialized injustice as such. The latter harms to African Americans are structural, according to Payne, not interpersonal; they include labour market disadvantages, poverty and housing segregation, among others.

Brown v Board of Education did nothing to address the structural issues. Indeed, it implied that 'psychic deficit' might be part of the explanation for the structural problems. In effect, a structural problem was addressed as a behavioural problem, and, as a consequence, the victim was blamed. Worse, according to Payne, this became a new Orthodoxy among white Americans, and, in this way, 'Southern attitudes' became generalized in a language that suppressed overt racism but reproduced its effects. So long as negative racial attitudes were not directly expressed, the disadvantages experienced by African Americans could be understood as deriving from their own (culturally derived) behaviours and not from discrimination.

In her minority opinion (supported by an editorial in the *Guardian*),[8] Lady Justice Gloster made the case for the 'collective harm' that gender segregation in a school represents for girls. She did so in the context that the main judgement included recognition that 'women have been and remain "the group with minority power in society" in terms of the distribution of wealth and influence' (*Ofsted v Al-Hijrah* 2017, §131). She went on to propose that single-sex education creates attitudes and sentiments that sustain later social networks where women lose out more than men and are disproportionately excluded from networks of power and influence. This, she argued, represents an outcome of the 'expressive harm' that segregation represents.

Notice that structural obstacles to gender inequality – for example, the organization of the working day and the availability of affordable child-care – are neglected in favour of interpersonal issues of sociability. Moreover, it is unlikely that a school serving a poor community has direct responsibility for the reproduction of interpersonal gender relations that diminish women's power and influence more generally. Of course, this is not to deny that women in poor communities, or Muslim women, in particular, do not also experience structural inequalities, including those deriving from patriarchal practices specific to their own communities, as pointed out by Southall Black Sisters, for example.

However, this then raises the issue of how best to mitigate such inequalities. For example, there may be cultural as well as structural constraints on women's employment opportunities. However, these can be offset by ensuring that girls secure good educational outcomes. This does not, in itself, entail disparagement of cultural attitudes, unless it is assumed that Muslim parents do not value education. In fact, one of the arguments levelled against Muslim parents and governors in Birmingham was that they were too zealous in criticizing schools for their failure to achieve better educational outcomes for their children (Kershaw Report 2014, §28). The point at issue, then, is the extent to which one community has become the focus of special attention.

Of course, Ofsted's argument that gender segregation is against 'fundamental British values', although not tested in the court, is prima facie difficult to sustain since it is a feature of many private schools, especially those favoured by the upper class and upper-middle class and involving the reproduction of their substantial privileges. Significantly, Ofsted sought to bring another case in 2019, having declared King David School High School, a co-educational Jewish faith school in Manchester, inadequate on the grounds of gender segregation. The school sought judicial review, but Ofsted quashed its own report before that could take place. The difference between it and Al-Hijrah was that they offered three streams, for boys only, girls only and, a third, co-educational stream. On this basis, the school argued that there was genuine choice, while the fact that there were pupils from Orthodox Jewish backgrounds in each stream meant that no religious or gender discrimination could be identified. Little reported outside the Jewish press; Ofsted returned to the task three years later, just as this chapter was being prepared for publication. It downgraded the school from 'outstanding' to 'inadequate' on grounds that girls in its separate stream were treated differently than boys in the separate stream and girls and boys in the co-educational stream.[9] Among the criticisms was that sex education was taught differently to the separate girls stream in line with parental wishes, and, therefore, they were inadequately 'safeguarded'. This serves to show that the issue is directed not only at Muslim schools but also other minority religious schools. It also serves to introduce my next case.

Parent protests against LGBT+ teaching

The most recent set of concerns has involved parent protests about teaching LGBT+ relationships in two primary schools – Parkfield and Anderton Park – in the same area of Birmingham as the other schools.[10] The protests took place during 2019 and received a lot of media attention.[11] The concerns of the parents were declared to be 'bigoted' and against British values.[12] One conservative local councillor called the protests a 'hate crime'.[13] The protests coincided with a government consultation about changes to sex and relationships education, with new guidelines planned for September 2020. This had already elicited responses from different religious groups. However, the protests were not straightforwardly about these proposals but about changes that had already been introduced without discussion.

At Anderton Park School, the school had seemingly adopted the approach to relationships education of an educational charity, *Educate and Celebrate*, to incorporate teaching about LGBT+ relationships. However, the curriculum was not discussed with parents, and both Ofsted and the EHRC declared that it was correct that this was not done. A spokesman for Ofsted stated, 'we support the right of school leaders to determine the curriculum as they see fit and in the interests of their pupils – free from hostile outside influence'.[14] The Head of the EHRC made a similar statement that primary schools should be free to teach LGBT relationships without consulting parents.[15]

In fact, the Department for Education guidelines (2019) state the opposite and do so by citing religion as a protected characteristic. They state:

> a good understanding of pupils' faith backgrounds and positive relationships between the school and local faith communities help to create a constructive context for the teaching of these subjects. In all schools, when teaching these subjects, the religious background of all pupils must be taken into account when planning teaching, so that the topics that are included in the core content in this guidance are appropriately handled. Schools must ensure they comply with the relevant provisions of the Equality Act 2010, under which religion or belief are amongst the protected characteristics. All schools may teach about faith perspectives. (Department for Education 2019, §s 19, 20, and 21)

It should be noted that reference to all schools does not distinguish between faith-designated schools and other schools.

At Parkfield, the teaching at issue was not primarily about sex and relationships education but concerned a curriculum called *No Outsiders*. This addressed the protected characteristics of the Equality Act 2010, with a particular emphasis on LGBTQ issues. However, it represented the school's approach to teaching 'fundamental British values' and the Prevent agenda. The school also had posters attached to the railings declaring its commitment to the Equality Act 2010, as well as a touchscreen for entry into the school on which visitors (including parents) had to indicate their adherence to the Act. The curriculum used lessons on gender identity and same-sex relationships to teach about diversity and difference more generally, including ethnic and religious difference. The latter was focused on the holocaust and that 'Christians are welcome here'. There was no discussion of Islamophobia. Nor, in the examples of different family types, was there any treatment of multigenerational families which would have been part of the experience of many pupils. It sought to introduce them to 'life in modern Britain', without their presence, or others like them, being acknowledged. The school was part of a multi-academy trust of four schools. Parkfield and one other school had over 95 per cent of pupils from a Muslim faith background, while the other two schools were white-majority schools. The curriculum was only introduced into the Muslim-majority schools. As in the case of Anderton Park, the parents had sought to be consulted, but in this case that was denied without that being in breach of guidelines because the curriculum was part of the teaching of 'fundamental British values'. This curriculum had been introduced precisely because of a concern of a deficit in this regard on the part of Muslim parents.

Conclusion

The question that needs to be asked is why religious liberty has proven hard to defend. One reason is the anomalous nature of religion itself in the context of 'equalities'. Those associated with gender, sexual orientation, disability, age and so on are easily justiciable as individual characteristics in terms of which redress can be sought for alleged discrimination in the provision of services. Religion is, in principle, about 'collective interactions'. It is not that 'religious discrimination' cannot be made equivalent to other forms of discrimination, but it is much more likely to be as an action brought by someone of no-faith seeking redress against a religious organization or by someone dissident in their faith claiming discrimination against other members. In this context, religious communities sometimes require special dispensation in relation to other protected characteristics. Thus, single-sex ordination for religious office is allowed, as is single-sex schooling (as we have seen, something advocated by the British upper-middle class and not just by religious communities).

As Julian Rivers (2020) has pointed out, one problem is that the form of equality that is of interest to religious communities is the equal liberty to live according to the requirements of their faith. This necessarily includes the liberty to hold that God intended marriage as a sacrament between a man and a woman for purposes of procreation, to repudiate divorce and to believe homosexuality is sinful. The requirement under law is *not to discriminate*, not to affirm. Yet it is precisely what 'communities of belonging' may affirm that is perceived as problematic from the point of view of groups self-constituted as 'communities of choice'. Ironically, secular liberals invoke their right not to affirm in declaring their freedom to describe religion as false.

For this reason, some secular liberals have begun to question religious liberty as a human right, arguing that a parent's right to educate their child in line with their own religious and philosophical beliefs has to be set against a child's right to choose their own idea of the good. Thus, Clayton et al. argue that 'Current legislation is too permissive to parents and insufficiently attentive to children's interests, in particular their interest in autonomy' (2018, 9). This is necessarily an argument, in principle, against religious liberty as normally understood. However, any incipient conflict with local religious traditions is rendered moot by an implicit recognition of Bellah's argument of the alignment between secular individualism and Christianity. Of course, in England, there is a practical reason for this concession; it would be far too expensive to take over the assets of church schools to run them on a secular basis.

Indeed, the current head of Ofsted, Amanda Spielman, has gone out of her way to indicate that any strictures about religion apply only to minority faiths. Thus, similarly to Clayton and his colleagues, she has argued,

> most children spend less than a fifth of their childhood hours in schools and most of the rest with their family. And so if children aren't being taught these values at home, or worse are being encouraged to resist them, then schools are our main opportunity to fill that gap. . . . This, I believe, was where the so-called Trojan Horse schools failed. Not only were there issues with promoting British Values in many of those schools, but in some cases members of the community were attempting to bring extreme views into school life. The very places that should have been broadening horizons and outlooks were instead reinforcing a backward view of society. (2017, np)

The problem, she proposes, does not lie with religion as such, and mainstream Christian religion was exempt from her strictures: 'one of [the] values as articulated in the definition of British values is "mutual respect for and

tolerance of those with different faiths and beliefs and for those without faith".
It is a happy fact that almost every Church of England school we visit takes
that value seriously' (2017, np). There was and is no evidence that this value is
not also endorsed by minority religious communities in Britain. Nor was there,
ultimately, any evidence that the 'Trojan horse' schools were deficient in this
respect, despite it being enshrined in media and government discourse.

I have suggested that the perceived problem of Muslim engagement with
the schooling of their children should be understood in terms of a legitimate
(multicultural) demand for equal participation in civic life. That it has not been
seen in this way is a serious limitation of liberalism and the 'reconciliation' of
potentially conflicting claims of right. Thus, Clayton et al. identify two legitimate
constraints on parental freedom: 'Parents' freedom to educate their children as
they prefer should be constrained by (i) children's interest in receiving their fair
share of educational goods, and (ii) the wider society's interest in the cultivation
of educational goods such as democratic competence, tolerance and mutual
respect' (2018, 5). Muslim children in Alum Rock have been denied their fair
share of educational goods as a consequence of false accusations of hostility to
values of 'democratic competence, tolerance and mutual respect'. The latter arose
as a consequence of prejudiced representations about the characteristics of Alum
Rock as a 'community of belonging', and it did so in the context of the community
taking steps to secure for their children their fair share of educational goods by
exercising their right to full participation.

A spectre is haunting Europe — the spectre of Islam and, more generally, of
diverse communities of belonging. Liberals are comfortable understanding the
mistreatment of religious minorities in terms of the protected characteristic of
race and ethnicity, as well as understanding it as a form of racism. Otherwise,
they believe that to treat it in terms of a right to religious expression is to endorse
conservativism. On the other hand, conservatives seem unable to embrace
minority religious communities precisely because their members are typically
poor and non-white. I have not had the space to address similar issues across
European countries. However, there is no reason to believe the situation in
England is unique and, in fact, there is growing hostility to Muslim citizens
across Europe based on secular liberal principles (as distinct from that directed
on religious grounds in, say, Hungary or Poland). This is evident in Denmark
and in France. Indeed, England is potentially aligning with France and its idea
of *laïcité*. Religious liberty is now at the heart of what it would mean for Europe
now to be just. It is time for Fortress Europe to lay down its arms against ethnic
minorities and their religious commitments.

Philanthropic hyphenated identity

Shia Pakistani–Scottish health activism in Scotland

Morteza Hashemi

Introduction

This chapter discusses the grassroots social activism and philanthropy of a community of Pakistani–Scottish citizens, marked by their Shia Islamic faith and darker skin. These activists are behind one of the most successful blood donation campaigns in Europe. The Imam Hussain Blood Donation Campaign (IHBDC) is the largest cross-ethnic blood donation campaign in the UK. It is a grassroots campaign run by young British Shia Muslims who work in close collaboration with NHS Blood and Transplant (in England) and the Scottish National Blood Transfusion Service (SNBTS) to involve Muslim communities in blood drives (Spellman-Poots 2012).

The IHBDC was founded in Manchester in 2006 by a handful of Shia Muslim university students. They found blood donation consistent with the spirit of Muharram, the month of commemoration of Imam Hussain, and in particular of his sacrifice and the spilling of his blood in the battle of Karbala in 680 CE. Imam Hussain, the grandson of the prophet, is a central figure in Shia Islam. In different cultural contexts of the subcontinent, Iran, Bahrain, Lebanon and Europe, the Shia have reanimated the story of Muharram and the murder of the Imam in the hands of the unjust ruler. The controversial Tatbir (Arabic: تطبير) or Ghame-zani (Persian: قمه‌زنی) is one of those rituals, which includes bloodletting and self-flagellation. It is controversial because many Shia authority figures see it against the teachings of Shia Islam. Thus, we have a situation where Tatbir is banned in Iran, while it is practised in some parts of Lebanon (Hashemi 2020a). Nevertheless, the point is that commemorating the sacrifice of Imam Hussain has always been tied to blood-related collective practices. The naming of the

IHBDC thus refers to a newly devised ritual of *donating* blood to honour Imam Hussain's sacrifice, this time in the UK. The campaigners' efforts have been received with considerable gratitude by the National Health Service (NHS) and British politicians. In 2019, the British prime minister gave the Points of Light Award to Mustafa Khan, the volunteer co-ordinator of the IHBDC in London. The UK government's website describes the IHBDC in this way:

> Supported by hundreds of volunteers, the 'Imam Hussain Blood Donation Campaign' has managed to generate over 4,000 blood donations; enough to provide blood for up to 12,492 adults or 29,148 infants. Mustafa organises the blood drives, which aim to increase the number of regular blood donors from Muslim communities, by hosting the drives in local Mosques and Islamic centres where both Muslims and non-Muslims can attend. (Points of Light 2019)

In November 2014, the Scottish Parliament passed a motion (code: S4M-11308) recognizing the philanthropic engagement of the IHBDC in Scotland. The motion acknowledged the Scottish Shia community's 'constructive effort to encourage Muslim residents of Edinburgh and the Lothian region to become more active in donating blood to help save lives' (Scott 2014). A few years later, in October 2018, the UK parliament also passed an Early Day Motion (EDM 1733) in support of the IHBDC and thanking the chairman of the Scottish Ahlul Bayt Society (SABS), Shabir Beg. The society is an umbrella organization of the Scottish Shia charities and cultural centres, and also organizes the IHBDC blood drives in Scotland. At its beginning, the IHBDC was held only during the month of Muharram. Currently, however, the blood drives are organized throughout the year and in relation to the demands of the NHS. During the Covid-19 pandemic and lockdown in 2020 and beyond, which led to a shortage of donated blood, the campaigners have contributed to community efforts to fight the pandemic by working with the NHS and donors to coordinate visits to the donation centres.

This chapter argues that the philanthropic engagements the Pakistani–Scottish community has organized in Edinburgh and Glasgow represent a struggle by a marginalized populace to restore an altruism to philanthropic activity, which is often undertaken for incompatible, economic motives. The by-product of such philanthropic work is the legitimizing of the dual identity of the Pakistani–Scottish community, a 'philanthropic hyphenated identity'. In other words, the activists and blood donors are designing a new, modern religious ritual of giving blood, which like many other rituals brings together the allegedly dichotomous aspects of social relations. In this case, the dichotomy is the anonymous altruism and the love of the neighbour on the one hand and building social capital on the other. This chapter discusses this process, based on an ethnographic study of the IHBDC (and, as the sponsor of the Campaign in Scotland, the SABS) from 2017 to 2020, as well as archived lectures given by the community activists.

Recapturing a more altruistic form of philanthropy

Social scientific studies of philanthropy have always refused to take charity uncritically at its face value. This section reviews philanthropic giving from the standpoint of several different theoretical frameworks. Drawing on Richard Titmuss, we begin by considering whether the blood donation campaigns of British Shia Muslims can be seen as indicative of a way in which ordinary citizens can reassert a form of philanthropic activity that is more altruistic than the philanthropy of the wealthy routinely unmasked by critical sociologists.

The problem with the altruism of the rich

The philanthropy of the rich tends to be debunked from a particular theoretical perspective; however, we need to be careful to distinguish such philanthropy from the philanthropy of ordinary citizens.[1] Frequently, an undifferentiated notion of philanthropy is juxtaposed with regulation. For instance, Linsey McGoey in her book entitled *No Such Thing as Free Gift* (2015) asks, '[w]hat's the best way to make sure that the poor have a share in a country's growing wealth: Regulation? Taxes? Philanthropy?' (McGoey 2015, 14). Do we need charities such as the Bill and Melinda Gates Foundation or more regulations and taxes for the rich? The typical answer to the question is formulated in an intriguing piece published in *Jacobin* magazine in 2015. The author tries to expose 'the flawed analytical framework' of movements such as Effective Altruism (1): 'Rather than solely creating an individualised culture of giving, we should be challenging capitalism's institutionalised taking' (Snow 2015). Thus, the duality of philanthropy versus regulation is aligned with the duality of individualism versus collectivism. The argument is that crafting a philanthropic identity is a game played by the wealthy individuals, from Hollywood celebrities to the owners of Silicon Valley firms (Maclean and Harvey 2020). As counter-intuitive as it may seem, the rise of philanthropy is not necessarily a sign of a healthy and humane society: 'Philanthropists themselves are often the first to admit that their philanthropy is aimed at preserving rather than redistributing wealth' (McGoey 2015, 28).

We can also think about this in terms of the long-term consequences of philanthropy for the well-being of ordinary citizens.[2] Individualized, philanthropic assistance might be substantial, but might also cause, or cover for, the retraction of existing governmental supports (McGoey 2015). Such retraction can easily be presented as support for civil society, for citizens' self-regulation or, in the words of David Cameron, for a 'Big Society' (2). Yet such individualized giving cannot substitute for the grassroots movements necessary to protect citizens' rights, such as the fundamental right to healthcare. Such rights can easily be imperilled by events like the Covid-19 pandemic and the subsequent financial crisis, which have required a powerful state response. Without a strong, state-provided safety net, citizens would be defenceless before the crisis. The altruism of the rich can be seen as a community-involved egoism, which can deprive ordinary citizens of the sense of unity they might gain by collectively fighting for their common good.

Yet scepticism about philanthropy is not restricted to the altruism of the rich and philanthro-capitalism (McGoey 2012). The very concept of a gift-relationship has been scrutinized by philosophers and anthropologists. In *Thus Spoke Zarathustra*, Nietzsche reminds us of the complexity of the gift-relationship: 'Great obligations do not make grateful, but revengeful; and when a small kindness is not forgotten, it becometh a gnawing worm' (Nietzsche 1986, 94). Gift-giving creates an obligation on behalf of the receiver, and the gift is thus a social phenomenon which incarnates interpersonal relations of obligation and indebtedness. Gifts are signs of the generosity of the giver, and as such they highlight a tacit responsibility for reciprocation, perhaps in the form of a favour or even direct compensation. Nietzsche's Zarathustra considers gift-giving an art, requiring some skill, of preventing the receiver from becoming conscious of this feeling of indebtedness (Schrift 1997, 3).

In a similar vein, Marcel Mauss, in his foundational text on gift-exchange, suggested that the gift-relationship cannot simply be understood as a relation of disinterested giving and receiving. There are underlying rules that govern the circulation of gifts, which Mauss showed already existed in archaic societies. Accordingly, he challenged the idea that market, as a social phenomenon, emerged after the invention of money (Mauss 1966). One of Mauss' goals was to show that, before finding its 'modern' form, markets already existed in the form of the gift-relationship. He also reminds us that there is an implicit danger in receiving, not only the pledge but also the exchanged object. In ancient Germanic languages, the word for gift means both a present and a poison. In certain circumstances, a present of a drink could well be a poison (Mauss 1966, 62).

This is an extreme example, but gift-relationships inherently involve some sort of ambiguity, confusion and uncertainty. They are open to interpretation and can initiate either an emotional bond and union or mutual hostility and intimidation.

Pierre Bourdieu challenges the centrality of reciprocation and mutuality in characterization of the gift. He highlights the insufficiency of both objectivist approaches, which see gift-relationship through the lens of market exchange, and subjectivist approaches, which emphasizes the individual intentions of the giver and receiver. Instead, he interprets gift-exchange in terms of a lag in reciprocity. With gift-exchange, there is an expectation of a delay in repaying the 'debt', and this is what distinguishes it from the economic phenomena of the market. While the receiver knows that the gift must be returned, they are not expected to do so immediately but only after an appropriate delay. Bourdieu sees in this practice a 'reality-denying reality' or a necessary fiction (Bourdieu 1992). At base, gift-exchange involves a collective transmutation of the 'inevitably interested relations imposed by kinship, neighbourhood or work, into elective relations of reciprocity, through the sincere fiction of a disinterested exchange' (Bourdieu 1992, 112). This idea fed into the development of Bourdieu's notion of symbolic capital.

Ralph Waldo Emerson and other figures of the Romantic movement also recognized a similarly fictional character to practices of gift-exchange, which they rejected on normative grounds. Emerson tried to unmask gift-exchange as an inauthentic 'intellectual trick' (Emerson 1950): 'Rings and other jewels are not gifts, but apologies for gifts. The only gift is a portion of thyself. Thou must bleed for me' (Emerson and Atkinson 1950, 403). The true and authentic gift for Emerson is love, which comes through suffering. Such suffering contradicts any expectation of a benefit from a gift given in return. The giver who incurs the pain of authentic giving exemplifies sincerity in practice. Giving a 'portion of oneself' is, from this Romantic standpoint, the ultimate form of philanthropy. For Emerson, however generous it may look, the philanthropy of the rich does not include 'a portion of oneself'.

Returning to the question of this section, what would the rich receive instead of their non-gifts? By a non-gift, the rich are gaining more, and in different forms. For instance, in their study, Mairi MacLean and Charles Harvey discuss types of contemporary entrepreneurial philanthropic identities.

A salient if under-researched feature of the new age of global inequalities is the rise to prominence of entrepreneurial philanthropy, the pursuit of transformational social goals through philanthropic investment in projects animated by entrepreneurial principles. (MacLean and Harvey 2020, 637)

Wealthy entrepreneurs craft philanthropic identities as a way of extending their presence, and soft-power, in the wider society (MacLean and Harvey 2020, 638). Such philanthropy aims at controlling civil society, not helping it flourish. Its mechanisms must thus be exposed and unmasked by sociologists as a mere whitewashing of selfish interests. Nonetheless, the recognition of the other forms of philanthropy characteristic of ordinary citizens is as crucial a task as exposing the self-interested 'giving' of the rich. The philanthropic activities of the marginalized, in particular, should not be interpreted as a way of subjugating others.

Particularity of skin versus universality of blood

Emerson's example of an honest gift is blood. Less metaphorically, through blood donation, we give our vital body liquid to others. This was one of the central themes of Richard Titmuss' groundbreaking book *The Gift Relationship: From Human Blood to Social Policy* (1970), published three years before his death. His question was this: could we find the gift-exchange mechanism that Mauss described at work in the medical care systems of an individualized, segmented and highly complex modern society? (Titmuss 2018, 176). Titmuss' fundamental thesis was that we should not underestimate the extent of gift-relationships with strangers in our diversified modern world. As he depicts it, the anonymous blood donation is a modern-day version of the classic gift-exchange, establishing a gift-relationship with fellow citizens.

In the 1970s, a decade before the advent of neoliberal politics, Titmuss already anticipated the difficulties of applying the laws of the market to blood (and tissue) exchanges. In his comparative study of blood donation systems in the United States and the United Kingdom, he suggested that if we define blood as a commodity that people can buy and sell, we will turn citizens into self-seeking economic agents. Within a market exchange, blood-sellers would identify their own benefit and happiness as separate from that of other people. Citizens would prioritize self-love over the love of strangers. Furthermore, by applying the laws of the market, one might deprive a society of mechanisms for 'transcending the good of self-love'. For Titmuss, the very mission of a policy-maker is to create an environment in which people will be compassionate towards strangers and fellow citizens, hence increasing social solidarity.

Besides the moral problem, selling blood endangers the clean supply of blood because such health policy encourages the emergence of a group of professional blood-sellers. Titmuss observed that untruthfulness among donors increases in the private sector. Voluntary blood donors, on the other hand, are less likely to donate contaminated blood. Titmuss' main insight was that the NHS plan to promote voluntary blood donation was also an appropriate policy mechanism for institutionalizing a gift-relationship among strangers, which would reinforce fellow-feeling in a society (Titmuss 2018, 207).

> What we do suggest [. . .] is that the ways in which society organises and structures its social institutions – and particularly its health and welfare systems – can encourage or discourage the altruistic in man; such systems can foster integration or alienation; to recall Mauss, they can allow the 'theme of the gift', of generosity towards strangers, to spread among and between social groups and generations. (Titmuss 2018, 190)

While Titmuss studied blood donation in its institutional settings in the United States and the United Kingdom, Copeman and Street have studied blood extraction (including blood donation and the political art of painting with blood) in its political context in India (Copeman and Street 2014). They suggested that one can draw a parallel between the Indian sanguinary politics and Gandhi's style of transformative fasting as a means of 'public positioning of self and cause' which promises a 'political purification' (Copeman and Street 2014, 213) and seeks to 'persuade from the moral high ground of political asceticism' (Copeman and Street 2014, 186). 'If fasting withdraws the body from the world, blood donation extends the body into it' (Copeman and Street 2014, 187). Those forms of activism can be distinguished in two ways: first, the political fast leaves some room for speculation and doubts about the honesty of the activist. But blood extraction is a more visually convincing demonstration of political commitment. A bag of blood is either filled with the red liquid or not. One can see the process of extraction as a political contribution. Second, there is a common misconception in the subcontinent that there are permanent and negative physical effects of giving blood. In the light of this misconception, any political activism which is related to blood extraction is seen as representing a 'deep-held commitment' (Copeman and Street 2014, 213).

A similar effort to locate a morally higher ground is behind the philanthropic blood donation of the Shia Pakistani–Scottish community. In this case, the morally higher ground is sought as the basis of a politically effective identity, which I will name a 'philanthropic hyphenated identity'. We can also look at it in this way: ironically, the philanthropic hyphenated identity of the marginalized is able to function only if the philanthropic activity succeeds in attaining a genuine altruism and purity of intention. Anonymous blood donation, and selfless community engagement through the NHS, is a kind of moral purification that can create a sense of moral obligation in the powerful, which compels them to recognize and acknowledge the presence and value of the marginalized bodies.

The concept of 'body politics' is mostly associated with feminist approaches but has also been extended to other aspects of the experience of less advantaged groups. The term encapsulates the idea that there is a deep-rooted struggle between individuals, institutions and governments over the regulation of bodies (Brown and Gershon 2019). Bodies with different skin colour, above all with brown skin, are regulated through migration policies, community programmes and integration guidelines, which draw boundaries between citizens and non-citizens, those who have rights versus those who do not (Mayblin 2019). The different skin-tone of ethnic minorities in Europe implicates their bodies as a constant and conscious part of their everyday struggle. Blood and organ donation and the sacrifice of a vital body liquid for the common good, by those marked by their darker skin colour, challenge such regulations from a higher moral ground. Through the grassroots blood donation campaign of the minority, the ethnically marginalized reclaim their skin and proactively turn their already problematized body into a battleground of their choice. The insertion of a hollow needle through the brown skin to draw the red blood is also a move in a moral battle for a universal truth. Under a particular-coloured skin there is a universally donatable substance. A universality is hidden under particularity, and a unifying truth concealed under a cover of plurality. As Janet Carsten shows, there are resonances between blood's material, medical and moral connotations (Carsten 2013, 144).

> The many possibilities that exist for inserting blood or other tissues into discourses which are politically or morally charged are suggestive of the capacities these bodily materials have for metaphorical extension. Even when it is apparently detached from its source, and contained in sample tubes or blood bags, blood nevertheless retains a symbolic potential. (Carsten 2013, 144–5)

Similarly, it could be argued that blood, and the somatic pain of donation, has the capacity to recapture a purer form of philanthropy from its corporate accretions. It could be seen as a salvage mission, rescuing the nominal purpose of charity from its manipulative functioning. On the one hand, the Bourdieusian 'delay' and 'lag' in reciprocation is not the essential part of the gift-relationships thus constituted with fellow citizens. On the other, the Titmussian institutional setting is important as a context for the transaction. Nevertheless, the IHBDC is about reclaiming control of the battleground over the donor's already problematized body.

Philanthropic hyphenated identity

'We are as Scottish as you are.' This was the final sentence in a speech by one of the members of the steering committee of the SABS in an Eid Al-Adha dinner party. The annual dinner was held in a meeting room in a luxury hotel on the Holyrood Road in Edinburgh. One could easily walk from the Scottish Parliament to the venue. Among the religious figures attending the dinner were (1) Leo William Cushley, Roman Catholic Archbishop of St Andrews and Edinburgh, (2) Colin Sinclair, Moderator of the General Assembly of the Church of Scotland, (3) Mark Strange, Bishop of Moray, Ross and Caithness and Primus of the Scottish Episcopal Church, (4) Dr David Pickering, Moderator of the National Synod of Scotland of the United Reformed Church, and (5) Syed Muhammad Suqlain Shah, the chairman of Darul-Ehsan in Scotland. The last named is a Sunni and Sufi Muslim figure. However, the Shia attendees were mostly from the community, with careers as teachers, employees, university students and small business owners. The contrast between the mostly white guests with powerful legislative or religious positions and the ordinary careers of the Scottish-Pakistani attendees is worthy of note.

Besides Abrahamic religions, the guests were united by a shared sense of appreciation of their Scottishness. The Scottish flag was displayed in the room, some of the guests wore kilts and the theme of national belonging arose in several of the formal speeches. The dinner was hosted by a young British Shia cleric and member of the SABS, Imam Sayed Ali Abbas Razawi. Before his concluding remarks, the Christian and Sunni Muslim figures delivered their formal speeches. In his lecture, a Christian figure humorously pointed out that the leaders of the different branches of the church in Scotland meet once per year – in the Eid Al-Adha dinner of the Shia Muslim community. In the initial invitation for the dinner, Nicola Sturgeon, the first minister of Scotland, was billed as the special guest. However, it turned out that she could not attend. Instead, she sent Ashten Denham, the Scottish National Party (SNP) Member of the Scottish Parliament for the constituency of Edinburgh Eastern, to represent her. Nonetheless, Sturgeon has appeared in other events organized by SABS, including blood drives. In her 2018 visit to an IHBDC blood drive in Edinburgh Donor Centre, Sturgeon said:

> I was pleased to be able to visit the Edinburgh Blood Donor Centre today to thank donors and staff, and to learn more about the valuable role the Scottish Ahlul Bayt Society plays in this campaign, by working to encourage the Muslim community across Edinburgh and the Lothians to give blood. ('First Minister of Scotland' 2018)

How has the small community of Pakistani–Scottish Shia Muslims been able to acquire this level of social and political recognition in Scotland? In other places, I have suggested that the SNP's role, through their active community-engagement initiative, is substantial (Hashemi 2020b). However, creative leveraging of the social capital obtained through their philanthropic activities also has some role to play in this success. The SABS' main efforts are focused on the well-being of the Scottish Shia, the blood donation campaign and interfaith dialogue with other religious communities (including Sikh, Sunni, Jewish and Christian). Yet these efforts are interconnected. A philanthropic engagement allows the acquisition of credibility and social capital, which is then ingeniously put to use for another effort. As with the gift-relationship, reciprocity and trust can be the foundations of social capital (Anheier and List 2006, 234), and the gift of blood can increase the social capital of the community within the larger society. The physical, somatic aspect of donation implies a sincerity that could be interpreted as a testament to a true allegiance to society. The empathy generated in this way is put to use in finding common grounds with other religious communities.

There are many intellectual strategies that can be adopted in interfaith and inter-religious dialogue. One approach reflects the secular understanding of tolerance. It assumes or seeks to secure a neutral public sphere, beyond any religious affiliation, within which the representation of groups with diverging affiliation will be tolerated. Another method, advocated by figures like Hossein Nasr, involves a comparative study of religions with the aim of discovering common, core principles. Such knowledge is thus both the knowledge of the sacred principles and itself a sacred knowledge (Nasr 2007). This approach is also known as perennialism. It goes without saying that only believers can adopt such an intellectual approach, and it is an inherently inner-religious attitude. For instance, one can find similarities (but also differences) between the theo-anthropological conceptions of blood in Christianity and Islam. While in the former, blood is linked to *sacrifice*, in Islam it is closely connected to *creation*. Hence, Catholic Christianity celebrates the sacrifice of the Mass, believing that the ritual bread and wine are transubstantiated into the body and blood of Christ. Yet, in Quran, blood is connected to the power of God, and His creation of man from a blood clot (Netton 2017, 86). The perennialist approach would then be to look for a hidden theme or principle beyond the pluralities of interpretations of God's miracle and creation. The core principles of the two Abrahamic religions could then work as a framework within which dialogue and agreement are possible.

Yet there is a third pragmatic theory of dialogue, which pursues interfaith dialogue by building on praxis. That is a dialogue which begins in gift, or some sort of 'pre-verbal' communication, which shows courtesy and serves to build trust. There are elements of this third method in SABS' strategy for interfaith dialogue. In a lecture, Imam Razawi explains the plan for dealing with the plurality of religions in the modern world and also the ways that one needs to look at multiculturalism. He believes that the virtuous life is, ideally, the embodiment of a constant movement from the world of multiplicity and plurality to the state of unity, which is the divine state:

> The message is that we first and foremost need to take care of our societies. Before spirituality came, before mysticism came, before a form of theology was developed, the thing that Moses does is to give us parameters. He said these are parameters to live by: 'I have made you restricted to a particular way. Otherwise, the being is scattered. You have thousands of ideas in your mind. I want to take you to unity and save you from this multiplicity.'

In other words, according to Imam Razawi, religions are there to give believers a map and a method by which to train themselves in pursuit of perfection. But how about the non-believers? This is an essential question because of the context of the lecture, given in front of a mostly non-Muslim audience. Imam Razawi recounts that Muhammad led people as a prophet for twenty-three years. As a prophet, he lived the first ten years with the polytheists in Mecca and thirteen years with Christians and Jews in Medina. Thus, he showed us how we can live with people who do not share our belief system.

> At the age of forty, he [Muhammad] gathered the polytheists, and he said to them that: 'you have seen my life. What would you say are two things about me which stand out?' They responded that 'the two things are that you are truthful and trustworthy.' These are the two fundamental qualities that are required to develop any society.

Imam Razawi continues by comparing this with a story from Confucius.

> Confucius once said to one of the kings: 'If you want to develop a cosmopolitan society, that is a society which is developed and well-rooted, there are three things that you need. Firstly, you need to give them food. If you do not feed them, they are not going to respond to you. Secondly, you should give them weapons to protect themselves. And thirdly, you must win their trust.'

There is a common theme in Razawi's interpretation of the strategies of interaction with others adopted by Moses, Mohammad and Confucius. That theme is about winning people's trust. Razawi suggests that such trust-building is one of the keys to, and foundations of, collaboration and common living in a multifaith society. Arguably, it comes before faith and any form of religious affiliation. As said earlier, blood donation has such a function for the Pakistani–Scottish community. For the same reason, on the SABS website one can see eight menu options. One of them is about the activities of SABS, the others are about Islamic articles and one is about giving blood, with the necessary information for booking a donation appointment. The way that the community leaders of the Shia Pakistani–Scottish community present it, blood donation is consistent with the symbolism of their denomination. They present it as a theologically meaningful gesture. It is also seen as a way of winning people's trust and establishing a philanthropic identity (and reputation). Thus, the IHBDC plays a central role in their activities across Scotland, and they actively try to attach their image to such philanthropic engagements. My extensive interviews with community members, donors and younger campaign activists also show that they have accepted the sanctity of this charity work. They approach it as a religious sacrifice or a gift to both the unseen God and the anonymous neighbour. Yet the by-product of creating social capital for community members is that it embodies the truth of their faith in a multicultural society.

As mentioned earlier, Ralph Waldo Emerson believed that '[t]he only gift is a portion of thyself', and the honesty of the relationship is based on the creed that 'thou must bleed for me'. In the mentioned Eid Al-Adha dinner, the IHBDC had pull-up banners placed around the venue. The official SABS banner also includes a Hadith from Imam Ali, the founder of Shia denomination and the son-in-law of the prophet: 'Man is either your brother in faith, or your equal in humanity.' The community takes pride in bleeding for their fellow citizens and wants others to acknowledge their hyphenated philanthropic identity. In brief, they are invested in the construction of an image of themselves as people who are able to go beyond the surface of the skin, people who are able to bleed for their fellow citizens.

Conclusion

There are many ways of crafting a philanthropic identity. The rich, Silicon Valley firm owners, celebrities and retired politicians extend their presence and relevance in society through a kind of limited, well-advertised giving. One thing the philanthropic identities of the wealthy have in common with those of the marginalized is that for both 'philanthropic identities are matters of consequence' (MacLean and Harvey 2020, 649). They are deemed to be successful when they make an impact on other people. Yet the differences are much greater than the similarities. I have suggested that the philanthropic hyphenated identity of Pakistani–Scottish Muslims is not economically motivated. It is more about acknowledgement, recognition and building trust between communities. Part of the Shia community in Scotland is heavily engaged in the blood donation campaigns and collaborations with the SNBTS. There are two aspects to their engagement. First, giving blood is an individualized, isolated and anonymous procedure. That means donors are not recognized as individuals, and they consider their donation an act of faith, and altruism, not something they might benefit from personally. It is an act of charity and sacrifice which should be concealed. The SNBTS guidelines on the anonymity of donation guarantee the hiddenness of the gift. Second, one of the objectives of the community of faith is to orchestrate the modern ritual of blood giving through the construction of a philanthropic hyphenated identity. This is a way of winning the trust of other communities through a vital gift that is also an engagement in body politics. Here, the philanthropy requires recognition and acknowledgement to be considered effective. The IHBDC is thus the result of an acute compromise between hiddenness and visibility. Furthermore, it represents a balance between religious practices and civic duty. Bleeding for others is an inner-religiously justified, and theologically consistent, act for the Shia, associated with the reference to Imam Hussain, his martyrdom and his sacrificed blood. However, the inner-religiously meaningful, modern ritual of giving blood is also associated with a search for the most universal aspects of religiosity and the establishment of a universal foundation for engagement with non-believers. Institutionally supported philanthropy provides such universal foundations. It goes beyond differences in belief systems. Through a newly devised religious ritual, the small Shia Pakistani–Scottish community is using the metaphorical connotations of blood to challenge prejudices based on their skin colour. The IHBDC reclaims the already problematized body of the 'minority' and goes beyond the skin to focus on the universal life-giving fluid, blood. Based on the universality attached to blood, and the universal admiration of philanthropy, these activists are able to craft and legitimize their own distinct philanthropic hyphenated identity.

An embedded minority

Young Alevis in Germany and their search for identity

Martina Loth

Introduction

Germany's recent role as a major host of refugees, many of whom are Muslims, masks a longer story of immigration dating back to the well-known Anwerbeabkommen (labour recruitment agreement). Since the 1960s, waves of migrant workers from countries, including Turkey, filled labour shortages in the industrial sector through a series of bilateral agreements. Nearly sixty years later, Germany has one of the highest Muslim populations in Europe with an estimated 4.9 million Muslims (Pew Research data 2016), more than half of whom (i.e. an estimated 2.8 million) are of Turkish origin, making the country home to the highest number of Turks outside of Turkey (Mikrozensus 2018). These significant numbers mask, yet again, a phenomenon that is difficult to measure but important to explore: the changes and challenges faced by individual Muslim migrants and their descendants, a demographic that is increasingly perceived with suspicion. It is at best an unfounded suspicion given that survey results from the Religionsmonitor initiative conducted by Germany's leading Bertelsmann Foundation suggest that Turkish migrants continue to develop and maintain multifaceted relationships and hence their social participation is improving.[1] An additional survey by Pollack et al. demonstrates that most people of Turkish origin in Germany feel like 'second-class citizens' despite their efforts to integrate (Pollack et al. 2016).

This study focuses on a particular minority group within Germany's 'larger' minority population: the Alevis. As Procházka-Eisl notes, 'The Alevis are a religious community on the periphery of Shia Islam. The name "Alevi" means "Adherents of ʿAli," alluding to Muhammad's son-in-law and cousin ʿAli ibn

Abi Talib, who enjoys extraordinary veneration among Alevis' (Procházka-Eisl 2016, 1). Despite the special worship of Ali, Alevis are not to be confused with Shiites and Arabic-speaking *Alawis* (Aksünger-Kizil 2018, 128; Vorhoff 1998, 237). The Bektaşi 'Alevism was developed in Central Anatolia during the 13th century by itinerant Muslim mystics' (Procházka-Eisl 2016, 1), with one of its most central figures, the itinerant preacher Hacı Bektaş Veli (Aksünger-Kizil 2018, 128). 'An ongoing discussion attempts to define the nature and identity of Alevism', whether it is a 'purely religious community, an ethnic identity, a political faction, or some special way of life', but '(n)either its scope, nor its content are clearly defined' (Massicard 2003, 125). Due to the absence of a codified, written religious canon, the religion has evolved in different directions. That is why, today, we can observe a spectrum of interpretations that include, and at times combine, religious, mystical, socialist, Kurdish-national or Turkish-national, philosophical or secular aspects (Spuler-Stegemann 2003), as well as 'a way of life mainly characterised by tolerance and critical-mindedness (aligned with) the very tradition of democracy' (Massicard 2003, 128).

It is worth noting that if Alevism were to constitute a religion sui generis (i.e. of its own kind and category), it would be the third biggest one in Germany after Christianity and Islam[2] (Kalbarczyk and Loth 2017, 89). Nevertheless, Alevis are often perceived in the popular German imaginary as 'Turkish Muslims'.

By showcasing the plurality among young Alevis in Germany, I give voice and visibility to individual strategies for confronting and responding to the growing climate of hostility facing those perceived as Muslims. Integral to the latter is the complex manner in which individuals seek to gain clarity and understanding of their own cultural identity in an introspective process of 'culturalization' that involves individualized definitions of Alevism juxtaposed with pressures from mainstream society and combined, at times, with those stemming from their own household.

Numbers: Significant differences between 'Alevis' and 'Muslims'

Further on, I take a deeper look at three central themes captured by the aforementioned surveys: integration, religiosity and acceptance. Using Pollack et al.'s survey[3] as a point of departure, I will focus on the identity formation of four Alevis in their early twenties.

While the general outcomes of the survey have been discussed extensively, no one has yet looked separately at the answers of those people who identified themselves as 'Alevi' (92 in total) in comparison with those who identified themselves as 'Muslims' (999 in total), of whom we can assume the vast majority follows Sunni Islam, as this group is significantly dominating.[4] However, as the question of whether Alevism should be categorized *within* Islam or *outside* Islam is one of the most debated topics in the German diaspora (cf. Kalbarczyk and Loth 2017, 89), we cannot exclude the possibility that a person of Alevi origin identified him- or herself as 'Muslim' when answering this question. Both Alevis and Muslims gave similar answers to the survey question 'However hard I try, I will never be accepted as part of German society',[5] but with slightly more agreement from the Alevis: 'Strongly agree' – 29.42 per cent Alevi versus 26.3 per cent Muslim; 'Somewhat agree' – 29.1 per cent Alevi versus 27.0 per cent Muslim.

However, the following results highlight how the Alevi experience is often defined in contrast (or at times in opposition) to Sunni Islam – a point often missed by members of mainstream German society and attitudinal surveys that conflate such categories:

- Alevis feel more 'content overall' about living in Germany than Muslims: 64 per cent of Alevis compared to 48 per cent of Muslims, as illustrated in Figure 5.1.

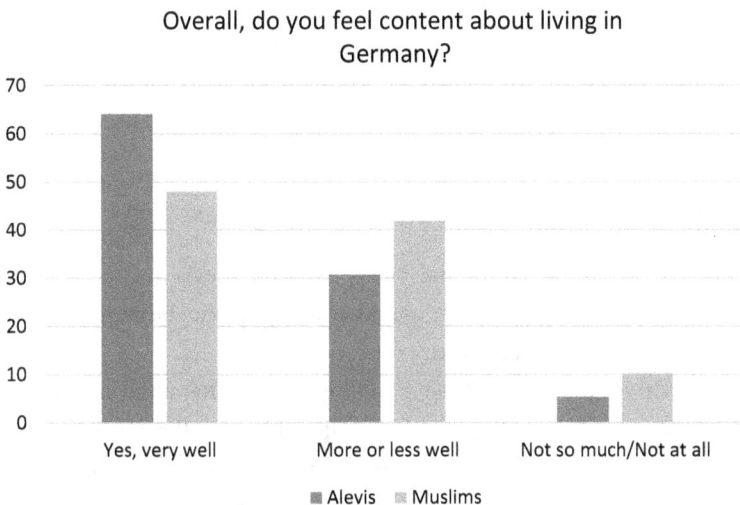

Figure 5.1 Satisfaction with living in Germany.

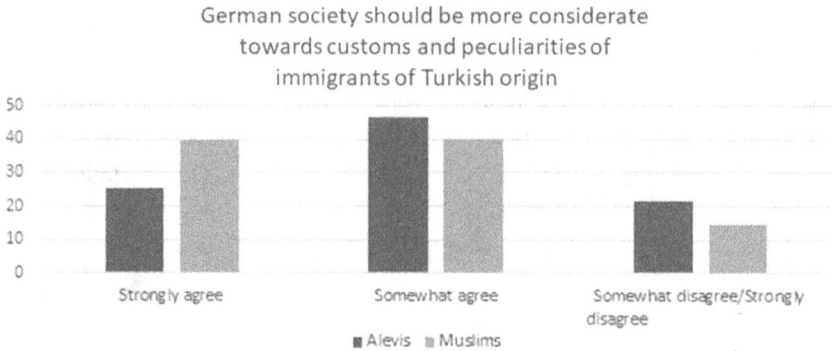

German society should be more considerate
towards customs and peculiarities of
immigrants of Turkish origin

Figure 5.2 Preserving Turkish culture in Germany.

- There is a significant difference in responses to the question 'German society should be more considerate towards customs and peculiarities of immigrants of Turkish origins',[6] to which only 25 per cent of Alevis answered with 'strong agreement' compared to 40 per cent of Muslims (Figure 5.2).
- The questions directly addressing controversial issues related to Islam in Germany also show significant differences between Muslims and Alevis: 34.7 per cent of Alevis stated that they 'associate fanaticism with Islam', while only 16.6 per cent of Muslims stated the same. The responses to the question associating Muslims with a 'readiness to use violence' were close to the first association with 'Fanaticism' for Alevis at 33.6 per cent, whereas only 10.45 per cent of Muslims marked it with a cross.
- The highest percentage of association with Islam was that of 'discrimination against women'[7] which was stated by more than half of Alevis (52.0 per cent) compared to only approximately a sixth (17.6 per cent) of Muslims (Figure 5.3).

Coming out of 'Takiye' in the German Diaspora

The contrast separating attitudinal views between Alevis and other Muslims presented in the three figures in the previous paragraph can be better understood by looking at the historical context.

To the Alevis, the establishment of the Turkish Republic meant a form of salvation from the oppression they suffered under the Ottoman regime. Historically, Alevism was founded amid the conflicts between the followers of the Prophet Mohammed. Alevis take a Shiite position by only accepting Mohammed's son-in-law and cousin, Ali, as the leader of the *umma*, thus

Association with Islam

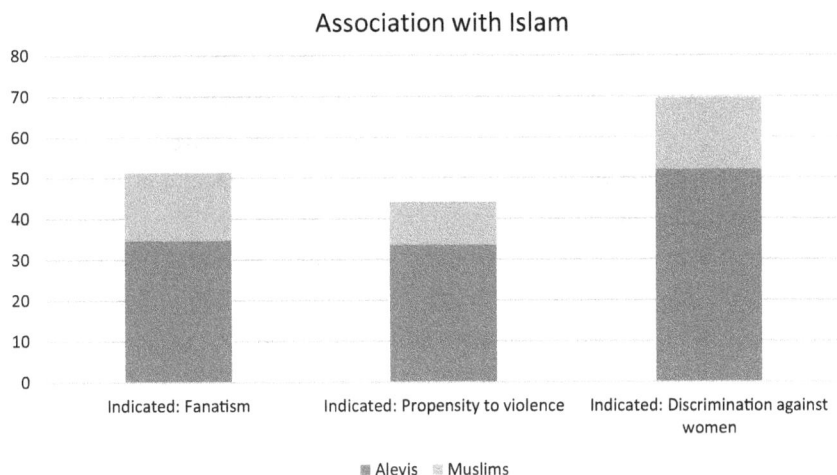

Figure 5.3 Association with Islam.

explaining the centrality of Ali in Alevi beliefs and culture. From these religious-historical roots, Alevism gave rise to what became known as an Anatolian Popular Islam in the fifteenth and sixteenth centuries (Dreßler 1999, 83), including a mystical understanding of religion that emphasizes a deeper spiritual message of Islam (Özyürek 2009, 236). The establishment of such an autonomous structure had political undertones at this time. Frustrated with the Ottoman central government, rural Anatolians allied with Persian Safavids – from whom the Alevis took some of their Shiite self-identity. However, bloody suppressions caused Alevis to flee to remote villages and due to this geographical separation, they developed their own socio-religious structures and cultivated a hostile stance towards the Ottoman Empire. This conflict-filled history helps one understand why Mustafa Kemal Atatürk, founder of the Turkish Republic (1923), is seen by many Alevis, past and present, as a saviour from pre-existing oppression and a champion of minority rights (Dreßler 1999, 83).

Although a form of secularism, called *laiklik*, consolidated the separation of religion and state in favour of minority groups in Turkey's republican era under Atatürk, the Turkish state 'conducted in practice a "see-saw policy"' towards Alevis. Their measures alternated between attempts to *include* Alevis, albeit that these attempts were operationalized for only a short time, and not only *excluding* them but actively seeking to eradicate them via a 'bloody defence'. The inclusion policy was based on the assessment that Kurdish Alevis, in particular, could help weaken and split the Kurdish camp, while the exclusion policy sought to mercilessly decimate the Alevis together with the Kurds (Spuler-Stegemann 2003, my translation).

Thousands of Alevis died in the Kurdish-Alevi region of Dersim (today Tunceli) within Atatürk's 'civilizing mission' to 'create a country with one language, one mentality and a unity of feelings' in 1937/38 (Dreßler 2008, 33). Hence, the Alevis' relationship to the Turkish nation and Kurdish culture is multilayered. In addition, it has been through a range of different phases of political, cultural and secular orientation (or identification) over time (Dreßler 2002, 175). For example, in the 1970s Alevis increasingly sympathized with leftist political movements[8] including anti-religious groups (Gorzewski 2010, 11) and were involved in the escalating polarization of leftists and ultranationalists (Dreßler 2008, 285). As a result, there were massacres in Maraş (also known as Kahramanmaraş, 1978) and Çorum (1980) and in Sivas (Massicard 2003, 31). Beginning in the 1980s, and especially since the Sivas massacre in 1993, where thirty-seven people were killed after an angry Sunni mob attacked an Alevi cultural event, Alevis have started taking a public stand defending their identity and gradually abandoning the principle of *takiye* (Kaya 2009, 60f; Sökefeld 2008, 9).

This development included a 'Coming Out of *Takiye*'. *Takiye* can be understood as a behavioural disguise aimed at keeping a low public profile, thus avoiding attracting attention within an adverse environment (Sökefeld 2008, 9). The word *takiye* comes from the Arabic *taqiyya*, which literally means 'prudence, fear' (Strothmann et al. 2012, 134). Along with this strategy, which had been practised and is still being practised in a limited way by Alevis in the German diaspora, came an assimilation process (Dreßler 2013, 276), resulting in a partial internalization of elements of Sunni religion and culture which would come to influence the following generation (Kaya 2009, 154). It is only in the last thirty years that initially a different cultural and more latterly a religion-focused orientation have become gingerly viewed as acceptable, despite lingering hesitation (Sökefeld 2008).

Hence, a striking contrast between Sunnis and Alevis is that while Sunnis migrated from a state-recognized majority position combined with an accepted public religious identity, Alevis came as a persecuted, marginalized and oppressed minority from the Republic of Turkey where their religious identity remains unacknowledged. On 26 April 2016 the European Court of Justice declared that Turkey was violating the right to freedom of religion (Art. 9) with regard to their treatment of the Alevis, as well as transgressing the ban on discrimination (Art. 14) (Aksünger-Kizil 2018, 136).

In Germany, however, the religious laws are much more favourable for Alevis than those in Turkey[9] for the basic reason that Alevis *are* officially recognized as a religious community – this recognition was even incorporated into religious education courses in several federal states in Germany from 2006. Politically,

Alevis are able to mobilize themselves in a way which would be unthinkable in Turkey (Massicard 2003, 185). At present, the young generation seems to play an important role in Alevi activism as they position themselves in an increasingly self-confident manner compared to the older generation and are integrated into a wider range of association activities (cf. Loth 2016, 180f). Gorzewski (2010) concludes that the transformation process among Alevis happened in accordance with the German context and shares the conclusion drawn by Sökefeld (2008) and Kehl-Bodrogi (2006): that Alevis are following a strategic orientation towards integration. Dilek Tepeli suggests that the often problematized diffusion of collective Alevi identity and inner plurality within Alevi discourses can actually be interpreted as an advantage for flexible identity formation in the context of adaptive diffusion and identity standards within main society. In contrast to Sunni Muslims, Alevis have a rather favourable stereotype within wider society, or nothing is known about them at all (Dilek Tepeli, in preparation). In short, one can argue that Germany has fostered a type of 'German Alevism' based on a newly found religious foundation (Kehl-Bodrogi 2006).[10] Yet, as previously mentioned, the categorization of Alevism *within* Islam or outside Islam remains one of the most debated issues in the German diaspora (cf. Kalbarczyk and Loth 2017, 89). Among the Alevi Youth Association (BDAJ e.V., *Bund der Alevitischen Jugendlichen in Deutschland* e.V), a subdivision of the umbrella organization Almanya Alevi Birlikleri Federasyonu (AABF; German: Alevitische Gemeinde Deutschland), the view that Alevism lies *outside* Islam is widespread (Loth 2016).

However, the aforementioned tensions at the end of the last century contribute to the existing variety of Alevi self-understandings. Bearing this historical juncture and the difficulties of establishing a coherent definition of Alevism in mind, one might wonder about precisely how history and collective memory converge in an individual's biography. In the case of this study, why does the singular positioning of adolescents in regard to Alevism matter?

A heuristic frame

Christel Gärtner points out that the 'religious identity of young adults constitutes itself depending on social and historical conditions, alongside levels of socialisation' (Gärtner 2013, 212f, my translation). From this point of view, the phase of adolescence is especially relevant, particularly regarding tradition and innovation in relation to religiosity (Gärtner 2013, 212).

Within individualized, pluralized and de-traditionalized societies, questions of identity are always connected to doubts and insecurities about who a person or a group wants to be. Late modern society offers a variety of options for action and lifestyles, which increase the importance of such identity questions (Straub 2000). While one might rightly argue that adolescence poses challenges to everyone, this study demonstrates that adolescents from immigrant families undergo a dual process of transformation: one stemming from their parents and the other from their place of origin (King and Koller 2006).

In the case of young Alevis, the complex and partly contradictory discourse about the definition of a collective Alevi identity may, as illustrated earlier, easily complicate this process. Century-old persecutions and discrimination (Yildiz and Verkuyten 2011, 246; Kaya 2009; Taşçı 2006) perpetrated by the Sunnis still play a major role within this Alevi identity discourse in the frame of *kollektive Verletzungsverhältnisse*[11] (Straub 2014). Considering these complexities, it is important to map the cultural, milieu-specific and, especially, religious differences from the parents' generation, while recognizing how these particular views still have a profound impact on the everyday life and identity issues faced by the youth. This is partly due to the transference of experiences, memories of marginalization and struggles for recognition within their families (see Kaya 2011, 154).

Sökefeld (2008, 33), Yildiz/Verkuyten (2011, 263), Taşçı (2006, 381) and Kaya (2009, 62) concede that Alevi identity for second-generation immigrants is still largely defined in contrast to Sunni identity. Even if the youth themselves have no experiences of migration and did not suffer directly from the same political and social conflicts their parents faced, they inherit these familial experiences indirectly through different conditions of socialization. The family dynamics, in which the experiences of migration and related aspects are condensed and transferred, must, therefore, be taken into account (see King and Koller 2006, 10 ff; see Mahçupyan 2017, 21; see also Straub 2014).

Perspectives from the ground

The individual narrative interviews analysed here were conducted in 2017 and 2018 in the aftermath of the attempted coup against the Turkish government on 15 July 2016 and the subsequent establishment of a state of emergency and constitutional referendum of 2017.

Together with my research collaborator, Dilek Tepeli, we reflected on our access to the field. Dilek Tepeli conducted group interviews among young adults of Turkish origin, considering questions of multiple belongings and psycho-social relations among young Alevis and Sunnis. The tensions among people of a Turkish background, mentioned earlier, were very much reflected within the interview process. As an autochthonous researcher, I was able to gain trust through my knowledge of Turkish language and culture, including specifics about Alevism, in view of my former interactions with and studies about Alevis. As I myself am not of Turkish origin, I also gained trust because I do not belong to a group perceived as potentially adversarial.

Due to her Turkish background, interviewees did perceive my collaborator with either trust or mistrust. This reaction was based on a perceived ambiguity in her religious or political sympathies. The lack of clarity around whether she identified with Alevism or Sunnism and her stance on President Recep Tayyip Erdoğan occasionally led to moments of unease among interviewees, especially when the group conversation addressed negative experiences with reference to the Sunni people or the rejection of Erdoğan.

The case studies

In the following, I will discuss four case studies of young Alevi adults in Germany. The first three cases all experienced *takiye* in their family and with the support of the Alevi Youth Association (BDAJ e.V., Bund der Alevitischen Jugendlichen in Deutschland e.V.) found a way to break with this tradition and become self-confident representatives of an Alevism which they easily connect to particular values identified as crucial for German society, such as democracy, openness and tolerance.

The fourth example shows, in contrast, that not practising *takiye* within a family does not necessarily lead to an unproblematic approach towards Alevism. Her close attachment to her Turkish-Kemalist-Alevi family makes it difficult for Handan to integrate into German society as well as into the Alevi youth organization.

First case: Umut, twenty-one years

Alevism as a political activity: 'You just do a lot for your faith'

Umut's[12] search for identity started in elementary school when he noticed that the teacher was talking about Islam, Judaism, Christianity, Buddhism and Hinduism without any reference to Alevism, which he was part of but had never explicitly learned anything about from his parents, who had little knowledge of Alevism and practised *takiye*. Umut's strong identification with Alevism started after a presentation at school on Alevism around the age of thirteen. This 'moment of religious identity arousal' can be seen as the beginning of a process, which finally allowed him to 'know *who* I am and to *where* I belong'.[13] He underlined the importance of this knowledge of identity and belonging in relation to the considerable number of young Alevis who 'unfortunately do not know anything about it'. In Umut's opinion, the core element and duty as an Alevi is to stand up as an Alevi. Within the self-image of Umut, who is affiliated with the Alevi Youth Association (BDAJ e.V., Bund der Alevitischen Jugendlichen in Deutschland e.V), aspects of transnational and intergenerational reference towards his Alevi identity are evident.

> (. . .) do also publicly announce, that I am Alevi. Although not in Turkey – I do not hesitate to say that I am afraid there – but in Germany, fortunately, we've got freedom of speech and religious freedom. And that's why I've participated in lots of demonstrations against Erdoğan or (. . .) various (. . .) Dersim[14]-festivals and also Dersim-seminars and you are around a lot; you just do a lot for your faith (. . .) I always think you can do a great deal, even if it's, for example, just this voting, going to the polls. This 'Evet-Hayır-Thing' (Yes-No-Thing, Umut refers to the constitutional referendum from 16th April 2017) (. . .) I've only got one vote, but this vote can change a lot, that's why you always need to take your chance and that's what I do.

First, it is worth noting how Umut self-confidently states his stance regarding Alevi identity in the public sphere and does not hide it as his parents or grandparents in Turkey did. Umut reports that his parents concealed their religious identity by practising *takiye* not only in Turkey but also in the German diaspora. Being opposed to this, Umut has freed himself from their collective praxis and broken with tradition. This means moving away from the former generation's method for coping with their minority position. In Turkey, however, such a change would not be possible for Umut because he would not be able to give up the practice of *takiye*. Accordingly, Umut relativizes his statement and adapts his behaviour to suit the degree of liberty or repression exercised in his environment.

However, Umut does also have some concerns about the focus of political activity: he has changed his membership in the Alevi community near his house to a membership in an Alevi community 60 miles away due to their wider range of political activities, which he appreciates a lot. But to his displeasure he observes a lack of ritual practices. In his former Alevi community, for example, he had regularly participated in the central Alevi communal worship service *cem*.

Second case: Duygu, twenty-four years

Individual interpretations: 'That you can develop your own opinion about it'

Duygu did not have any knowledge about Alevism until she was a teenager. Like Umut, Duygu is a member of the Alevi Youth Association, where – together with her Alevi peers – she is gaining knowledge about Alevism which was not forthcoming within her family. Nonetheless, she is being confronted with the issue of a 'missing' knowledge transfer from one generation to the other. Duygu interprets Alevism as an undogmatic religion. As with Umut, Duygu's parental generation continues to practise *takiye,* and there was a time in her life when there was no dialogue with her parents' generation about her family's Alevi origins. With the support of the youth organization, Duygu is breaking this tradition. She openly talks about how she found out about being Alevi and speculates about why her parents had not told her:

> I think it was because in Turkey Alevis had been tortured and beaten up and burned, chased, you know, just like the Jews, and they (my parents) were afraid that something could happen to me.

This comparison with the Jewish history of suffering links Alevism and Judaism on a relational level and connects the two groups regarding their collective experiences of inferior status and persecution throughout different historical periods.

Therefore, Duygu's religious self-perception is closely related to the experiences of violence and suffering of her parents' generation. Non-transmission and secrecy permeate the inner space of the family. In consequence, Duygu has independently initiated the process of 'becoming-Alevi' in joining the Alevi community, which has also led to further knowledge acquisition within her immediate family.

Duygu re-interprets her missing knowledge in a form which allows for her individualization:

> . . .and I do always argue about the fact that Jesus was a Jew, you know (. . .) and that his disciples are Christians and that in our case it could have been the same, I mean, why not, you wouldn't know; it is not written on paper or something like that and the written things are not always a hundred per cent true either. And that's why, I mean, I appreciate the fact that within our religion you can develop (. . .) your own interpretation.

In order to make her stance plausible, Duygu draws another comparison to Judaism, this time to the Judeo-Christian tradition. This comparison seeks to better explain Alevism and the reason why Alevis are not necessarily Muslims. It is her attempt to explain something unclear and ambiguous, namely her interpretation that the central figure for Alevism – Mohammed's cousin Ali – was a follower of Sunni Islam. The comparison between Jesus, the Jew, and his Christian disciples aims to make this apparent incompatibility plausible and helps Duygu position herself as an Alevi *outside* Islam, even if this narrative does not necessarily reflect historical facts.

Her criticisms, on (missing) written texts and their supposed authenticity, strengthen her position: written religious documents do not necessarily have to be true, which is why it is no disadvantage that Alevism lacks doctrines fixed in writing and their attendant dogmas. By re-interpreting a supposedly problematic aspect as something creative and emancipatory, Duygu attributes a positive value to her religion. To Duygu, the flexibility inherent to understanding Alevi identity signifies an enrichment rather than a disadvantage. Her perspective offers almost endless possibilities for interpreting and re-interpreting Alevism as guided by convertible understandings. However, the hesitant way that Duygu presented her positive understanding in the interview may also be an indication that this diverse spectrum of possible interpretations can also make it difficult to find a particular orientation.[15]

Third case: Dilay, twenty-one years

Modern Alevism: 'We can *reject pork meat, but we are not obliged to*'

Twenty-one-year-old Dilay was born in Turkey and came to Germany together with her two younger siblings at the age of 6. Her parents emigrated from an Alevi-Kurdish-dominated region in Turkey because of threats from both the Partiya Karkerên Kurdistanê (PKK, Kurdish Worker's Party) and Turkish soldiers. With hope for a better life, the father left his little shop behind and moved to Germany.

Dilay has never come to terms with her family's difficult past, and, preferring not to address the topic, she declares: 'I almost cannot remember my childhood, I would say. So, what had happened in Turkey also remained in Turkey I guess.' She later adds: 'Eventually, everything turned out to be good.' For Dilay, this phase is part of the past and clearly located within Turkey. In Germany, the family found release and the possibility of a better future. For Dilay, the decision to migrate and its process are thus considered a success story. The dangerous and highly conflictual situation in Turkey was left behind and a safe place was found in Germany.

Until the age of sixteen, Dilay had not explicitly known that she and her family were Alevis. Together with her dad, she *had* visited the Alevi community of her hometown from time to time, but nobody had framed it as an 'Alevi' place, and, in retrospect, she states that she was not particularly attracted to the place and was therefore not very interested back then.

The 'trigger' moment was when a Sunni school friend asked her:

> 'Well, are you actually going to Mosque?' To which Dilay responded: 'I have never been to a mosque', an answer which irritated the Sunni friend who wondered whether Dilay's parents had neglected to teach her that she should regularly visit the mosque. In the subsequent confrontation with her parents, Dilay was surprised by their answer: 'You don't need the mosque and the Koran in your religion, you are Alevi'. Her parents did then 'briefly explain to me what Alevism meant'.

Until this 'turning point', Dilay had thought she was a Muslim and never questioned it. However, she *had* experienced 'othering' from Sunnis. Unable to understand the reasons, her Sunni friends had told her 'this girl doesn't do anything (. . .) she is so atheistic'. That is why she felt more 'comfortable' among Christian friends and (happily) attended church regularly.

After this 'turning point', Dilay self-confidently distinguished herself from both Sunnis and Christians. She started to feel comfortable among new friends of Alevi origin: 'I felt so much (more) connected, it was kind of an "Aha-moment". Now I've got a religion as well, I can tell something about it.' Whereas before, she had (implicitly) felt a 'deviation' from the two congregations she had known up until that point – Christianity and Sunni Islam – she now attained an understanding of herself as belonging to a confessional group, and a very special denomination at that, which makes her feel unique.

Dilay was very happy when, only shortly after reaching this 'turning point', she encountered a board member of the Alevi community of her city and, as it turned out, there were several other, potentially like-minded, young Alevis 'keen on' learning more about Alevism:

> . . .and I was like: yeah, but I don't know anything about Alevism. And he replied: Well, none of them know anything about Alevism, you can just come. . . . Then I went there, and I learned, they learned Alevism like a school lesson somehow, for several weeks, and we also did exercises and homework and that is how we learned the lang-, I mean the religion. And I found it so interesting because it was totally different from what I know from Sunni Islam or Christianity.

The interpolation of the utterance 'lang-' can be interpreted as a Freudian slip of the tongue. It indicates that Dilay might understand her access to Alevism as the learning of a language. She would not even have to have a foreign language in mind, but rather the *ability* to speak, to articulate explicitly what has been established implicitly within her family within a 'cultural habitus'.[16] The new group of Alevi peers is very meaningful within this context because a language only makes sense when it is spoken to a counterpart. The communitarization within the group can be understood as having empowered this part of Dilay's identity, which had remained in the background until this point.

To Dilay, in Germany, Alevis are a minority within a minority (see Introduction), and young adults like her need to learn the 'Alevi language' as Alevism plays a major and (highly) religious role in their lives. In complete contrast to this, Dilay points out that Alevism only plays a very minor role in Turkey. She refers to her cousin from her hometown as a point of reference and reports his statement: 'We have got an Alev- Cultural Association, but not more than that.' Dilay continues by interpreting the cousin's words: 'So, they maybe only go there to have fun, but afterwards they leave again. It is nothing religious.' Dilay also proudly recounts how her cousin wondered about her numerous participations in *cem* ceremonies in Germany (that she posted about on Facebook). This is in itself remarkable, First, because Dilay didn't participate in the only *cem* ceremony which took place during the ten months of my data collection, due to a parallel seminar organized by the Alevi Youth Association in another city on the topic of inclusion. Second, Dilay's rather devaluing understanding of her cousin's Alevism is not understood reciprocally by the cousin himself: he is not jealous of Dilay's different approach to Alevism in Germany but rather sincerely puzzled by her high commitment for Alevism shared on Facebook.

When it comes to Dilay's characterization of 'German' Alevism, she points out the following 'core elements': 'nature, gender (equality), being humanistic and tolerant towards other religions' and she considers herself 'rather as one of the "not-Islam-type"'. To Dilay, Germany represents the 'top' example of having achieved the goals with regard to her (Alevi) ideals of 'tolerance' and 'openness' and does not need to 'improve' anymore. 'Why should anything be changed here in Germany? Everything is already very free, open and tolerant.' Turkey, on the other hand, seems to be a hopeless case to Dilay, as Alevi identity seems only of minor importance to the people. But she does not want to 'dig deeper into' the underlying reasons such as oppression and fear and distances herself with the help of 'space and time': 'but you don't live in Turkey, so it's hard to understand'. The reasons for *takiye* might lie in 'much earlier times': 'I don't know why [*laughing*] maybe due to much earlier times, where they had to reveal everything and so on.'

When asked about her experience of Alevism in school, Dilay comes up with an explanation of her newly achieved knowledge which turned into a concrete and religiously framed interpretation. She proudly explains that Alevis are modern, tolerant and free, as they do not have a Koran or any other holy scripture: 'I mean we are modern, we accept everything (. . .) because everyone has to decide for themself on their own', including the choice over whether to consume pork and alcohol or not.

Fourth case: Handan, twenty-one years old

Clear understanding of Alevi Affiliation: 'I have always known about it, the whole family is Alevi in our case'

Whereas Umut, Duygu and Dilay explicitly found out about their Alevism as teenagers, Handan never had to ask whether Alevism might be her category of religious belonging: 'I have always known about it, the whole family is Alevi in our case.' Handan does not report having any experience of *takiye*. Rather, she remembers that when she was about four years old, her father had a tattoo of the Alevi sword-symbol *zülfikar* done on his arm. In comparison to the other cases who are of Kurdish origin, Handan is part of another minority: she is a Turkish-Alevi in favour of Atatürk, understanding Alevism as located *within* Islam, and she openly shares these views with everyone.

Handan's parents both come from the same Sunni-dominated region in Central Anatolia. They are first cousins as their mothers are sisters. Handan's father came to Germany as a little child because Handan's grandfather wanted to find work in Germany. Handan's mother arrived for the wedding when she was almost eighteen years old. This means that the (arranged) marriage not only followed the endogamy rules of traditionally organized Alevi communities (cf. Aksünger-Kizil 2018, 129) but continued the traditions specific to the family's Turkish origin. Hence, even in a diasporic setting, the continuity of a (special) socio-cultural tradition of a minority group can be observed. Handan has difficulties maintaining friendships because her parents do not let her go out after 8.00 pm. That is also why she has not been able to start an apprenticeship, either as a stewardess or in a café, and is without a concrete job perspective at the moment. She blames her parents for these limitations because, in her understanding, Alevis should be more 'relaxed' compared to Sunnis, who she considers more 'strict'.

The significance of her Turkish-Alevi identity is closely linked to her belief in miracles, as illustrated by her visits to religious sites in Turkey. To Handan, the Alevi pilgrimage place Hacıbektaş in Nevşehir, not far from her hometown, holds a powerful significance. In her understanding, Hacıbektaş is a 'pure' Alevi site. For Kemalist Alevis, Atatürk's visit to Hacıbektaş on the 22 and 23 of November 1919 signifies a 'crystallisation point within Alevi myth creation' as it is seen as a symbol of the alliance between Bektaşi Alevis and Atatürk (Dreßler 1999, 94). Hacıbektaş is at the centre of many disputes, with multiple different groups claiming it as an important place for sustaining their cultural identity, whether they identify as Sunni or Alevi (Massicard 2003, 130). Nevertheless, Handan is very much inspired by the miracles which occur at the site and which she experienced herself during various visits since early childhood. She believes in the powers of the 'holed stone' (*Delikli Taş*) which enables 'good' people to climb through even if they have corpulent bodies, while preventing slim persons of 'bad character' to climb through it. Her belief in the Alevi ritual *cem* creates her biggest desire for her near future: Handan wants to participate in a *cem* for the first time in her life, over the course of becoming a 'regular' member of an Alevi youth group and hence the Alevi community.

Handan's understanding of familiar Alevi belonging is so strong that she considers the decision of her aunt and cousin – who live in the same German town and are related to both Handan's mother and father – to convert to Sunni Islam as an act of betrayal. The aunt, the only relative who was married to a Sunni man, had maintained her Alevi way of life until the death of Handan's grandparents, who had been 'holding the family together' according to Handan. A conversation with her cousin, who until then had been like 'a sister' to Handan, reveals Handan's understanding of an intertwined religious and national identity.

> Together with her husband my cousin (. . .) keeps saying: 'Why do you like Atatürk? (. . .) he hasn't done anything for Turkey!' '(But) we say, he managed to make the Ottoman Empire go away'.

From Handan's perspective, in leaving Alevism for Sunni Islam, her cousin also left the Kemalist approach for one centred on Erdoğan. Hence, we can observe that the dichotomies Atatürk-Alevism versus Erdoğan-Sunnism are being constructed here. Handan does not manage to come to a more liberal standpoint but takes the cousin's choice very personally. This issue represents a rift between them: 'I cannot change what is on her mind with regard to Erdoğan, and she cannot change it on my side.'

Conclusion

The previous four cases capture more than just the experiences of four young adults wrestling with issues of identity in the midst of socio-political flux affecting both Germany and Europe's contemporary social fabric. Instead, they also map in a representative fashion the diversity of individual experiences within an important minority group whose ties with Islam, whether tenuous or tight, or with previous manifestations of Alevism under *takiye*, are rarely subject to scrutiny. In the first case, we can see how the constraints of Umut's parents and grandparents, with regard to the difficulties they faced as Alevis in Turkey, shaped his mindset. However, we also see how he eventually came to emancipate himself from the particular value of *takiye*, by taking agency and giving a presentation about Alevism in school on his own. Later, he was enabled to further develop his Alevi identity with the help of the social relationships he created in the Alevi Youth Association.

The second case, Duygu, also found a way to overcome *takiye*. She juxtaposed her newly acquired understanding of her heritage group with the knowledge she obtained through being socialized within the German school system: the knowledge about the Jewish experience and the comparison of Jesus and Ali as founders of new religions. She is open to complementary narratives and underlines 'non-purist' and 'non-dogmatic' aspects within Alevism. This is how she positions her understanding of Alevism *outside* of Islam.

Dilay's religiosity also enables her to gain differentiation and uniqueness. She proudly presents her newly acquired knowledge in her school by giving a 'liberal' answer to the question of whether Alevis are allowed to eat pork. In what seems a superficially simple process and rationale, she distances herself from Sunni Islam, which strictly categorizes pork as forbidden (*haram*). At the same time, her rhetorical underlining of her religious attitude to contrast with her Alevi cousin in Turkey might also be a strategy to avoid a more complex confrontation with her family's reason for leaving Turkey.

These three cases share a common pattern of 'successful' dual transformation (cf. Heuristic Frame, King/Koller 2006): by actively connecting with Alevi roots which hitherto were in the background of the respondents' lives. They all experienced so-called epiphanies via meaningful discoveries but later re-interpret Alevism in a different way to their parents or grandparents, who practised a concealed version of their faith through *takiye*. The conscious distancing from the practice of former generations comes, however, through a simultaneous creation that can be fairly described as an innovative, unique and personal approach compatible with the values of mainstream German society.

The end effect stands in sharp contrast to *takiye*: instead of hiding, young adults present their Alevi identity assertively with the backing and encouragement of the Alevi youth group (BDAJ). The first three cases featured earlier make use of their position as an embedded minority. By operating in a context of religious freedom, they stand up for the rights of Alevis and other minorities, giving public visibility to their practically unknown religion and attempt to distance themselves from Sunni Islam – a group that in some ways acts as an 'inconvenient other' for being better known but more negatively perceived by Germans. They proclaim Alevi values they see in line with those from Germany, such as democracy, openness and tolerance. In addition, they act as messengers for the belief that Alevism can be interpreted *outside* Islam. Duygu even interprets the genesis of Alevism and its religious founder Ali in a manner analogous to Jesus and Christianity, which despite high numbers of secessions from the church still enjoys high levels of popularity in terms of cultural roots among German mainstream society. It is worth noting that for two of the cases (cases 1 and 3), schools have acted far beyond their formal roles as educational institutions to serve also as important conduits for socialization and identity formation. It is, precisely, in school where Umut and Dilay start to feel particularly irritated and somehow as if they 'don't fit'. While Umut notices the absence of his religion in the curriculum, Dilay is confronted by a Sunni classmate who wonders: 'Why are you not a version of me?' Consequently, it is also school – where Umut gives a presentation on Alevism which changes his whole life by bringing his Alevi identity from the background to the centre of his everyday life – from whence he goes onto Germany's streets to fight for the rights of Alevis in Turkey. Dilay responds to the curiosity of her teacher and classmates about Alevism with her newly achieved knowledge, which developed into a concrete and highly religious interpretation. For her, Alevism's 'core elements' centred on modernity and freedom, leaving the choice to its followers to reject or tolerate pork meat, in contrast to the Quranic tenet. However, all three cases do also show that despite the clear rhetoric, some insecurities about their Alevi identity remain: Umut is nostalgic for original Alevi rituals, Duygu expresses scepticism about any religious (written) documents and Dilay constructs an idealized version of Alevism.

Lastly, this study's fourth case (Handan) shows that having a clear understanding of Alevi affiliation alone is not sufficient to attain a positive standing as part of the embedded minority. On the one hand, she has difficulties in understanding non-Kemalist approaches. On the other hand, Handan has not yet had the chance to go through the transformation processes of (migrant) adolescents (cf. King/Koller 2006). This process needs a balanced 'adolescence triad' consisting of the young individual, family *and* peer groups (King 2013, 111). Peers help to 'bring up new room to maneuver' (Hummrich 2011, 71) to enable the intergenerational relationships between the adolescent and their family to be 'thwarted, complemented, corrected, questioned and widened' (Hummrich 2011, 111). The Alevi youth group, with its subgroups of friends, proved instrumental for the development of the three former cases (Umut, Duygu and Dilay) but is notably missing in Handan's case. Instead, Handan remains very attached to her traditional family. The latter, in turn, shapes expectations that are difficult to fulfil in Handan's life in Germany without isolating her from possible peers.

Yet Handan's desire to become part of the Alevi youth group is just as real as her feeling of 'embarrassment' for being different and thus standing out from the group. On reflection, she is able to find an assertive tone about herself vis-à-vis the group. Her words stand as an important reminder of not only the rich plurality within Alevism in Germany but the fundamentally syncretic character of Alevism across time and space.

'Christian culture' and its others

Culturalized religion, Islam and confessional Christianity in the Netherlands

Daan Beekers

In the run-up to the 2017 national elections in the Netherlands, the upcoming far-right populist politician Thierry Baudet sent out a tweet in which he advocated a 'revaluation' of Christianity. This tweet – phrased, as if to underscore the point, in Latin – earned him an invitation to join a debate on the topic in a televised talk show. There, he identified himself as an 'agnostic cultural Christian' and argued that one doesn't have to 'literally believe' in Christianity's doctrines to recognize the relevance of Christian values for Western society.[1] He said that because the Dutch have tried to 'radically break' with these values in recent decades, 'we have orphaned ourselves, we have become detached from our roots'. Christianity, he pointed out, can provide us with a sense of who we are and of what binds us in this time of 'identity crisis'.

And this is where Baudet's full ideological message reared its head: a renewed focus on our Christian tradition, he said, is particularly important 'now that we are faced in the Netherlands with a very self-conscious, *totally* different culture – Islam – that does manifest itself, with very different values, where freedom of conscience does not play a role, the equality of men and women is very different, separation of church and state is not acknowledged'. Baudet argued that given our current 'inability to define our own identity' in relation to 'this huge challenger that has arrived here', we need to become aware of 'the sources of *our* civilisation'. These words rather blatantly made clear that his call to revaluate Christianity was motivated above all by a desire to resist Islam.

The television programme had also invited a couple of confessional Christian public figures to join the conversation – I use the term 'confessional' here to denote active membership to a particular religious group and adherence to a particular religious creed. Having listened politely to Baudet's exposition, they showed little enthusiasm for his extolment of Christian tradition. Frank Bosman, a Roman Catholic cultural theologian and public commentator, said he believes that Christianity is essentially defined by the commandment of love. For him, this means that the religion teaches us to love the other and allow them to lead their own lives. This, he said, pertains to Dutch Muslims in particular. 'So how can you base yourself on a revival of Christian norms and values and at the same time use that as a kind of leverage to push Muslims out of the door? I feel abused as a Christian by this… imperialist politics!', he exclaimed. Baudet could count on little more approval from Carola Schouten, at the time a Member of Parliament for a confessional Protestant Christian party (ChristenUnie) and currently the minister for poverty policy. Being a Christian, she said, is not only about the kinds of ideas and inspiration that Baudet talks about but also about attempting in one's everyday life – 'with the Bible in one's hand' – to do good. She remarked: 'You cannot talk about Christian culture without also talking about the person it was named after, and how He defines the good life.'

Culturalized religion appears to be on the rise. Many parts of the world witness the appropriation of religion as a source of belonging, heritage and cultural identity. In a review of the literature on this topic, the sociologists Avi Astor and Damon Mayrl (2020, 209) define culturalized religion as 'forms of religious identification, discourse, and expression that are primarily cultural in character, insofar as they are divorced from belief in religious dogma or participation in religious ritual'. As these authors note, 'culturalized religion' is a tricky concept since it could mistakenly be taken to imply a neat separation between 'cultural' and 'non-cultural' religion or, for that matter, culture and religion (210). Indeed, it can be argued that belonging and cultural identity have been essential parts of religious life at all times. Moreover, the mobilization of religion as culture does not rule out a committed personal faith.

Nevertheless, looking specifically at Western European countries that have seen a steep decline of institutionalized Christianity, there is an increasing reorientation on Christianity in which the emphasis is put not on belief and doctrine but on culture, identity and heritage. This pertains, among other phenomena, to political debates about Europe's alleged Christian identity (Marzouki, McDonnell, and Roy 2016), a revived interest in Christian art, history and architecture (Isnart and Cerezales 2020) and the appropriation of religious symbols – such as crucifixes – as tokens of national culture (Joppke 2013). What makes these engagements with Christian religion distinctive, Astor and Mayrl argue, is that its cultural or symbolic elements are brought to the foreground, while its connections with traditional or conventional religious forms 'lend it rhetorical, emotional, and political weight' (2020, 211). This does not mean that this is not 'real' religion but rather a re-worked engagement with religion under secular conditions (Astor, Burchardt, and Griera 2017, 126–7; Astor and Mayrl 2020, 211–12).

As the statements of Thierry Baudet demonstrate, the emergence of discourses and practices of culturalized religion in Europe raises an important question about processes of inclusion and exclusion: If European cultures are defined in Christian terms, then who is included and who is excluded from that symbolic realm? Indeed, in current debates about diversity and belonging, the dynamics of culturalization (Duyvendak, Geschiere, and Tonkens 2016), be it in religious or other terms, surfaces as a primary language for determining 'self' and 'other'. In terms of the inclusion or exclusion of religious communities in particular, the literature on culturalized religion in Europe – covering a wide variety of social phenomena, orientations and practices – has focused on two important developments: the exclusion of Muslims through political discourses that equate European culture with Christianity (Van den Hemel 2014; Marzouki, McDonnell, and Roy 2016; Brubaker 2017; DeHanas and Shterin 2018; Strømmen and Schmiedel 2020) and the privileging of Christianity through public narratives and judicial rulings that define Christian symbols and objects as national 'culture' or 'heritage' (Joppke 2013; Oliphant 2015; Astor, Burchardt, and Griera 2017; Coleman 2019; Baumgartner 2020).

In this contribution, I aim to connect these two areas of inquiry. I focus on the Netherlands, which offers an interesting context to study this phenomenon given its almost proverbial secular culture. The Dutch tend to pride themselves on their liberal and secular values. Ever since the 1960s, strongly anti-ecclesiastical positions have pervaded popular culture in this country (Van der Veer 2006; Van Rooden 2010; Duyvendak, Geschiere, and Tonkens 2016). Yet, in the last couple of decades, the Netherlands has also seen an increasingly widespread reorientation on Christian culture and history (Van den Hemel 2014; 2017; Beekers 2017; Meyer 2019). In what follows, I argue that the culturalization of Christianity in the Netherlands sits uneasily with confessional religious communities, not just Muslim but also Christian ones. In contrast with findings in several other contexts (e.g. Oliphant 2015; Astor, Burchardt, and Griera 2017; Isnart and Cerezales 2020), the promotion of Christian heritage in the cases I focus on here is spearheaded less by Christian actors and organizations than by secular ones. What is more, confessional Christians are at times even understood to jeopardize the preservation – and public accessibility – of Christian heritage.

This chapter, then, interrogates the complex and ambivalent relations between culturalized Christianity and confessional religion – both Christian and Muslim. I examine two quite different manifestations of culturalized Christianity: the mobilization of Christian identity in political – especially far-right populist – discourses and the revaluation of Christian heritage in debates about closed and repurposed church buildings.

Before I continue, a brief clarification of my use of terms may be helpful. In this chapter I employ the terms 'identitarian Christianity' and 'heritage Christianity' to refer to these two manifestations of culturalized Christianity.[2] These reflect distinct, although partly overlapping, approaches to the religion, and my aim is to shed light on the continuities and discontinuities between them. 'Culturalized Christianity' is used as an overarching term that includes – but is not limited to – both of these approaches. By contrast, 'confessional Christianity' denotes an engagement with faith marked by active church membership and religious practice: a commitment to Christian dogma, rituals and (communal) practices that can be distinguished from an exclusive focus on religion as cultural identity or heritage.

Identitarian Christianity

Let me return to the televised debate featuring Thierry Baudet for a moment. Several aspects stand out: the first is the way in which Baudet decouples 'culture' from 'belief', passing over Christian doctrines and focusing on the religion as a source of identity and belonging. His Christian interlocutors reject this move to focus selectively on what might be called the 'high culture' of Christianity at the cost of its teachings and moral prescriptions. Of course, not all confessional Christians in the Netherlands would assent to Bosman's plea to love the 'Muslim other' – antagonistic or ambiguous sentiments towards Muslims can be found among segments of the Christian population too (see e.g. Balkenhol and Van den Hemel 2019; Van den Hemel 2020). Yet most confessional Christians would object to Baudet's strict separation between religious culture and doctrine. Second, Baudet unabashedly invokes Christianity as a means to demarcate a 'Western self' over and against a 'Muslim other'. He juxtaposes Dutch or Western society, which he describes as uncertain about its identity, with 'Islam' – defined as 'self-conscious', 'manifest', 'totally different' and a 'huge challenger'. Finally, Baudet seems to effortlessly pair Christian culture with liberal and secular values such as gender equality and the freedom of expression. This is remarkable because during the cultural struggles following the 1960s, such liberal values rather tended to be pitted over and against Dutch Christian traditions (Kennedy 1995; Righart 2004; Van der Veer 2006).

This 'identitarian' (Zúquete 2018) mobilization of Christianity and its distinct elements outlined here are representative of a larger trend in far-right populist politics in Europe (Marzouki, McDonnell, and Roy 2016; Brubaker 2017; DeHanas and Shterin 2018; Strømmen and Schmiedel 2020). Whether it is the Rassemblement National (formerly Front National) in France, the Lega Nord in Italy, Fidesz in Hungary or the Schweizerische Volkspartei in Switzerland, far-right populist parties have increasingly employed references to Christian culture and symbols in their political messaging (Marzouki, McDonnell, and Roy 2016). This reorientation on Christian culture is also increasingly found among more mainstream right-wing, conservative political actors (Van den Hemel 2014, 2017; Roy 2016). These political actors make use of a populist 'political style' that opposes the righteous 'people' to both 'others' and 'elites' (Moffitt 2016, 43–4; DeHanas and Shterin 2018, 180). In European contexts, the 'others' referred to are usually minority groups with a migration background, especially those identified as Muslims. In far-right populist narratives, they are understood to threaten the culture, tradition and security of 'the people'. Meanwhile, 'elites' are accused of betraying their own culture by indulging in cosmopolitan and liberal ideologies (Marzouki and McDonnell 2016; DeHanas and Shterin 2018). Against this background, Christianity has emerged as a potent symbolic resource for defining European cultures and distinguishing these from – especially Muslim – post-migrant cultures.

Rogers Brubaker (2017, 1199) argues that the Christianity mobilized in these populist politics is not what he terms a 'substantive' one. It is an identitarian Christianity that focuses on 'symbols of belonging' rather than 'practices of worship'. In Europe's secularized context, he suggests, '[i]t is precisely the ongoing erosion of Christianity as doctrine, organisation, and ritual that makes it easy to invoke Christianity as a cultural and civilisational identity, characterized by putatively shared values that have little or nothing to do with religious belief or practice' (1199). What is more, populists' references to Christian identity coincide with a promotion of liberal and secular values, including freedom of speech, gender equality, gay rights and philosemitism (1194). As Olivier Roy similarly argues, right-wing populists set out to defend Christian identity by promoting secular and progressive values that 'the Church itself does not support' (2016, 198).

Brubaker (2017) posits that this seemingly contradictory politics follows above all from a heightened concern with Islam. As antagonism towards Islam has increasingly become a 'master frame' for national populist movements in Europe (Vossen 2011, 180), Brubaker suggests that populists selectively embrace liberalism, secularism and cultural Christianity as means of demarcating their national and European cultures and setting these apart from those of Muslims (2017, 1204). The emphasis on Islam, he posits, has inspired a move in Northern and Western European populisms from nationalism to civilizationism:

> The definition of the constitutive other in civilizational terms invites a characterization of the self in the same register: the preoccupation with Islam calls forth a corresponding – and increasingly explicit – concern with Christianity, understood not as a religion, but as a civilization, as coextensive with 'the West', or with what used to be called 'Christendom'. (Brubaker 2017, 1200)

In this analysis, Christianity is presented by and large as an empty signifier. As Brubaker summarizes the populist narrative: 'Crudely put, if "they" are Muslim, then "we" must, in some sense, be Christian' (1199). Other scholars have similarly argued that the role of Christianity in this populist politics 'seems to be almost entirely identitarian and negative' (DeHanas and Shterin 2018, 178) and that most right-wing populist parties in Europe 'are Christian largely to the extent that they reject Islam' (Roy 2016, 186).

Religion and the desire to ground 'native' culture

However, the interpretation of identitarian Christianity as merely negative or devoid of content is debatable. It is not self-evident that self-identified secular political actors characterize European civilization in terms of Christianity rather than, say, the Enlightenment or liberal secularism. Indeed, in the Netherlands, which constitutes a central case in Brubaker's analysis, earlier right-wing conservative discourses that were already concerned with Islam tended to emphasize the secular and liberal principles of Dutch or Western culture, and the Dutch 'emancipation' from religion (Prins 2007; Mepschen, Duyvendak, and Tonkens 2010; Sunier 2010; Verkaaik 2010). The prevailing sentiment in these discourses was that the strict morals of Muslims, in the words of Peter van der Veer (2006, 119), 'remind the Dutch too much of what they have so recently left behind'. Given this earlier – and in many cases continuing – focus on secular freedom in response to Islam, I argue that the invocation of Christianity among right-wing populists cannot be sufficiently explained by pointing towards widespread concerns with Islam alone.

In his work on the political mobilization of notions of Christian – or 'Judeo-Christian'[3] – culture in the Netherlands, Ernst van den Hemel (2014, 2017, 2020) addresses this shift in right-wing discourses about religion. He argues that the emergence of appeals to (Judeo-)Christian tradition is inadequately understood if it is seen as mere populist opportunism or criticized for being inherently contradictory – even if such critiques are often justified. He posits that these appeals should be taken seriously as a conservative, rhetorical practice that self-consciously crosses the boundaries between the religious and the secular. These narratives about Christian culture, he explains, are consistent with a longer tradition in conservative ideology of appealing to – and retrospectively constructing – tradition as a means of grounding the community. It is 'a performative-linguistic act, an invocation rather than a description, that has as its goal the simultaneous defence and construction of a community that is perceived to be under threat, by appealing to a tradition that cannot be grasped in rational, objective terms' (Van den Hemel 2014, 68). Religion provides what might be called a 'heavy' cultural resource for the formulation of an essential and indeed almost transcendent sense of tradition. In this way, culturalized Christianity gives a felt substance to national identity while at the same time construing Muslims as inherent 'others' for whom this identity is ultimately unattainable. As Van den Hemel (2017, 17) has it: 'Religion, defined as part of a framework of heritage, tradition, and national identity, is a suitable way to "ground" culture firmly both in its (religious) past, and in a present in which one needs to believe in the superiority of secular majority culture.'

Thus, right-wing conservative actors in the Netherlands and elsewhere in Europe appear to be increasingly embracing notions of religious culture precisely because these are felt to provide a more solid foundation of national identity than secular and liberal values such as gender equality, individualism or freedom of speech. Frits Bolkestein, a leading conservative Dutch politician at the end of the last century who manifested himself as a guardian of secular values, provided a telling illustration of this sentiment. In an interview he gave after his retirement from active politics, he deplored the disappearance of Christianity as the 'connective tissue' (*bezielend verband*) of Europe, and he expressed his worry that secular phenomena, such as the Constitution, fell short of providing such a meaningful connection.[4]

Identitarian Christianity also carries specific content in a more intellectual sense. When elaborating the relation between Christianity and secularism, those advocating the significance of Christian identity occasionally point out that they are not talking about contemporary religious practice but about the cultural roots of European societies. The relation is presented as a genealogical one: Christianity and, more broadly, Judeo-Christianity are perceived as the unique source of the liberal, democratic and secular values of contemporary Europe. From this perspective, the Christian tradition has allowed Europeans to take leave of religion, to become secular, whereas Islamic tradition is seen to prevent Muslims from becoming truly secular and embracing principles such as the separation of church and state (Van den Hemel 2017, 10; cf. Brubaker 2017, 1200). This narrative presents a simplified version of scholarly understandings of the cultural-historical relationship between – particularly Protestant – Christianity and secularism (see e.g. Gauchet 1997; Asad 2003; Taylor 2007). Many political actors invoking Christianity, however, are not making a nuanced genealogical argument that situates religion as the past cultural foundation of secularism. Rather, they stress the importance of Christian symbols – such as religious festivals, crucifixes and Christian sites – for the safeguarding of European identities *today*. They are engaging less in an intellectual interpretation of cultural history than in a politics of belonging that centres on distinguishing a European 'self' from a Muslim 'other'.

The identitarian appeals to Christianity are situated within increasingly prevalent sentiments of nativist – essentially white – nostalgia in the Netherlands and elsewhere in Europe. As Jan Willem Duyvendak (2011, 2) has pointed out, many of those who seek to reaffirm national identity 'dig deeper and deeper into the national past, fuelling nostalgia for a time when populations were – supposedly – still homogeneous'. Olivier Roy (2016, 197) argues in this context that references to Christian culture enable the promotion of 'an idealised and ahistorical notion of a harmonious community life that existed before the elite and bad "others" began to endanger the prosperity, rights and wellbeing of the good people'. This nostalgia for a lost home has coincided with what Dutch scholars have termed the 'culturalization of citizenship', a process in which values, morals, emotions, symbols and tradition, including religion, have come to play an important role in defining what it takes to be a citizen (Duyvendak 2011, 92; cf. Schinkel 2008; Geschiere 2009, 24–5). In the Dutch context, this means that in order to be seen as a 'good' citizen, migrants and their descendants have to demonstrate that they adhere – not just rationally but also emotionally – to the 'progressive moral consensus' of the majority population (Duyvendak 2011, 87–94). In the process, liberal achievements have come to be depicted as inherent, 'natural', features of Dutch culture rather than 'products of an ongoing contingent, historical, progressive social struggle' (Mepschen 2018, 21).

It is against the backdrop of these processes of nativist nostalgia, culturalization of citizenship and naturalization of culture that 'Christian tradition' has increasingly been embraced as an alleged foundation of Dutch identity, perceived to be under threat from Muslims and multiculturalists (Van den Hemel 2014). This has contributed to a primordialist take on religion that, while distancing itself from religious beliefs and communities, presents Christianity as inherent to Dutch 'native' identity and Islam as essentially 'other'. In this context, identitarian Christianity represents a shift, albeit a gradual and partial one, in dominant discourses on religion in the Netherlands from a liberal–secularist narrative that construes religious communities – be they Christian, Muslim or other – as lagging behind in a purportedly universal process of secularization to a more reactionary nativist narrative that stresses the perceived incompatibility between Islam and Western – secular and post-Christian – culture (Beekers 2021, 12–14). It thereby feeds into processes of racializing Islam, by which a heterogeneous set of people are, because of their physical and cultural characteristics, perceived as members of an essentialized group that is attributed with supposed inherent traits (Meer 2013; Garner and Selod 2015; De Koning 2016). In short, what makes narratives of Christian culture particularly effective in identitarian politics is the double work they perform in 'othering' Muslims on the one hand and grounding 'native' identity in a presumed homogeneous past on the other.

It is illustrative to consider the different ways in which Islamic heritage in Europe tends to be treated. Charles Hirschkind (2016), for instance, has shown that the Islamic heritage of Al-Andalus tends to be resolutely relegated to the past in scholarly and popular discourses in Spain. While many Spaniards now acknowledge the significance of the Muslim period for the country's history, they simultaneously maintain that it is almost entirely irrelevant to their lives today (2016, 215–19). Here, the Islamic past can only enter the registers of nostalgia, myth and romanticism. Hirschkind argues that these registers 'police the [region's] temporal walls, ensuring that no foreign (i.e. Middle-Eastern) elements cross the border where they might make a claim on the present social, political, and religious order' (215), just as 'the fences set up on the borders hold back the influx of North Africans seeking to enter Spain' (218).

Responses from the side of confessional Christian politics

More often than not, Christian leaders and institutions in Europe express scepticism about political appeals to culturalized Christianity (Marzouki, McDonnell, and Roy 2016). While some might welcome the renewed political interest in their religion and a number of conservative Christian organizations themselves promote notions of Christian national identity (see e.g. Balkenhol and Van den Hemel 2019; Van den Hemel 2020), many Christian actors are wary of what they see as a political instrumentalization of their religion. They take issue with a culturalized interpretation of their religion that glosses over central Christian beliefs, doctrines and ethics. In their perspective, this approach to Christianity misses the point because it barely engages with what confessional Christians understand to be the essential tenets and moral teachings of their religion. In the words of Gert-Jan Segers, a prominent Christian public figure and presently leader of the aforementioned Protestant Christian party (ChristenUnie): this kind of politics boils down to 'a Christian culture without Christians'.[5]

When both far-right populist and more mainstream conservative Dutch politicians came out in defence of purportedly Christian symbols such as Easter eggs and phrases such as 'Merry Christmas' (in response to, among other issues, a retail shop that was accused of re-naming 'Easter eggs' as 'hide-and-seek eggs' – seen as an attempt at accommodating Muslim sensibilities), none of the confessional Christian political parties supported these appeals to protect Christian symbols. They rather expressed scepticism about these newfound concerns with Easter among secular politicians, who otherwise show little interest in maintaining Christian practices or promoting Christian moral issues (Van den Hemel 2017).

An exchange in 2015 between Geert Wilders and Kees van der Staaij, leader of the Dutch Orthodox Protestant party (SGP) illustrates some of the main points of contention between identitarian and confessional Christian politics (cf. Van den Hemel 2020). The SGP represents strictly Orthodox Christian communities, defends Christian privileges and expresses reservations about the public presence of Islam (Van den Hemel 2020). Nevertheless, its understanding of religious politics differs crucially from that of far-right populist parties such as Wilders' PVV. In this debate in parliament, Wilders talked about defending Christian values, and SGP's Van der Staaij challenged him to name some of these values.

> Wilders: One of these Christian values is that we stand up for our own
> people. . . . Standing up for our own people means that we – every Christian
> should take a leading role in this respect – have to prevent that our country

Islamises. What is more Christian than that? . . . Your party, your people and the Christian values in the Netherlands will be the first victims if Islam gets its way.

Van der Staaij: You don't have to convince the SGP of the importance of Christian values. Yet what I actually see in Europe and the Netherlands today is that lots of people in this culture oppose the Christian past. From the PVV, too, I didn't find support when typical Christian issues were at stake, such as the protection of life or safeguarding the day of rest. . . . How do you mean Christian values?[6]

What is striking here is not only that confessional politicians such as Van der Staaij object to the appropriation of Christian culture by right-wing populists but also that these populists, in turn, criticize confessional politicians and organizations for not doing enough to defend that Christian culture. For Wilders and like-minded political actors, safeguarding Christian identity essentially means abating the growth and influence of Islam in society. In that regard, Wilders has criticized not only Christian parties but also churches in the Netherlands for being too 'soft' on Islam (Van Kessel 2016, 70).

The turn to heritage Christianity

Calls to revaluate the significance of Christianity for Dutch culture are not limited to populist politics. In recent years, public intellectuals, writers and opinion makers have increasingly turned their attention to Christian tradition, arguing for the need to preserve the memory of the religious past, safeguard knowledge of Christianity or revive values based on the religion.[7] This reflects a broader development in public narratives in the Netherlands – and elsewhere in Europe – whereby Christianity is increasingly reframed as heritage and, in many cases, (re-)appropriated as national culture (Joppke 2013; Astor, Burchardt, and Griera 2017; Meyer 2019). Scholars writing on this phenomenon have pointed to processes of privileging Christianity, as opposed to other religious traditions, through legislation at the national or European level, and the ways in which Christian institutions have actively propagated these processes (Oliphant 2012; Joppke 2013; Astor, Burchardt, and Griera 2017). By contrast to this apparent symbiosis between states, judiciaries and Christian actors, it has struck me that in the Netherlands the most vocal proponents of Christian heritage tend to be self-identified secular, or non-religious, people who often explicitly distance themselves from Christian beliefs and institutions.[8]

An evocative example of this stance on Christianity is provided by the Dutch novelist Nicolaas Matsier (pen name of Tjit Reinsma). Born in 1945, Matsier grew up in a Protestant family. While he abandoned faith during his teens and now describes himself as an atheist, he nonetheless harbours a strong interest in Christianity. He published books on both the Old and the New Testament and he translated *The Book of Genesis* by the American cartoonist Robert Crumb. In an extensive interview with a leading Dutch newspaper he remarked that he has become 'deeply convinced of the value of Christianity as cultural factor number one in our civilisation and in our thought. . . . Christianity runs through our veins. When it comes to human rights, we are talking about a development that sprang directly from Christianity.'[9] When the interviewer asked him whether he was sure that he had abandoned faith, Matsier answered:

> I find many forms of faith primitive. I'm absolutely unsympathetic to pure orthodoxy. Those people take texts literally that shouldn't be taken literally. Those people don't understand what it means to read. But I can find it intensely sad that the Christian culture has gone to shreds and that people don't know anything any longer, that the magnificent, iconic buildings of any medieval village or city have in some sense become meaningless, that people no longer understand that, when they are lost, it suffices to walk up to a church to know where you are. Literally. Because a church is oriented. So you know the choir is placed on the east and the entrance to the church on the west. I find it really sad that those churches are empty. Of course, I know I don't go to church and I won't easily do so in the future. But at the same time there are lots of things that we are throwing away. That's what I have come to think. We throw away the cultural continuity with a tradition that is, by itself, not necessarily foolish or criminal.[10]

Matsier's narrative on Christianity is marked by a strong sense of loss, not of his childhood faith, but of a Christian culture with its particular modes of knowledge, architecture and know-how. His sense of a lost Christian past is an – at least partly – idealized one. For instance, the architectural principle of orientation is far from universally applied to churches in the Netherlands (indeed, if you are really lost, it's a safer bet to orient yourself on the nearest mosque).

While Matsier does not share the stark anti-Muslim rhetoric of the populist politicians discussed earlier, his and their views of the significance of Christian culture overlap when it comes to the strict separation between faith and culture, nostalgia for a lost past and perceived importance of Christianity for national and civilizational identity. With regard to this last point, Matsier decries the 'carelessness' with which the Dutch have treated their national history, arguing that 'cultural and historical heritage' is crucial for 'our identity'.[11] Different from those political actors blaming Islam, Matsier seems to identify secularization and excessive libertarianism as the main culprits of the Dutch disregard of their cultural and religious traditions. That said, he does contrast Christianity with Islam (referring to the former's 'egalitarian' spirit) and points to the 'culture shock' caused by the immigration of people 'who hail from the Bible Belts of Morocco and East-Turkey'.[12]

Repurposed churches, diversity and Islam

The fate of church buildings, touched upon by Matsier, is one of the foremost issues in debates about religious heritage in the Netherlands. This is not surprising given the staggering pace of church closures and conversions in this country. Since the 1970s, more than a thousand church buildings have been repurposed and hundreds of others have been demolished.[13] These processes of material transformation provoke fervent and often emotionally charged public debates, in which local residents, politicians, church leaders, heritage activists and others express distinct ideas about what should happen with these buildings (Beekers 2017; Meyer 2019). It seems no exaggeration to say that recent years have seen the emergence of something of a religious heritage industry in the Netherlands (Beekers 2017, 164) and elsewhere in the 'Western' world (Badone 2015; Astor, Burchardt, and Griera 2017; Coleman 2019; Burchardt 2020, chap. 5).

The Dutch government that served between 2017 and early 2022, a coalition of neoliberal secular and confessional Christian parties, invested in the preservation of heritage, with a special focus on 'monumental churches'.[14] The minister responsible (representing the liberal secular party D66) explained in a newspaper interview: 'In the field of heritage, churches play an enormous role when it comes to the recognisability of the landscape. If you know in these times where you are coming from, if you have that firmly under your feet, you can also cope with more transformation [*vernieuwing*] as a society'.[15] Here, again, we find the notion that an awareness of one's religious past is especially important with regard to ongoing social changes. The minister does not say what changes she is referring to, but in the light of ongoing debates about immigration many would interpret these words as pointing to increasing cultural diversity.

The connection between Christian heritage and religious diversity is particularly apparent when church buildings are converted into mosques. In the Netherlands, it has been estimated that there are around twenty-five mosques housed in former church buildings.[16] The (potential) repurposing of churches as mosques is an often contentious issue that, in line with changing public opinions regarding Islam, has become increasingly uncommon since the 1990s.[17] Since then, the reuse of church buildings by non-Christian religions – including, most notably, Islam – has been ruled out by the Dutch Roman Catholic Church and is generally considered undesirable by the Protestant Church in the Netherlands (Beekers and Tamimi Arab 2016, 143). In this respect, church-related actors take up ambivalent positions regarding the relation between Christian culture and Islam. While, as shown earlier, many Christian public figures reject identitarian appeals to Christian culture aimed at excluding Muslims, Dutch church authorities have become largely averse to the idea of selling their church buildings to Muslims – a stance that seems to reflect the prevailing negative climate towards Islam.

During my ethnographic research on abandoned and repurposed church buildings in Amsterdam and Utrecht,[18] I learned that the stances of 'ordinary' Dutch Catholics and Protestants on reusing churches as mosques are more diversified than those of the church authorities. While some find this kind of reuse unsuitable or even painful, others have no objections, often pointing out that they prefer churches to be preserved as 'houses of God' over repurposing them as, for example, shops or bars. Many Muslims I have spoken with share this latter position. Strikingly, in local discussions on the reuse of urban churches, the option of converting the building into a mosque – whether or not this is a likely course of events – always tends to be mentioned sooner or later. Different from the widespread transformations of church buildings into apartments or social centres, the potential repurposing into a mosque – just like repurposing into, say, a night club or a trampoline park – sparks people's imagination. Thus, even when Islam does not play a prominent role in debates about the redevelopment of a particular church building, it tends to be inevitably part of these deliberations as a background referent, a kind of implicit – or shadow – presence.[19]

Repurposed churches, Christian communities and religion critique

During my fieldwork on the reuse of churches in Amsterdam and Utrecht, I have found that antagonism towards Christian communities and organizations was often expressed more explicitly than anxieties about Islam. It was quite common that those who advocated the preservation of church buildings criticized church authorities and Christian communities for hindering their conservation efforts. In these narratives, confessional Christianity is not only set apart from culturalized Christianity but also, remarkably, perceived to jeopardize it. In the remainder of this chapter I will demonstrate this by briefly discussing the reuse of the Saint Willibrord Church in Utrecht. While this is an exceptional case because the building was bought, rather than sold, by a Catholic institution, the accompanying local debates offer a sharply focused lens on the more widespread tensions between 'heritage religion' (Burchardt 2020, chap. 5) on the one hand and religious communities and institutions on the other.

In the spring of 2017, a controversy erupted in Utrecht around the sale of the Saint Willibrord Church in the city centre. Unusually, the prospective new owner wasn't an entrepreneur impatient to convert the church into a trendy hotel, lofts or wine-bar but a conservative Catholic fraternity that wanted to refashion it as a place of religious worship. In previous years, the church had been run by a cultural association that rented it out for concerts, theatre plays and civil weddings, while it continued to be used by a Catholic congregation.[20] Now, the prospective buyer, the Society of Saint Pius X (SSPX), argued that the site should return to its proper use, that of a consecrated Catholic Church. SSPX is an internationally operating society of priests, founded in 1970 by Archbishop Marcel Lefebvre. It takes an anti-Modernist approach, criticizing the outcomes of the Second Vatican Council and holding on to the Tridentine Mass (the traditional liturgy of mass in Ecclesiastical Latin). It has had a troubled relationship with Rome.[21] The cultural association running the church, consisting of around ninety volunteers who organized cultural activities and guided tours, strongly disapproved of the sale. As reported by several media at the time, the spokespersons of these volunteers argued that SSPX was going to profit from the substantial renovation of the church building, which was partly paid by public funds. They were also concerned that the building would become inaccessible for a broader public after the sale. The volunteers moreover disliked the fact that the fraternity would cancel non-religious activities in the church, and they worried that the LGBTQ+ people among them would no longer be welcome as tour guides. In their eyes, the sale heralded the end of the building as a place of cultural creativity and cultural attraction. A local broadcaster, which described the fraternity's plans for the church as 'rigorous', quoted a spokesperson of the cultural association who said that the church will 'move back in time for about twenty years, perhaps even longer'.[22] These arguments garnered support from prominent authors and artists from Utrecht as well as sympathy from most local political parties.[23]

The position that these volunteers articulated was a characteristically secular one. They pitted values such as cultural expressivity, sexual freedom and tolerance against a religious perspective that was placed back in time. The emphasis on the threat that conservative religion is seen to pose to sexual liberty and tolerance of LGBTQ+ people, and the idea that religion threatens to take us back to an earlier and more intolerant past, is distinctive for contemporary secularist discourses (for the Netherlands, see Van der Veer 2006; Mepschen, Duyvendak, and Tonkens 2010; Knibbe 2018). It is striking that what was at stake in this explicitly secular position here was a Christian site that was built – and now reused – for religious worship.

This secular sentiment was also apparent in a debate in the Utrecht city council about the sale of the church – which was effected in the end. During the debate, one of several in the course of 2017, a representative of the Social Democratic Party who was critical of the transaction remarked: 'We all agree that this is a beautiful church with great monumental value. Even stubborn Protestants and anti-church people like me think so.' He characterized SSPX as an 'extremely conservative' group that has made anti-Semitic and homophobic statements in the past. Most representatives of other political parties shared this discomfort with the Catholic fraternity but emphasized they could do little to prevent the sale. The alderman pointed out that this was also a question of the separation of church and state. And in the end, he said, the most important concern for the city council was to safeguard the monument and to keep it accessible for a broad public. A representative of the Green Party expressed a position that was widely shared across the political spectrum: 'It is important that people can still feel: this is my monument.'

Here we see how a church building is claimed as a public site, a monument that should be freely accessible – an aspiration that is seen to be threatened by a religious community. While this case is rather exceptional in the current Dutch context in that a church building is brought *back* to its religious purpose, the disagreement between those who approach church buildings above all as houses of worship and those who approach them as monumental heritage sites is much more common. Often, this disagreement comes to the fore when local residents and heritage associations set out to preserve abandoned church buildings through projects of renovation and run up against the Christian owners of these sites who set particular conditions for their transformation, express concerns about their potential 'unworthy' reuse or at times even favour demolition over repurposing of the buildings (Beekers 2017). Similar conflicts arise around the multiple use of – usually Protestant – church buildings, for instance when members of a congregation have to contend with, and negotiate, the use of their worship space for artistic expositions that are open to members of the general public (Kuyk 2018).

The transformation of the Chassé Church in Amsterdam, which I followed during my fieldwork, further illustrates such contention. While the diocese of Haarlem-Amsterdam originally wanted to demolish the church building and sell the land (it held that the building could not be profitably reused and it needed the funds for the restoration of the remaining central parish church), neighbourhood residents spoke out strongly in favour of preserving and repurposing the site. Eventually, the demolition plans were cancelled, and the building was converted into dance studios, a hotel and a café (Beekers 2017). When I later interviewed the spokesperson of the local committee that had advocated the preservation of the building, he emphasized its historical relevance. 'The building is also important from a cultural-historical perspective', he said. 'It has a function as a memory of the past. . . . The fact that churches have to close down is in itself not a bad thing. But it is a bad thing when you demolish these buildings, because when you do so you also demolish your history.'

These words reflect a view that is widely expressed in today's debates around abandoned church buildings in the Netherlands, namely that these sites have a historical and cultural function that extends beyond their particular use for religious purposes (for comparable ideas in Scotland, see Cotter 2020, 169–71). In this perspective, church buildings – and the Christian religion to which they refer – have become important markers, not necessarily of lived faith, but of history, culture and heritage. This view has implications for ideas about who has legitimacy to decide about the fate of church buildings (cf. Cotter 2020, 171). Indeed, the spokesperson of the local committee felt that the neighbours of the Chassé Church have more to say about the new use of the abandoned church than the former church-members, whom he described as the mere 'historical owners' of the church.

Conclusion

The culturalization of Christianity comes in many forms. Its two manifestations discussed in this chapter differ in terms of their content, motivation and political implications. While the identitarian mobilization of Christianity is characterized by anxieties about Islam and often fervent anti-Muslim politics, local debates about the reuse of church buildings are rather driven by concerns about the preservation and public availability of what is perceived as cultural heritage. Despite these differences, both of these renditions of culturalized Christianity are characterized by antagonism towards religious 'others'. In identitarian Christian politics this is clearly articulated through negative sentiments and often outright xenophobia towards Muslims, thus deepening antagonism towards an already marginalized social group. In local contestations around Christian sites it is more commonly expressed through a – more or less explicit – critique of Christian institutions and communities. While this form of antagonism tends to be more subtle and does not question people's belonging in the same way as identitarian Christianity does, it can have a deeply felt impact on those involved.

At first glance it seems contradictory that those advocating the preservation of Christian (material) culture regularly clash with confessional Christian actors. These conflicts, however, highlight the differences between heritage Christianity and confessional Christianity as separate – though not mutually exclusive – modes and moods of enacting religion. Heritage Christianity and culturalized Christianity more broadly entail a reconfigured engagement with Christian tradition – often by self-identified non-religious, secular or atheist actors – that focuses on religion as a source of cultural heritage, identity, art, history and/ or belonging. While confessional Christians and church communities may acknowledge and value these dimensions of Christianity, they often put a greater emphasis on religious creed, belief and rituals of worship. They generally value church buildings primarily as houses of God or community spaces rather than cultural monuments. As cases like the Saint Willibrord Church and the Chassé Church demonstrate, these divergent values can – and often do – lead to conflicts of interest. This recurrent 'stand-off' between heritage and confessional Christian positions may be particularly manifest in a country like the Netherlands, which is characterized by a predominant secular culture, a strong post-1960s tradition of religion critique and the absence of a state church or an unequivocally dominant Christian denomination. Similar observations have been made elsewhere (for instance, in Quebec; see Burchardt 2020, chap. 5), whereas more symbiotic relations between heritage discourses and church institutions have been identified in other places (see e.g. Oliphant 2015; Astor, Burchardt, and Griera 2017; Isnart and Cerezales 2020).

While the manifestations of identitarian and heritage Christianity discussed here differ in terms of which religious 'others' they oppose, and how and to what extent they do so, this chapter has also exposed an important continuity across them. What many actors across the spectrum of culturalized Christianity in the Netherlands share is a desire for rearticulating one's sense of self – for recovering one's roots and belonging in the face of processes of social transformation, cultural diversification and the decline of organized Christianity. Notions of Christian culture – and solid, material and iconic Christian sites (Knott, Krech, and Meyer 2016) – appear to provide a 'heavy' resource within such quests for cultural belonging, even for those who explicitly reject Christian beliefs and institutions or pursue a secular political agenda.

Indeed, culturalized Christianity is ambiguously related to secularism. For one part, it often dovetails with a secular politics that rejects religious practices and values. For another part, the renewed interest in Christian culture appears to be motivated, at least for some, by a dissatisfaction with the wholesale denunciation of religion that has become common practice in the Netherlands since the 1960s. Those who express this position worry that by having moved away from the church, the Dutch have also taken leave of a major repository of meaning, identity and community. These proponents of culturalized Christianity strive towards a continuity of religious tradition that does not necessarily entail a continuity of ritual practice – a type of religious engagement that can be described as 'belonging without believing' (Hervieu-Léger 2000, 162).

The depth of feeling that characterizes such attempts at retrieving a sense of belonging may help explain the fervent antagonism towards religious communities described in this chapter. Confessional Christians, who often set other priorities than those emphasizing cultural belonging, may be seen to jeopardize not only the preservation of heritage but also the reassertion of identity that can be found to underlie such preservation efforts. Muslims, on their part, have to bear the brunt of attempts at demarcating a Dutch or European self in terms of a Christian past that is positioned, either explicitly or implicitly, over and against an Islamic 'other'. Those seeking to destabilize the epistemological borders around Fortress Europe, then, will need to critically think through ways of engaging with Christian culture that could be inclusive rather than exclusive, empower minoritized religious communities rather than brand them as the enemy and enable inviting rather than restrictive modes of belonging – even if, in the final instance, conflicting interests based on distinct understandings of religion may never be entirely avoidable.

Shaken identities

A refused handshake and its politicization in Switzerland

Martin Bürgin

From the classroom to the political arena

In spring 2016, a local incident at a Swiss secondary school became the source of transnational media coverage, national political activism and a cantonal legislation process. At the secondary school of Therwil, a rather small town in the Canton of Basel-Landschaft, counting approximately 430 students living in Therwil and the surrounding villages, two teenage students refused to shake hands with their female teacher.

In their perception of Islam, the two Muslim boys reportedly argued, a handshake with a woman would transgress their religious conviction. They justified the refusal of the handshake, referring to the teacher's sex and/or gender. Accordingly, they did not refuse to shake hands with their male teacher. At the level of the local school as well as in the following debates, this disparity was largely interpreted as sexual discrimination against the female teacher and a violation of the school's gender equality policy.

In order to take both interests – religious diversity and gender equality – into account, the local school management mediated a temporary code of conduct, which ought to ensure the equal treatment of female and male teachers and ought to be in accordance with the religious regulations, postulated by the students and their parents. The involved parties agreed that the two students address their teachers for the future with another form of appropriate and respectful greeting. This form of greeting however had to be applied to all teachers, independently of their sex and/or gender. In other words, the agreement forbade the students to shake hands with male teachers as long as they refused to shake hands with female teachers. Although a practical modus operandi was established, the school management brought the case to the attention of the cantonal department of education, expressing the wish for guidelines on how to deal within analogous situations henceforward.

Meanwhile, the discussion of the subject left the narrow sphere of the local and cantonal educational system. When a studio audience attendee on a Swiss television political talk show called *Arena* referred to the case – in an episode broadcasted under the lurid title *Angst for dem Islam* (*Fear of Islam*) – the incident was brought to public attention. Although spoken in Swiss German, which is neither spoken nor understood in all parts of the country, *Arena* was at the time the political talk show that gained the highest number of viewers, reaching a market share of almost 20 per cent of all television programmes broadcast in Switzerland, including non-political programmes and foreign channels. Subsequently, news media picked up the incident. Talk masters, journalists and politicians commented on the case, linking and expanding it with discourses on migration, diversity, integration, assimilation, cultural boundaries, Islamophobia, foreignness and citizenship. The local incident of two Muslim students refusing to shake hands with their female teacher – catchily addressed as the *Therwil case,* the *Handshake Affair of Therwil,* the *Therwilian Handshake Affair* or simply the *Handshake of Therwil* – became the subject of a nationwide political debate.

The handshake – a common, but certainly not comprehensively applied, salutatory practice at Swiss schools – was declared to be an old-established custom, an expression of courtesy, a symbol of Swiss values and, as the minister of justice expressed, an essential part of Swiss culture.

With over 450 media articles from local newspapers to broadcasters like *Al Jazeera* and publications like *The New York Times*, with a transnational audience the Therwil Affair gained – be it as a controversial topic or a bizarre oddity – the status of a media affair (Stahel 2021). The extensive media coverage, as well as the demand of political measures postulated by politicians of influence on a national level, in turn put pressure on the regional authorities and politicians in the Canton of Basel-Landschaft. This resulted in a legislative process to modify the educational law as well as the cantonal constitution.

The Therwil Affair also had an impact on the academic world and became a subject of several enquiries in different disciplines. Petra Bleisch reflected the affair within the scope of professional ethics in the educational system (Bleisch 2016). Jurists Fabienne Bretscher (Bretscher 2017), Anne Kühler (Kühler 2018a, b, 2021) and Laila Hersi (Hersi 2018) discussed the case in the perspective of comparative and constitutional law. Lea Stahel focused on the media scandalization and the concept of collapsing contexts in networked publics (Stahel 2018, 2021). Bryan Turner and Rosario Forlenza included the case in a survey on the politics of Europe's religious borders (Forlenza and Turner 2019, 9). Christoph Baumgartner reconstructed arguments of different handshake debates in several countries, considering motives from Islamic legal discourses, which he illustrates as the basis of the refusal to shake hands, and turns to a normative disquisition of the matter (Baumgartner 2019). Rafael Walthert, Katharina Frank, Daniela Stauffacher and Urs Weber used the affair as a case study for a systems-theoretical analysis (Walthert et al. 2021). Mirjam Aeschbach discussed the relationship between culture, religion and gender in the debates around the case as a process of culturalization (Aeschbach 2021). Philipp Hetmanczyk examined different concepts of diversity within the debate and their implications for the politicization of public schools (Hetmanczyk 2021). The present chapter (like Bürgin 2021) explores the relationship between law, religion and the politics of remembrance. It analyses the political debates in the mentioned cantonal legislative process, verbalized in its central documents; it contextualizes implicit and explicit imaginations of belonging, expressed in the parliamentary and governmental bills; and it shows how collective memories are used to mobilize political action.

Symbolic law and the politics of alterity

In June 2017, the cantonal government of Basel-Landschaft presented a legal bill to change certain provisions in cantonal acts and the cantonal constitution. The bill was a reaction on four motions submitted by political parties and Members of Parliament. It suggested the installation of a so-called *primacy of civic duties* (over ideological perceptions and religious commandments) in the cantonal constitution and the expansion of the legal basis of educational law towards *an obligation to inform the authorities in situations when problems of integration should occur.*

The primacy of civic duties was a concept which was installed in the national constitution in 1874. As a product of culture war politics, it was initiated by the, at the time, liberal-radical majority and directed against the Catholic-conservative minority. On a nationwide level, this relic of the nineteenth-century politico-denominational conflict was removed from the constitution in 1999. It was a law that lost its applicability over time. In twentieth-century jurisdiction, individual freedom of religion and freedom of thought were usually regarded as legal interests of higher value. Moreover, when the liberals lost their dispositive of power, it was no longer clear how civic duties should be defined and what exactly these duties include (Kühler 2021). Anne Kühler reads the primacy of civic duties as a symbolic constitutional norm and as a product of symbolic legislative procedure. With reference to Peter Noll, she considers *symbolic* in contrast to the *instrumental function* of law and in contrast to the legal effectiveness of law, stressing the *intentions of the lawgiver* as the relevant constituent of symbolic law (Noll 1981, 347–8). From a history of religion perspective, it is of interest how such *intentions* were underpinned with historical narratives and related to potent topoi of remembrance cultures.

Memories of the culture war period, however, differ in different political camps. They are associated with conflicting narratives. If one reads the primacy of civic duties as a symbolic constitutional norm, it may be worthwhile to discuss the major readings of the culture war period and the constructions of political identities associated with it.

First, however, the government council's proposal shall be read with regard to the dichotomization of collective identities it contains. It is evident that the bill is marked by the discursive order of the public debate on the refused handshake in Therwil. On two pages the government expatiated on the 'initial situation' that had led to the effort to modify the cantonal constitution and the education law. These two pages consist of seven paragraphs, containing four passages in which the government resorted to the practice of othering, a key element of identity politics (Jensen 2011; Spivak 1985). The first passage can be translated as follows:

> Particularly in view of the increasing immigration of people to Switzerland with different ethnic and religious backgrounds, it is essential that these people respect the rights, values and socially accepted customs that apply in our country. (Regierungsrat 2017a, 3)

In this passage, the others are characterized as a rather opaque mass ('these [immigrant] people [. . .] with different ethnic and religious backgrounds'). This is accompanied by the expectation that *these others* must respect the 'rights, values and socially recognised customs that apply in our country'. The nature of these rights, values and customs, though, is not revealed to the readers. The passage does not clarify their concrete characteristics, nor does it provide a definition of the terms in use. Another passage of the bill indicates that

> [o]ur liberal state and societal order, built on a humanistic but also secular foundation, is being challenged [through] religious fundamentalist motivated behaviour. (Regierungsrat 2017a, 3)

The distinction of the *own group* from *the other* is intensified, as their achievements are seemingly questioned by *the others*. In this configuration, one's own identity is constructed and accentuated through otherness. The government continued this dichotomous perspective when, a few sentences further on, it described the challenges 'the society as a whole' was facing:

> The questions raised are currently of concern to society as a whole. How does society deal with the increasing heterogeneity of the population without losing its values and thus its self-understanding and identity? How does a democratically constituted, secular, pluralistic, liberal and adaptive society deal with anti-liberal or even totalitarian individuals and groups who refuse dialogue and integration? (Regierungsrat 2017a, 3)

The fourth passage, in which explicit othering is practised, now takes the argumentation into the school context:

> In connection with the increased influx of persons with foreign citizenship, some of whom have different cultural and religious backgrounds, which differ strongly from Switzerland's traditional Christian-occidental, but today also secularised humanistic values, conflicts occasionally arise – as the incident mentioned at the beginning shows. Not only, but especially in the field of education, the state has a legitimate interest and the right to protect and enforce the values on which its order is based. (Regierungsrat 2017a, 4)

In the first three passages, the description of *the other* undergoes a continuous intensification: from immigrants with different ethnic and religious backgrounds, to persons who question the social order through religious fundamentalist motivated behaviour, to totalitarian individuals and groups who refuse dialogue and integration. The own group, on the other hand, is first described as an entity with a liberal state and societal order built on a humanistic foundation, then as a democratically constituted, secular, pluralistic, liberal and adaptive society, whereby these attributes are implicitly denied to *the others*. At the same time, the phrase of an increasing heterogeneity of the population due to migration implies the image of a previously less heterogeneous society that – to stay within the logic of the argument – had to deal less with the question of how to act in order to preserve its values, its self-image and its identity.

In the fourth passage, the description of the others is eased again. *The others* are thus described more or less analogously to the first passage as persons with foreign citizenship with partly different cultural and religious backgrounds. The description of the *own group*, however, is expanded. Their values are no longer described as merely secularized humanistic.[1] They experience a remarkable expansion in the additional description as traditionally Christian-occidental. Through this expansion – as will be shown subsequently – different commemorative topoi are served.

Collective identity and collective commemoration

The recourse to a common past, in which the currently 'valid values, rights and [...] customs' are rooted, serves – like the practice of othering – the construction of a collective identity. In *Les cadres sociaux de la mémoire* from 1925, Maurice Halbwachs emphasized the social structure of memory: What finds its way into memory is generated through communication and social interaction within a group and is thus a group-specific product. This group-internal memory, in turn, acts as an identity-forming factor that enables the production of identity through alterity.

The collective memory is neither a static nor a homogeneous entity. Remembrance changes with the respective present; it evolves in its specific historical and cultural context. Within a specific group, a variety of shared memories may exist; various social groups imagine the past in different ways. Aleida Assmann – who shaped the term 'functional memory' (*Funktionsgedächtnis*) – pointed out that parts of the collective memory are cultivated actively and open for manipulation. Its contents are used selectively and strategically, especially by political players. In doing so, memories would be subjected to a perspectival use and serve to legitimize or delegitimize political power (Assmann 1999). In reference to Lévi-Strauss' concept of bricolage (Lévi-Strauss 2013, 29–48), Guy Marchal characterized the selective and strategic usage of the past as 'Gebrauchsgeschichte' or 'imagologische Bastelei', wherein images of the past are 'used again and again to legitimise one's own positions historically' (Marchal 2007, 13). In a collage-like manner topical images can be arranged, interpreted and reinterpreted. The imagery that is meaningful for the self-understanding of a community is not based on historical reliability or verifiability. Rather, it represents

> a construct, a *bricolage* into which a very specific set of images, concepts and symbols has been composed. But these are only adopted insofar and in those ideal connections as they can be an identificatory *signifiers*. [. . .] The specific selection and weighting, the arrangement of the imagological bricolage, takes place out of the respective different experience of identity. (Marchal 1992, 47)[2]

The government's bill can exemplarily be read along the concepts of Assmann and Marchal. In such a reading, the past recalled in the draft is selective in nature and subject to a strategic calculation. In addition, it can be insinuated that the authors of the bill relied on a certain set of images and terms that they considered to be suitable for the mobilization of majorities in the cantonal parliament.

When the government evoked the image of a formerly less heterogeneous society in which no one had to fear for 'the loss of values, self-image and identity', the government concealed the extent to which Swiss history has been shaped by conflict, especially with regard to religious–political questions. From the 1520s to the end of the eighteenth century, the Old Swiss Confederacy was divided into a Protestant and a Catholic camp. Members of these two camps fought four confessional wars and a multitude of regional denominational conflicts. In addition, there was continuous structural violence and persecution against Jewish, Baptist and Anabaptist communities. From the late eighteenth century to the late nineteenth century, what Olaf Blaschke called the 'second confessional age' (Blaschke 2000), the country was divided – sketched here in an ideal-type manner along the lines of the history of ideas – into a liberal (modern) and an anti-liberal (anti-modern) camp. The former followed the ideals of the French Revolution; the latter opposed these ideals and the social upheavals associated with them. The liberal camp advocated a secular state that would curb the influence of religious players in education, politics, the economy and the public sphere in general. The conservative camp pleaded for a federalist state that would leave sovereignty over school matters in the hands of the cantons. Associated with this was the question of whether clergymen could remain employed as teachers in public schools and whether it was mandatory to use secular teaching materials provided by the government. For the conservatives, the state should not interfere in religious matters, respond to social change with hesitation and leave sovereignty of education with the church. The relationship between the two camps was formed through processes of social and cultural differentiation.

These took place in private and public spheres, within political disputes and armed conflicts (Holenstein 2014; Mesmer 2006; Hettling 2006).

As conflict-ridden areas of experience, these disputes are still transmitted in conflicting narratives. Both (ideal-typical) camps and their successors – or those parties and individual protagonists who claim to be their successors – refer to their own historical narratives (Metzger 2019; Mohn 2013, 57–8). The government of Basel-Landschaft confronted the two camps and their respective narratives in an ambivalent manner. The primacy of civic duties, which the government wanted to incorporate into the cantonal constitution, carries a strong commemorative burden: its inclusion in the revised federal constitution of 1874 was precisely a product of the culture war politics between the liberal and conservative camps. In sketching the picture of a formerly less heterogeneous society, the government, however, eviscerated the conflictual nature of the intended amendment.

The bill presents the 'values of the past' as lived continuities. Although there is reference to a change in these values (from 'traditional Christian-occidental' to 'today also secularized humanistic values'), this remains without historical contextualization. The associated disparities and fracture lines remain obscure. Meanwhile, the two ciphers 'Christian-occidental' and 'secularized humanist' or 'secular, pluralist and liberal' can be interpreted as references to the respective remembrance cultures of the liberal and conservative camps. If one reads the bill as an imagological bricolage, these two ciphers form – in terms of Marchal – a set of images, terms and symbols intended to evoke ideational associations among the Members of Parliament. As Marchal explained, only those ideational associations that are read as identificatory signifiers are absorbed. The arrangement of the imagological bricolage, the specific selection and weighting, is carried out on the basis of political affiliation. The actual ruse of the bill, seen from the perspective of remembrance politics, lies in the manner in which it unites the narratives of both camps.

The liberal narrative

The bill submitted to the parliament paraphrases essential passages from two motions submitted by the liberal fraction (*FDP-Fraktion*), which called for a constitutional amendment. In a motion called 'Enforce the right to education!', the liberal party (*Freisinnig-Demokratische Partei. Die Liberalen*) interpreted the refusal to shake hands as an act that was rooted in 'archaic values' and as an expression of a 'fundamentalist and militant ideology':

> The Therwil refusal to shake hands with female teachers is not an adolescent escapade by two pupils, as it is sometimes trivialised. Also, it is about much more than decency or the disregard of self-evident Swiss customs. With their behaviour, the youths are implementing a fundamentalist and militant ideology that diametrically contradicts our state and social order, which is based on personal freedom, legal equality and the equality of women and men. (FDP 2017a, 12)

Personal freedom, equality under the law and equality of women and men are articulated here as the pillars of society. If one replaces the equality of women and men with the rather old-fashioned concept of fraternity, rooted in times of male hegemony, it turns into the triad of *Liberté, Egalité et Fraternité*, the slogan of the French Revolution, which is essential for the self-perception and historical self-positioning of the Swiss liberals. Of course, one might ask whether the very essence of personal freedom would not guarantee the right to refuse a handshake. The liberals, however, refrained from doing so. They focused on gender equality and equality before the law. In their second motion 'state law before religious rule', the liberals claimed:

> The refusal to shake hands with female teachers at a Therwil school raises fundamental questions that go beyond the school and education sector. Religious freedom does not provide a right to evade civic duties laid down by the state. That is valid law. However, this no longer seems to be sufficiently clear. Militant fundamentalist circles are increasingly attempting to promote their archaic values, which contradict the liberal-democratic state and social order, by means of an extensive interpretation of religious freedom. This has to be stopped resolutely.

Here, the liberals stated that state law should take precedence over religious regulations. By describing Switzerland's state and social order as liberal–democratic, the FDP staged its own memory-cultural location and associated it with its motion: the liberals as founders of the modern federal state and the defenders of this state against illiberal and archaic religious forces in the nineteenth century as well as in the present. The liberals demanded the implementation of the aforementioned priority of civic duties in the cantonal constitution. They referred to the constitution of the canton of Aargau and to the federal constitution of 1874, which contained analogous provisions:

> Section 11, subsection 2 of the cantonal constitution of Aargau explicitly states that ideological views and religious rules do not exempt from the fulfilment

of civic duties. An analogous provision existed in Article 49 of the old federal constitution of 1874. (FDP 2017b, 14)

What the liberals called the 'old federal constitution of 1874' meant the revision of the constitution of 1848, the first constitution of the modern state. Both versions were products of the conflict between the two dominant camps of the nineteenth century described earlier, the liberal-radical and the Catholic-conservative camps. The constitution of 1848 was written and put into effect after the state-forming civil war (*Sonderbundskrieg*) between liberal and Catholic-conservative cantons. The constitution of 1874 in turn – and this was particularly the case for the primacy of civic duties – was a product of culture war politics of the 1870s (*Kulturkampf*). Both constitutions served as guarantors of the liberal-radical majority of the time and were directed against the Catholic-conservative minority. They served as a genuine dispositive of power.

The constitutional revision was characterized by exceptional laws to the disadvantage of the Roman Catholic Church. Culture war politics in Switzerland implied opposition to the *syllabus errorum* enacted in 1864; resistance to the dogmas of the First Vatican Council, to papal infallibility and the papal primate of jurisdiction; the closure of numerous monasteries and the confiscation of their properties by radical-liberal-governed cantons; within the Catholic Church, the confrontation between supporters and opponents of the Catholic Enlightenment; the establishment and promotion of the Old Catholic Church (in Switzerland: *Christkatholische Kirche*); the expulsion of two bishops loyal to Rome who questioned the state authority in the radical-liberal-dominated cantons overlapping with their dioceses; the expulsion from office of those clerics who declared their allegiance to the two deposed bishops; and – as the climax of the escalation spiral of culture war – the severance of diplomatic relations with the Holy See (Stadler 1996; Clark and Kaiser 2003; Bürgin 2019).

Already the constitution of 1848 banned the Jesuits and the affiliated societies from any activity in state and church (Art. 51). In the revision of the federal constitution of 1874, the articles directed against the Catholic Church were expanded: Art. 51 specified the prohibition of the Jesuit Order with an explicit interdiction of activities in church and school for members of the Jesuit Order; Art. 52 prohibited the establishment of new monasteries or the restoration of abolished ones; Art. 50 made the establishment of dioceses subject to federal approval; Art. 75 excluded Swiss citizens of clerical status (including ordained Protestant pastors or Old Catholic priests) from being elected to the national council (the large chamber of the federal parliament). The advocates of these religious–political amendments justified the derogatory restrictions on freedom of faith and conscience as measures to preserve religious peace and protect the young democracy. In the liberal narrative, the aim was to defend Switzerland's liberal and democratic order against religious zealots – whom they identified primarily in the ranks of the Jesuits, the monastic orders and Catholic-conservative politicians. In the liberal narrative, the purpose was the defence of Switzerland's liberal and democratic order against *ultramontane* influence (controlled from beyond the Alps) and religious zealots – whom they identified primarily in the ranks of the Jesuits, the monastic orders and Catholic-conservative politicians.

With references to culture war politics and the claim for the reinstatement of the primacy of civic duties, the FDP fraction enacted itself as the historical heir and legal successor of the nineteenth-century culture warriors. The FDP adopted its predecessors' lines of argumentation but shifted the religious–political distinction: it was no longer the Catholic-conservatives who were described as illiberal and externally controlled forces, but the two Muslim pupils who refused to shake hands with their female teacher. According to the liberals, they represented the 'militant fundamentalist circles' who wanted to 'promote their archaic values, which contradict the liberal-democratic state and social order, by means of an extensive interpretation of religious freedom'. The government adopted the perspective of the FDP fraction and backed its demand to incorporate the primacy of civic duties in the cantonal constitution. However, the government refrained from taking up the liberals' historical narrative and concealed the historical origins of the article in its bill. In the government's bill the societal order of the *own group* was described not only as liberal–democratic – as in the motion of the liberals – but also as a Christian-occidental. Thereby, the government referred not only to a commemorative topos of the liberal narrative but also to one of the conservative narrative.

The conservative narrative

The topos of a Christian-occidental Europe has become heavily charged in terms of remembrance culture and identity politics. The concept of a Christian Occident (*Christliches Abendland*) is a core element of conservative narratives and anti-liberal visions of Europe (Pöpping 2002; Faber 2002; Forlenza and Turner 2019; von Stuckrad 2006). The term was shaped to a significant extent – particularly in the Swiss reception – by Frédéric Gonzague de Reynold, an influential thinker of Swiss conservatism in the first half of the twentieth century. The implications of the term will therefore be illustrated along the lines of his writings. What is described here as the conservative narrative, however, does not derive from the culture war of the 1870s but is to be read as a response to it in the context of the formation of political and confessional milieus in the early twentieth century. As will be exemplified by the work of de Reynold, the concept of a Christian Occident was set up as an antithesis to the culture war narrative of the liberal camp.[3]

As a proponent of a hierarchical order in the Roman Catholic Church, he considered papal infallibility and papal jurisdictional primacy to be self-evident. He appealed to the Roman Catholic Swiss citizens to adopt the church's doctrines as their sole guidance in all aspects of life, especially in politics. This included a defence of the *syllabus errorum* of 1864, the list of eighty theses that Pope Pius IX condemned as erroneous (Mattioli 1994b, 86–7).[4] For him the most urgent task of the present was not the modernization of Catholicism but the catholicization of the modern world. The political culture of the liberal federal state of 1848 he characterized as a betrayal of the *sacred principles of Catholicism* (Mattioli 1994b, 85–9). In his treatise *L'Europe tragique*, published in several editions, he articulated a fundamental critique of modern Europe, which had been suffering since the French Revolution from the aberration of liberal civilization (de Reynold 1934). His admiration went to the Portuguese *Estado Novo* under António de Oliveira Salazar, in which he saw the embodiment of an *Etat chrétien* (de Reynold 1936). Yet, he believed, the contours of a new world were emerging on the horizon. A world in which Christian monarchies and other authoritarian systems would prevail. The age of democracies he considered to be over. If Switzerland wanted to assert itself in the new world order, it would have to overcome its democratic form of government, transform itself into an authoritarian regime headed by a dictatorial *Landammann* and in doing so – according to Gonzague de Reynold – find its way back to its true heritage (Mattioli 2007, 196).

With these claims, he became – at least for a while – a pariah in liberal academic circles. He soon found himself isolated in Bern, where liberalism and Protestantism dominated. He drew the consequence and bid farewell to his professorship in Bern. He toyed with the idea of taking up an offer made by the Italian minister of justice Alfredo Rocco and accepting a professorship at the *Sapienzia* in fascist-ruled Rome. When he received a call soon after to the Catholic-conservative University of Fribourg, which lured him with a chair – tailored to him – for the *Histoire de la civilisation à l'époque moderne*, he accepted (Mattioli 2007, 194).

In Fribourg, he began to work on the monumental seven-volume work *La formation de l'Europe*. Under the impression of the war's turn in 1943, he reconsidered his vision of a new European order. Henceforth, he devoted himself to the exploration of what he called 'the essence of Europe's origins and future developments' (de Reynold 1944, 32). His core thesis, which runs through all seven volumes, was anticipated already at the outset: the essence of Europe resides in Christendom. The ideal state of European culture he saw achieved in 'the age of Christendom' in the thirteenth century. The world of the polis in ancient Greece and Hellenism was central to the development of this ideal type because 'they brought culture to Europe'. Roman antiquity, in turn, gave Europe the 'idea of the empire'. Nevertheless, it was not until Charlemagne that 'the empire was established under the sign of Christendom', to which 'Europe owes its existence, its soul and the very essence of its civilisation'. Thereby, he distinguished between a true and a false Europe. The true Europe he located in the Occident, in Romanic and in Germanic Europe. Slavic Europe, by which he also meant the non-Slavic-speaking countries and regions of Eastern Europe, he described as a barbarian world, which existed beyond the borders of European civilization. Europe, he wrote (and meant occidental Europe), was only a small continent, but it was the actual 'centre and navel of the world'. For de Reynold, it was exclusively in Europe that a 'culture of a universal character' had emerged (de Reynold 1944, 36, 55, 74). Gonzague de Reynold postulated not only the cultural superiority of occidental Europe over the rest of the world. He simultaneously abnegated the historical significance of other religious and areligious influences on the cultural development of Europe.

With his Christian-determined and Eurocentric view of history, de Reynold met the pulse of his time, as Aram Mattioli pointed out (Mattioli 2007, 201). The layout and principal assumptions of *La formation de l'Europe* expressed the occidental self-perception of conservative circles during the Cold War. During the ten years in which the European integration process was launched – from the establishment of the Council of Europe (1949) to the Treaty of Rome (1957) – de Reynold was considered one of the leading scholars in European history. His concept of a Christian-occidental Europe served as a conceptual framework for the Christian conservative parties in post-war Europe, directed (explicitly) against the 'godless communists' in Eastern Europe and the 'increasing Americanization of culture' as much as (implicitly) against the liberal and Social Democratic Parties in Western Europe (Mattioli 2001, 196).

While de Reynold associated the term 'Christian' above all with Roman Catholicism, the term was used in a broader sense in the debate about the Therwil handshake. Apart from members of the Christian Democratic People's Party (CVP), whose right wing stands in the tradition of the Catholic-conservatives, politicians of the traditionally Protestant-Reformed national-conservative Swiss People's Party (SVP) or the Evangelical national-conservative Federal Democratic Union (EDU) referred also to the concept of a Christian Occident as the guiding principle. Although it cannot be assumed that the three parties are still bound to clearly defined confessional milieus or that Christian ethics, however defined, guide the political actions of the representatives of these parties,[5] in terms of memory culture, however, they can all be located in the conservative camp, in intentional demarcation from the liberalism of the nineteenth century.

The bill as an imagological bricolage

The governmental bill can be read as a multiple bricolage. Written and edited as a patchwork by the government members (from different political parties) and their staff, it integrates demands, arguments and concepts from three parliamentary motions, whereby the government council either adopted their positions – sometimes in the form of entire passages without declaration – or took a critical stance on them. Moreover, it can be read as an imagological bricolage in the sense of Marchal, as a condensate of different historical narratives and commemorative topoi.

Resembling a conundrum, the bill triggers different associations depending on the political position of its readers. From the perspective of the history of ideas, the liberal and conservative narratives are antithetical to each other, as explained earlier. In the liberal narrative, the conservatives are the antagonists; in the conservative narrative, the liberals are the antagonists. In the government's bill, however, the conflicting historical narratives are united. Liberals and conservatives are not presented as opponents. As antipodes the bill arranges the two Muslim pupils who refused to shake hands with their female teacher as symbolically charged agents of a 'fundamentalist religious', 'anti-liberal' and 'totalitarian' threat (Regierungsrat 2017, 3). Against them, both liberals and conservatives can present themselves in accordance with their respective narratives as 'defenders of a liberal, humanistic and secular order' or as 'guardians of Switzerland's traditional Christian-occidental values'.

The culture war of the nineteenth century is associatively countered by an assumed culture war of the twenty-first century, which is staged as a conflict between the state and the 'local values' against a threat from anti-liberal and fundamentalist-religious Muslim migrants. The extremely vague and open-ended description of 'local values' in the bill allowed politicians from different camps to link their own political positions and historical narratives to the bill. The imagined threat and the associated othering serve to establish a political identity that unites the liberal and conservative camps with their respective different party-political remembrance cultures.

The refused handshake thus becomes a politically charged symbol of an ideal civic order that is challenged by migration and cultural diversity. Such a symbolic interpretation can only be understood on the background of a discourse that has been established in Switzerland in recent decades, in which 'Islam' is formulated as a projection screen of increasingly xenophobic politics, in which religio-political positions and politics of migration are interwoven. Within this discourse, legal terms – the primacy of civic duties – may serve as markers of identity politics. After all, law is a product of cultural and social processes of negotiation and differentiation.

Conclusion

In recent decades, all over Europe, public schools became sites where issues of religious diversity were negotiated. Several debates had their cause at the level of school regulations related to religious clothing of teachers or students. Others concerned school-provided services and facilities, such as food offered in school canteens or the availability of prayer rooms. The objection against certain teaching materials and contents by concerned parents and the manifold social interactions among pupils or between pupils and their teachers define other situations in which issues of religious diversity become contested and negotiated. The list of incidents related to school regulations, facilities, curricula or classroom interactions is long and ranges from incidents concerning whether or not headscarves for students and/or teachers should be allowed; if yoga and meditation are appropriate practices for recreational breaks between school lessons; if schools have to provide religiously specific diets in their cafeterias or should not be permitted to provide them; if students can be excused from co-educational sport lessons or sex education due to religious reasons; if creationistic concepts should be taught in biology classes; or how to prevent religiously discriminatory behaviour in the classroom.

In many cases, such incidents tend to take the form of political conflicts and leave their local environment of the schoolhouses in which they happened. They show a tendency to become issues of national and sometimes international debates concerning the relationship between religious diversity and secular school; moreover, they serve as starting points to launch copious debates on religious freedom, cultural values, migration politics, national identity, liberalism or the limits of the latter. The increase of religious diversity is perceived and portrayed as a challenge to – however defined – national and cultural values and identities. Such perceptions rest upon the configuration of public schools as institutions in which collectively shared concepts, orders of knowledge and specific political values, ethics and worldviews are taught – implicitly or explicitly – as constitutive and integral elements of a common culture and identity of a given society. As such, it is hardly surprising that public schools have been and continue to be the subject of culture war debates.

Considering the nature of societies as heterogeneous and fluid entities with a multitude of individuals and social groups, public schools are particularly sensitive areas, wherefrom issues of religion and identity – locally debated as everyday occurrences – emerge very quickly into affairs of wider political interest. The Therwil Affair is a paradigmatic case of such a politicization. It illustrates how religion and non-religion are addressed in the context of migration politics as markers of exclusion.

Swiss critics of an open migration policy rarely emphasize an affiliation of Switzerland to Europe when it comes to joining the European Union or mobility rights within the continent. In the Swiss context, the metaphor of Fortress Europe used in the title of this anthology could be adapted as Fortress Switzerland. Concerning the idea of Europe as a domain with a shared collective culture, which must be defended against foreign influences coming from beyond Europe, the same politicians however would certainly agree that Switzerland is a European country. Albeit imagined as a country that is not a mere part of the metaphorical fortress, but forms its centrepiece, while the surrounding countries rather appear as outer walls and trenches. Within this discourse, the nature of the shared collective culture is secondary. The politics of othering, the reference to those who remain (or ought to remain) outside the wall, obviates the need to clarify the question. The allusion to alterity is the wall that keeps the fortress stable.

8

Debating Irish identity

Religion, race, nation and the construction of Irishness

Hazel O'Brien

Religion, race and nationality in Ireland

The Republic of Ireland's[1] rapid economic and social change since the 1990s has transformed Irish society. Mass immigration and increasing ethnic diversity have forced Ireland to confront what it means to be Irish in the contemporary era. These trends have driven increases in religious diversity which now exists alongside a simultaneous decline of Ireland's traditional faith, Catholicism. This chapter synthesizes ethnographic observations on the experiences of Irish Mormons as a religious minority, with analysis of recent high-profile incidents relating to race, religion and exclusion in Ireland. It questions if and how nuanced understandings of diversity have been incorporated into dominant frames of Irish identity.

What are the mechanisms through which Ireland's traditional definitions of belonging are being sustained in the contemporary era? Ireland's creation of the modern nation state confirms that Ireland has been constructed as an ethnic state to support the development of a strong national identity (Fanning 2012). Evidence of this abounds but is well articulated by Brannigan (2008, 230):

The Irish state and Irish society have mobilised figures of racial difference – the 'black babies' in need of Irish charity, travellers and Jews demonised and vilified, Hungarians, and latterly Romanians, Nigerians, Chinese and others abused and denied rights of citizenship and equality – in order to legitimate an implicitly white, nationalist, usually Catholic, masculine and heterosexual identity. 'Race', in this context, does not mean an essentialising discourse of collective biological, cultural, or historical genealogy, but the persistent circulation of ideologies of cultural difference and relation based upon what Fanon calls the 'racial epidermal schema' of identity.

In Ireland we can see that religion works with and against concepts of race and nation to construct and maintain appropriate cultural understandings of the category of 'Irish', from which some groups are denied full access. Wilde and Glassman (2016, 409) observe in a US context that 'just as inequality in the United States is complex, so too is its relationship with religion. Accepting this premise has important implications for our understanding of politics.' My research with Mormons in Ireland indicates that even as a mainly white religious minority in a majority-white country, they do not escape these processes of marginalization. Although clearly racialized religions such as Islam may more obviously illuminate the entanglement of racial and religious exclusion in Ireland, those religious minorities who are majority-white and majority Irish-born are also excluded. Thus, this chapter contributes an alternative approach to the discussions of religious exclusion discussed in many of the other chapters of this volume by offering observations on how majority-white religious minorities are both privileged and marginalized within a European society that has built collective identities based on specific religious and racial experiences.

Davie (2000) has observed that religious diversity and religious tolerance are distinct, and we must try to understand how both operate if we are to comprehend contemporary European religion. Throughout this chapter it will be evident that although Ireland's diversity is increasing, its tolerance for this diversity may not be. Ireland's religious, national and racial history continues to shape its present in ways which exclude particular groups from narratives of national belonging. Ireland's understanding of national belonging is not simply based on race, nor is it a simple response to recent mass immigration. Rather, it is based on a complex intermingling of race, religion and nationality which has been sustained into the current moment where it can now be utilized strategically for political gain, or be articulated in new, more visible ways through twenty-first-century technologies such as social media. Further on, I offer a brief overview of how a rhetoric of conservative exclusion came to dominate Irish politics by centring the role of religion, race and nation in Ireland's social development.

Exclusion and the Irish cultural landscape

Ireland's political development has been unusual in some respects. Ireland's independence from Britain shaped Ireland's political landscape in ways which we can still see evidence of today. After independence and the subsequent partition of Northern Ireland, a brief but bitter civil war occurred which has shaped Irish politics up to the present (Whyte 1976; Ferriter 2004). For almost all of Ireland's history post-independence, one of two centre-right political parties has held power – either Fianna Fáil or Fine Gael. With the history of each party reaching back to opposing sides of the early-twentieth-century civil war, their obvious similarities in economic and social policies have until recently not been enough to overcome these historical deep divisions. This has left Ireland as somewhat of an 'anomaly' (Garner 2007, 110) across Europe, where typical left-right political divides shape nations' political systems (Ferriter 2004). As a result of Ireland's 2020 general election where left-wing party Sinn Féin scooped 24 per cent of first-preference votes in Ireland's proportional representation system, there is some evidence that the dominance of the civil war parties in Irish voting preferences may be breaking down in favour of the left-right split we often see elsewhere. However, it is too early to tell if this is a sustained shift in Irish political patterns, or a reactionary response from the electorate due to frustrations at the effects of their government's economic and social policies.

What we can say with some certainty is that until recently Ireland has avoided the political representation of far-right populism which we can see within the political system of its European neighbours (Garner 2009; McGinnity et al. 2018). This is not to say that there is no far-right political presence in Ireland. There are a number of far-right groups and/or political parties currently operating in Ireland, such as the Freedom Party and the National Party, whose slogan of 'Ireland belongs to the Irish' demonstrates their exclusionary policies towards migrants and those deemed outside of their construction of Irish. However it is notable that despite concerns of a far-right surge in the recent 2020 general election which would reflect trends seen across Europe, these parties accumulated less than 2 per cent of first-preference votes (McDermott 2020).

Nonetheless, there does appear to be a shift in Ireland towards a vocal rather than a silent conservatism. In defining populism, whether conservative or otherwise, Mudd and Kaltwasser (2014, 379) maintain that populist ideologies often describe society as segregated into homogeneous but opposing groups – the 'pure people' and the 'corrupt elite' – while Brubaker (2017, 5) agrees with Mudd and Kaltwasser (2014) that populism also lays 'claim to speak in the name of the people'. As this chapter demonstrates, who 'the people' are defined as often involves the reduction of a nation's complex history to a matter of 'us versus them'. In Ireland's case, 'the people' are constructed as Irish-born, white and Catholic with the consequence that all others are defined as a hostile group outside the realms of belonging. Such populist rhetoric is making visible the tradition of conservatism in Ireland, which has a long legacy.

The dominance of centre-right Fianna Fáil and Fine Gael throughout Ireland's political history speaks to a deep social and economic conservatism that could be characterized as a quiet conservatism. The 1990s and 2000s particularly marked a shift towards neoliberal policies as Ireland's economic success hurtled towards becoming the infamous 'Celtic Tiger'. These policies exacerbated an exclusionary state construction of Irishness, as seen through immigration decisions which created a hierarchical system of immigration with white, European, English-speaking graduates given the most favourable treatment and working conditions in contrast to those migrants of a different background (Loyal 2003). Ireland's 2004 citizenship referendum, which resulted in changing Irish citizenship eligibility from birthright citizenship to a system based on descent, is also often cited as evidence of an Irish political establishment that desired to create a restrictive legal and symbolic interpretation of Irishness through citizenship. The emotive and xenophobic political rhetoric surrounding the referendum further underlined that exclusionary conservatism was legitimized at the highest levels of Irish government. That the proposal was easily passed by the electorate has been thought to be reflective of racist and exclusionary attitudes towards migrants living in Ireland at that time (Garner 2007, 2016; Lentin 2007; Fanning 2016).

Ireland's asylum system, introduced in the 1990s and known as Direct Provision, has also been heavily criticized by those who maintain that it is designed to prevent integration and dehumanizes asylum seekers by physically and symbolically separating them from the Irish population (Breen 2008; Loyal and Quilley 2016). Direct Provision further underlines Ireland's problematic relationship to outsiders, and its continuance in the face of criticism implies a quiet acceptance of this on the part of the general public. Thus, we must understand that a lack of far-right political representation in Ireland should not be mistaken for a lack of conservativism in Ireland. Indeed Loyal (2003, 74) argues:

> Underlying the celebrated liberal values of freedom, choice and opportunity which are supposedly intrinsic to the cultural renewal ushered in by the 'new Ireland', is the harsh reality of capitalist production, exclusionary nationalism and growing xenophobia, in relation to both the state and the general populace.

Throughout 2019 and 2020 anti-immigration movements became more visible in Ireland due to a number of incidents which received widespread media coverage.

These incidents may reveal to us something of the contemporary nature of populist conservatism outlined earlier. In September 2019, protests against plans to house 250 asylum seekers in a local hotel began in Oughterard Co. Galway, a small rural town in the West of Ireland. While many locals were keen to emphasize that their concerns were about the problematic nature of the Direct Provision system itself, or about the effects on local services of a sudden influx of large numbers to a small rural town, it also appears that racism and a suspicion of outsiders may also have played a role in these protests. Such analysis was confirmed through comments by local Independent TD[2] Noel Grealish at a meeting held with locals to discuss the issue. He stated that most African asylum seekers were 'sponging off the system', that a Direct Provision centre would 'destroy the fabric of Oughterard' and, reportedly, that the only persecuted group in Africa were Christians who were being targeted by the Islamic State (Clarke et al. 2019; McGee 2019). His comments were met with applause. Similar protests have also been held elsewhere amid accusations that far-right groups are manipulating such protests to amplify their views to a wider audience (Gallaher and Pollack 2019).

In November 2019, a local Fine Gael by-election candidate Verona Murphy commented that some asylum seekers 'have to be deprogrammed' and that they were 'possibly infiltrated by ISIS and we have to protect ourselves against that' (McCarthy 2019). Murphy was deselected as Fine Gael's by-election candidate in the aftermath of these comments, ran as an Independent and was ultimately unsuccessful. However, just a few weeks later in the February 2020 general election she was successfully elected to Dáil Eireann[3] as an Independent candidate. In both the Grealish and Murphy cases, they have sought to associate the Other (asylum seekers) with a racialized religious extremism. Specifically, this perpetuates understandings of racial and ethnic minorities as religious fundamentalists, and more generally, as a threat to the Irish way of life. Such comments show no understanding of the diversity and heterogeneity of asylum seekers in Ireland and confirm that racial, ethnic and religious minorities in Ireland continue to be constructed as a homogeneous and dangerous Other by public figures whose voices not only represent their constituents but are legitimized and given authority as public representatives. In 2022, the open welcome provided to Ukrainian refugees to Ireland fleeing the Russian invasion clearly emphasized divisions in Irish responses between the mostly white European Ukrainians and other asylum seekers who are often not European, white or Christian. That Ukrainian refugees were not placed into the Direct Provision system created a two-tier asylum system with clear racial, religious and cultural distinctions between them.

We could conclude that there is an emergence of exclusionary discussion towards minorities in Ireland, and this may be part of a slow move towards a populist 'Fortress Europe' ideology in Ireland as seen elsewhere in Europe. However, I suggest that the dominance of centre-right parties in Ireland's political system, coupled with the construction of the Irish State around Catholic social conservatism, indicates that this trend is nothing new. Rather, the Irish State and Irish values have long centred around a clear understanding of Irish belonging, and those outside this definition have always struggled for full acceptance into the national narrative. From this perspective, the recent high-profile incidents described here are not an emergence, or even a resurgence of narrow boundary-making in Ireland. They are an adaptation of a long-established Irish fear and suspicion of the Other, coupled with a strong need to assert powerful limits around understandings of 'the Irish' which predominantly seek to exclude those who are not Irish-born, white or Catholic. Viewed from this perspective, recent events in Ireland illustrate the argument of Mondon and Winter (2020) who maintain that far-right discourse is incorporated into mainstream politics.

Catholic nation-building

We cannot speak of the creation of Ireland's conservatism without an analysis of the role of the Catholic Church as Ireland's dominant religion in that construction. An all-encompassing influence of the Catholic Church on Irish social, cultural, political and economic landscapes continued for all of the nineteenth century and most of the twentieth (Inglis 1998; Ganiel 2016). As early as 1845, the Catholic Church was known as 'an independent power bloc to which the British state had decided to bequeath the task of civilising and socially controlling the Irish people' (Inglis 1998, 103). Such power, Inglis (1998) argues, resulted in a Catholic monopoly over Irish morality as Catholic values came to imbue the Irish sense of self and to serve as a clear boundary marker in understandings of national and ethnic identity.

Post-independence from the British, the new Irish Free State continued to carve a clear and bounded national identity through the reinforcement of associations of Irish national identity with Catholic religious identity (Whyte 1976; Smyth 1995; Kearney 1997; Kenny 2000). This is evidenced by the strong influence of key Irish Catholic leaders in the creation of Ireland's 1937 Constitution (Kenny 2000; Tanner 2001). Through control of education, health and other welfare functions in the early twentieth century, the Irish

Catholic Church wielded both institutional and symbolic power which served to create and sustain an intermingling of Irish and Catholic values. The extent of the success of this Catholic nation-building project is what makes Ireland unique across Europe (Fanning 2014a), where many nations have used religion and ethnicity to support nationality. 'An unofficial Church-State alliance permitted ecclesiastical dictatorship and political democracy to live side by side without any sense of incongruity' (Fanning 2014a, 51).

Though numbers self-identifying as Catholic have dropped from 95 per cent in the 1960s to 78 per cent in recent times (Central Statistics Office 2012, 2017), it is evident that Catholicism continues to shape Irish understandings of religion and of Irish belonging through cultural identity maintenance. Although many argue that Ireland is now 'post-Catholic', I agree with Ganiel (2016), who argues that post-Catholic Ireland does not infer an outright rejection of the institutional church but rather a new engagement with it. Ganiel (2016) argues that adherents to other religions in Ireland still articulate their religious identities and experiences through a framework of Irish Catholicism, something I also find in my own research on Mormonism in Ireland. Additionally, Inglis (2007) argues that we are now increasingly in an era of cultural Catholicism where many self-identified Catholics do not adhere to the teaching of the Catholic Church but claim that identity nonetheless, seeing it predominantly as a symbol of Irish belonging. Thus we can see that the 'religious habitus' (Inglis 1998, 2) of Irish culture has adapted. Irish Catholicism as a form of institutional religion may be in decline, but it continues to serve an important function in supporting a homogenous interpretation of Irish national identity and belonging.

Colonial Complexity: Sustaining the white Irish Catholic myth

The conventional construction of Ireland as white, Irish and Catholic (Lentin 2001, 2007; Garner 2009, 2016) has long excluded those who do not fit these criteria. In Ireland, 82 per cent of people identify with the census category of 'white Irish', and another 8 per cent as 'Other Irish'. Nine per cent of the population identifies with 'Other white', meaning that Ireland remains overwhelmingly a white-majority country (Central Statistics Office 2017). According to prevailing discourse, to be Irish is to be white, a discourse which continued even after Ireland's first encounters with mass immigration in the late 1990s (Ignatiev 1995; Lentin 2001, 2007, 2012; Morrison 2004; Fanning, Howard and O' Boyle 2010; Fanning 2014b; Joseph 2018). Such manifestations of the category 'Irish' has been actively supported by the nation state. Ireland has been constructed as a 'racial state' (Goldberg 2002) in which Irishness has been fashioned as white and incorporated into the nation state itself (Lentin 2007). Whiteness in Ireland has been created as ethnically and racially homogeneous and has been normalized and made invisible to scrutiny (Lentin 2012). This continues despite Ireland's recent growing diversity in which 18 per cent of the country identify outside of the core identification of 'white Irish' (Central Statistics Office 2017). Between 2011 and 2016, there was an 87 per cent increase in the numbers of those with dual Irish nationality, while 11.6 per cent of the population was non-national in the 2016 census (Central Statistics Office 2017). Thus, though Ireland is still a white and Irish country, it is quickly diversifying.

As Ireland struggles to adapt its self-perception to reflect its changing reality, its relationship to its own past is also in a process of flux. While acknowledging that the collective memory of history is always in the process of being re-imagined (Poole 2008; Berger 2011; Zerubavel 2011), nonetheless Ireland's modern face as a 'liberal, progressive and multicultural' nation (Kuhling and Keohane 2007, 66) incorporates a 'repression of historical memory and a denial of many aspects of Irish history, in particular the Irish experience of trauma, diaspora, and colonialisation' (Kuhling and Keohane 2007, 66). A postcolonial analysis of Ireland's development of communal identity highlights the significant influence Ireland's history as a colonized territory has had in shaping the modern nation state, its collective memory and its sense of self. Importantly, this perspective argues that Ireland's colonial trauma has assisted in maintaining a closed attitude towards outsiders, and a suspicion or even fear of those beyond the 'safe' category of Irish (Kirby, Gibbons and Cronin 2002; Moane 2002, 2014; Kuhling and Keohane 2007).

In many ways we can see Irish history come full circle. It has been noted that the Irish were racialized by the British as an 'alien' (Mokyr 1985, 291) and 'primitive race' (Brantlinger 2004, 199), with such attitudes exacerbating the pitiful British response to the 'scarring' (Cohen 1996, 513) Irish Famine. This may partly explain the development in Ireland of a closed and suspicious attitude towards many outsiders. However, the development of this Irish character has facilitated the Irish to do to others what the British once did to them – to demonize, exploit and exclude. The Irish relationship with those deemed to be outsiders is made visible in the contemporary era through the treatment of asylum seekers and refugees, migrant workers and religious minorities. It illuminates how this half-forgotten traumatic memory lingers unexamined in the modern era, affecting the ways in which Irish society manages rapid immigration and growing diversity. By incorporating a postcolonial lens to understand Ireland's communal imagining of nation, race and identity, we can make visible the ways that Ireland's colonial past continues to shape its present.

Yet there is much about Irish identity and Irish nationalism which is not unique (Malesecic 2014). In spite of Ireland's weaving for itself a national myth of exceptionalism (Inglis 2014), Irish nationalism also has much in common with other European nationalisms: emerging in a similar historical period, using similar strategies for success, and undergoing a twenty-first-century resurgence (Malesecic 2014). Connected to this, it is important to note that despite Ireland's dark history of colonization, it has also benefited from its position at the heart of the European project as a wealthy, educated, white and English-speaking country. As an EU member, Ireland is part of a 'Fortress Europe' system of policy creation, and this ensures that Ireland is complicit in the exclusion of those from the Global South. Thus, Ireland is simultaneously a country with a traumatic history of occupation and colonialization, *and* a wealthy European country whose social structures sustain a view of the Other as a resource to control and exploit. The complexity of Ireland's experiences may go some way to contextualize the contradictory pictures emerging of contemporary Ireland, a modern liberal democracy which resists inter-culturalism and marginalizes diversity.

Understanding the complex construction and maintenance of 'Irishness' as incorporating both religion and race is an important component in comprehending Ireland's contemporary nationalisms. The racialization of non-Catholic religions in Ireland has accelerated as numbers of adherents to religions such as Islam and Pentecostalism have increased. Research with adherents of racialized religions is a particularly strong field of growth in the Irish study of religions. Importantly, the growth of these religions in Ireland has been primarily fuelled by immigration (Maher 2009; Cosgrove et al. 2011; Kmec 2017; Ritter and Kmec 2017; Röder 2017), and so these religions are positioned as 'migrant religions', facilitating perceptions of adherents to these religions as less than fully Irish. This is visible through studies of religious minorities in Ireland who have a strong African-Irish adherence such as Ireland's Pentecostal communities, which note that racism is a commonplace experience for these groups (Ugba 2008, 2009; Maguire and Murphy 2012, 2015). Similarly, research with Ireland's Muslim communities highlights how they navigate negative perceptions of Islam in Ireland as a racialized faith (Carr 2011, 2016; Scharbrodt 2015). Such research first confirms that those who are not white in Ireland are racialized as 'other' and are subject to marginalization and discrimination. Second, in the case of racialized religious identities, their religious and racial differences intermingle and become entwined, supporting outside perceptions of the individual as an 'outsider' (Carr 2011, 578).

Thus, Ireland's racialization of religious minorities constructs both majority and minority groups as homogeneous, positioning them as inherently distinct from each other, while masking the heterogeneity within each group. These marginalizing processes are not unique towards religions whose membership is predominantly Black, Asian or minority ethnic. Ireland has a long history of excluding religious minorities who like the majority population, are white Irish. This is evident in the treatment of Ireland's various Protestant communities (Ruane and Todd 2009; Crawford 2010; Nuttall 2015; Walsh 2015; Röder 2017). and as I have noted elsewhere, this is due to a colonial trauma which leads Irish people to associate all forms of Protestantism with the old British occupier (O' Brien 2019). In this respect, listening to the experiences of majority-white religious minorities in Ireland, such as Ireland's Mormon community, can allow us to appreciate how contemporary religion operates in an Irish context where Whiteness is a taken-for-granted category.

What can Irish Mormonism tell us about religion in Ireland?

Mormons in Ireland are a majority white, but also a diverse religious minority. While they are majority-white Irish, the religion has more racial and ethnic minorities among its membership than is reported among the general population in Ireland. Thus, they serve as a useful case study to explore the interconnections of religion, race and nation in modern Ireland. Mormonism has been present on the island of Ireland since 1840 but has struggled, particularly in the Republic of Ireland. Historically, Protestantism in Ireland was associated with British colonizers, leading to a legacy of mistrust towards it. Walsh explains that 'Protestants, with their historical connection to processes of English colonialization and their alternative understandings of religion were seen as tainted, foreign, and heretical' (Walsh 2015, 75), while Ruane and Todd argue that 'Irish Protestants saw themselves as Irish, but in a different way from the Catholic Irish' (Ruane and Todd 2009, 4). As a result of these othering processes, Harris (1990, 8) observed the following regarding the differing development of Mormonism in Northern Ireland and the Republic of Ireland: 'The [Mormon] church is growing much more rapidly in the north than it is in the predominantly Catholic south, where religion and patriotism-being Catholic and being Irish-are intertwined, where leaving the Catholic church is almost synonymous with defecting.'

The church's focus on Northern Ireland and the easier reception that Mormonism received there had a lasting effect. According to recent church figures, there are 5,358 members in Northern Ireland and 3,071 members in the Republic (The Church of Jesus Christ of Latter-day Saints, no date).[4] Perhaps because Mormonism is a majority-white religion it has been suggested that it has been viewed by the Irish as just another form of Protestantism (Card 1978). However in the Irish context this is not a positive assessment and may go some way to explaining how and why Mormonism has struggled in Ireland despite some key commonalities with Catholicism such as a focus on the family and conservative views on issues such as abortion, same-sex relationships and sex outside of marriage.

The development of Mormonism in the Republic of Ireland has been directly influenced by the religious, cultural and political meanings behind Ireland's common understandings of the categories of 'Catholic' and 'Protestant', and a cultural suspicion of the Other. I have found that Irish Mormons in the contemporary era continue to be 'othered' by a majority society which views their religion as a branch of Protestantism which is not to be trusted. Such attitudes are further confirmed by research which finds high levels of stigma and marginalization among eight majority-white religious minorities in Ireland, including Mormons (Cosgrove 2013). Questionnaire findings from this study indicate that 68 per cent of the respondents reported being personally discriminated against on the basis of their religion in the preceding five years. Forty-one per cent indicate they had experienced between two to four discriminatory incidents in the previous five years. For the Mormon subset of the sample, this figure was 79 per cent. Though Mormons were less likely to have concealed their religious identifies than other majority-white Irish groups such as Scientologists, almost half of them had concealed their identities in the last five years and the high levels of discrimination they report appear to indicate that revealing minority religious identity even as a white Irish person, is associated with higher levels of discrimination. Eighty-one per cent of the general sample responded that they felt the perception of small religious groups in Ireland was negative. Such findings confirm that minority religions are constructed by the majority society in negative terms. Though minority religions with a predominantly white Irish membership experience the benefits of white privilege that facilitates them to conceal their religious identity if they want to, nonetheless the negative experiences they have had illustrate that a number of white 'outsiders' also exist within the Irish religious landscape.

My own research with Mormons in Ireland identifies that the negative aspects of life as a religious minority can be somewhat mitigated by choosing to remain less visible. My research involved a year's ethnographic fieldwork with two Mormon congregations and thirty in-depth interviews, and identified the risks involved for those Mormons who choose to emphasize their religious differences. Mormons spoke of being singled out and mocked at social occasions, being spat on, and being verbally abused as a result of their religious identity becoming 'visible'. For some it was during their time as missionaries, when distinctive clothing and name-badges identified them to the public. For others, it was when those at social occasions were told about their identities by others. I spoke with one young woman in her twenties who recalled being publicly humiliated due to her faith:

> I remember there was one night we went out for the Twelve Pubs at Christmas [a pub crawl] and I was standing there chatting away . . . nothing had come up about religion at all. And this guy pulled my arm up like this [she raises her arm high in the air] and said, 'this is the one with the weird religion' and I was like, 'what are you doing?' I was like, 'that's so mean'. I was so drop-kicked by it that I actually left. I just thought, why? Why? It's not like I had a *Book of Mormon*. I was just out for a normal night, and that's what I get.

Experiences such as these led to many Mormons I knew adapting their identities so as to ensure their religious status did not attract unwanted attention. Practising Mormons do not drink alcohol, and many reported to me that their sobriety was a key flashpoint in an Irish cultural milieu where consumption of alcohol is seen as a sign of sociability and is done to achieve belonging. Within this context, one participant told me in quiet tones of his guilt about lying as an identity management strategy to ensure his religious identity remained hidden:

> If I'm somewhere on business and I don't want religion to come into things, and they'd ask me if I want something to drink, sometimes I don't make a big deal; I don't drink but I won't say it's about religion I'll say 'I just don't drink for health reasons' or whatever. But I don't always have to bring it up' 'no because I'm Mormon', which probably I should do all the time.

It must be noted that being able to remain hidden in plain sight and masking one's difference from the majority if and when one chooses is part of the privilege of Whiteness which is not accorded to all religious minorities in Ireland. Within Irish Mormonism, such advantages are made possible more frequently due to its majority-white membership. These adherents are simultaneously advantaged by their racial position in the social hierarchy, yet disadvantaged by their religion.

The stigma created by Mormon abstention from alcohol within a wider culture in which alcohol and the pub are important aspects of cultural identity (Stivers 1991; O' Brien 2017) connects to another aspect of the marginalization of Irish Mormonism from dominant constructions of Irishness. It is often when individual's religious identities are perceived to have breached Irish cultural norms that negative reactions occur. Many Mormons told me that there was a 'right' and a 'wrong' way to be religious in Ireland, and one had to be careful to perform religiosity the correct way in order to avoid being viewed as 'too holy' or a 'holy Joe'. One participant told me how she perceives Irish society's attitudes towards religion in the contemporary age:

> It's just a trendy thing to be spiritual, but if your spirituality is involved or associated with a religion it's kind of like, my experience is that people, undermines your spirituality. It's like you are following a set of rules as opposed to being a free spirit following your spiritual journey. You have aligned yourself with something that's outside of yourself.

The reference of a rejection of institutional religion underlines that the relationship of the Irish to religion, and to Catholicism specifically, is changing (Inglis 2007; Ganiel 2016). One must identify as Catholic to be viewed as Irish, but it should be a *cultural* and not religious belonging.

As active expressions of religiosity are feared and distrusted among the Irish population, there appears to be a presumption that members of a religion which demands high activity such as Mormonism, will be seeking to avail of any opportunity to convert others to their religion. Such attitudes cause Mormons in Ireland to retreat, to become even more quiet about their religious identity for fear of others' perceptions of them. Sometimes the issue of sobriety and concern of being thought to be too 'holy' combine, as in the experience of the participant further whose story illustrates how others are highly sensitive to any mention of religion in public:

> I don't even go out of my way [to talk about religion] when I am at family functions. They all know, they all know, of course they know, but I don't go out of my way to talk about it. Because then it's kind of like, 'she rams her religion down people's throats' . . . even when you're trying to be nice about it, and *they* are asking the questions.

Yet interestingly in cases of conversion to Mormonism, the convert's family and friends became more familiar with the basics of Mormon doctrine and culture as time goes on which often then leads to strict enforcement of what they perceive Mormonism to be. One man told me about his family and friends' reactions to his everyday behaviour:

> If they ever saw me doing something that Mormons wasn't supposed to do they'd say 'Mormons aren't supposed to do that!'. I'd get annoyed and I'd start cursing at someone, and they'd say 'Mormons aren't supposed to curse'. . . . It's much easier if you have a stereotype than an individual. If they expect me to be a Mormon all the time, and they class me as a Mormon, and their view of me is as a Mormon, then that's all I am. I'm also Irish, I'm also doing research, I'm also obsessed with computer games, you know? So, Mormonism is just one part of who I am.

It seems to me that this phenomenon reflects a need in Irish society to enforce cultural and religious boundaries and to gloss over the nuances and complexities of life as a minority. Many participants told me that life as a religious minority in Ireland involved coming to terms with this experience; 'being ok with not being understood'.

Participants told me of Ireland's generally poor levels of religious literacy, and of how this low level of knowledge often means that Mormons get confused with other majority-white religions; 'are we Mormons, or are we Jehovah's Witnesses, or are we Christians, or whatever'. This exacerbates a hierarchical othering process in which Catholicism, and increasingly, cultural Catholicism, is viewed as white Irish, religions such as Islam or Hinduism are seen as not Irish and not white, while Mormonism and the Jehovah's Witnesses are viewed as white, but not Irish. Such simplistic categorization clearly overlooks the inherent complexity of Ireland's religious experience.

Where Irish attitudes towards religious minorities appear to lack nuance, others have told me that, in contrast, Irish expressions of racism are often subtle. One Black African Mormon who had previously spent some time living in Germany told me that before arriving in Ireland he had been warned by friends that in Ireland 'racism is too high'. Yet when contrasting Germany and Ireland he told me: 'if you have been in the country where racism was just direct to you, and then you see that here racism is just, it's not direct, it is there but not direct.' I clarified further by asking 'it's underneath the surface?' 'exactly', he replied.

This 'underneath the surface' form of Irish racism speaks directly to the traditional nature of Irish exclusion as discussed at the start of this chapter. Ireland does not have a strong support for explicitly far-right political parties, yet the mainstream political system is easily able to enact exclusionary polices which marginalize those outside dominant understandings of Irish. Similarly, it seems that at a micro level racism may not always be 'direct', but nonetheless its consistent quiet existence still excludes those it targets and shapes their own understandings of their place in Irish society. This is illustrated in how the above participant spoke about the Irish racialization of religion and about the assumptions made about his religious identity based on his race. He told me that Irish people often assume that because he is Black, he must be Muslim. He spoke about highlighting his biblical name to Irish people as a way to signpost to others that he saw himself as Christian, and that he was certainly not Muslim. In this way, he uses Christianity as a way to create commonality with the wider Irish population who already viewed him as an outsider due to his race. His need to distance himself from Islam further demonstrates the hierarchies of religious and racial categories which exist in contemporary Ireland.

Other Mormons confirmed the difficulties of negotiating Irish people's perceptions of them. A participant originally from Eastern Europe spoke to me about the challenges in finding the right time in the conversation to reveal his religious identity. He tells me of an awkward situation with an acquaintance, which involved firstly fielding questions about his nationality before the conversation turned to religion:

> I had a few chats with this guy from the gym and we talked about, we didn't get to the part to tell him that I'm not Orthodox. So, I have to restart that conversation! Because he was more concerned about 'what do you think about this, like all these Muslims, what do you think?'

Here, we can see that his co-conversationalist had assumed because of his nationality that he was Orthodox Christian. He hadn't managed to 'get to that part' of challenging that particular assumption. One can only imagine that he may be more hesitant to do so now that his acquaintance has revealed his anti-Muslim sentiments.

As part of my research, I spoke with a South American Mormon couple who have lived in various European countries and who are now settled in Ireland. They provided me with interesting insights into cultural processes of exclusion and belonging across Europe. They argued that although Ireland has its own historical and political reasons for its conservative understanding of 'Irish', these trends are also part of a wider European culture which is quite different to what they grew up with in South America. For the purposes of this chapter, I have labelled these two participants as A and B and given the very small nature of the Mormon community in Ireland and the need to protect anonymity, I have not identified their specific nationality.

A: Europeans are more and more closed for everything. So, they restrict their thoughts to their traditions, to their county, to their accents, to the region, to the type of food.

Hazel: You think that is Europe-wide, not just Ireland?

A: It's all of Europe is like that, and that also affects religion because people are more open-minded in many ways [in country of origin], and so the traditions are respected, but it's not part of your nationality.

B: When we came to Europe, I thought that with the European Union and everything; in my mind I thought that everything was sorted. I had two interesting experiences. One was in Italy; I was living in a small town and later on I realised that people refer to me as 'the foreigner' . . . but that's okay-I was a foreigner. But the funny story is that one day they were saying that the new teacher was coming, and they said, 'a foreigner, she's a foreigner'. And I thought oh maybe she's from Spain or whatever. And when she came in, she was from a city that was 50 km away! And they call her the foreigner.

A: She had a different dialect.

B: So that is the way. Then I get to Ireland, and I work. We are a multinational [company] so you can have your flag printed and have it above your computer . . . I have this Spanish co-worker from Barcelona, from Catalonia, and I go up to her and I give her the Spanish flag and she looked at the flag and she said, 'what are you giving this to me?'. I'm like, 'you're from Spain?' and she is like, 'no I'm from Catalonia'. So, I was like, oh my goodness, I thought that everything was sorted here! We didn't have that in [country of origin]. In [country of origin] we are all [nationality]. You don't have the choice.

B's observation that in their home country religious traditions 'are respected, but it's not part of your nationality' acutely confirms the role religion specifically plays in the maintenance of particular forms of European nation-building. More generally, this conversation reminds us that although Ireland has its own specificities around nationality, race and religion, it is also part of broader patterns of exclusion and conservative interpretations of tradition which are visible across Europe.

Conclusion

This chapter has demonstrated that Ireland's exclusion and racialization of religious and ethnic minorities are part of a broader trend which is evident across Europe yet is also uniquely created to reflect Ireland's collective identity which has emerged as a result of specific historical experiences. As a wealthy EU member, Ireland enforces and supports Fortress Europe policies which exacerbate the marginalization of those outside traditional understandings of 'European'. Ireland is also undergoing an adaptation in its expression of xenophobic discourse; though it still has no far-right political representation, far-right groups are more visible and mainstream politicians espouse related views and enact restrictive policies designed to reinforce a narrow interpretation of Irishness. In this respect, Ireland is part of a broader system which seeks to strengthen boundaries around Europe by positioning asylum seekers, non-EU worker migrants or adherents of Islam as dangerous.

What makes Ireland distinct is its recent history as a colonized country, and how these experiences have shaped Irish national identity around Whiteness and Catholicism as a direct response to its experiences at the hands of imperial power. Ireland's contemporary demands for assimilation of difference and exclusion of minorities are not new and reflect a young nation state which is still working to create its sense of identity in the midst of profound societal change. The lived experiences of Mormons in Ireland illustrate that though the words of politicians Grealish and Murphy may be antagonistic and designed to grab headlines, they are not anomalies. Rather, they illumine a quiet and persistent xenophobia which sits beneath the surface in Ireland and works both explicitly and implicitly to marginalize expressions of Irishness which do not conform to dominant narratives. On the one hand, these observations imply that there may be fertile ground in Ireland for far-right movements to grow further. Yet on the other, Ireland appears to be committed towards reworking its cultural hegemony of white, Irish and Catholic to include a public face of progressiveness that, on the surface at least, decries such exclusionary rhetoric. Can this superficial commitment to diversity grow enough to replace the deeply rooted exclusionary conservatism which has so firmly shaped Ireland's social structures and sense of self? We must perhaps wait and see.

Anti-Islam politics, Christianity and identity in the Finnish public sphere

Tuomas Äystö

Introduction

Most religion scholars probably know Finland as part of the Nordics – countries that are often considered among the most secular places on earth. However, of the Nordic countries, Finland has experienced secularization slower than the others. The membership of the Lutheran Church is, as of January 2022, at 66 per cent in Finland, with a downward trend mirrored in other Nordic countries (see Furseth et al. 2018, 42–52).[1] The membership rate is similar in Norway, Iceland and Denmark, but markedly lower in Sweden (55.2 per cent in 2020). According to International Social Survey Programme (ISSP) (2018) data, the number of people believing in god is 55.6 per cent in Iceland, 46.7 per cent in Finland, 36.9 per cent in Denmark, 36.5 per cent in Norway and 30.7 per cent in Sweden. The potential explanations as to why Sweden can be viewed as the most secularized Nordic country, why Iceland is on the other end of the spectrum and others between the two involve, for example, differences in the pace of societal modernization, economics, political power relations, immigration rates and legal factors (see Furseth et al. 2018).

While the unique position of the Lutheran Church is increasingly questioned in Finland, Finnishness and Lutheranism are still often thought to be culturally intertwined (Hjelm 2014; Tervonen 2014). This comes up regularly in the political discussions regarding Islam and religious diversity, which is the focus of this chapter.

Finland has always been a country of emigration. Stories of relatives moving to the United States or Sweden, for example, are circulated in many Finnish families. Large-scale immigration to Finland did not occur until the late 1980s, when some of the refugees from Vietnam arrived. The 1990s saw refugees from

Africa and the Middle East, and from that point onwards, the Finnish public discussion also began to change. Islam was previously addressed mainly via economic language in the media (Martikainen 2008, 66–8). The arrival of a visible Muslim minority population, as well as some high-profile international incidents where the role of religion was highlighted, such as the Iranian revolution (1979), the Salman Rushdie controversy (1988 onwards) and, later, the 9/11 attacks (2001) and the Jyllands-Posten cartoon controversy (2005–6), moulded the discussion in the direction where Muslim immigrants and their religion are viewed as a threat to the secular or Christian Finland.

This transformation of the discussion was, in many ways, also connected to the rise of the securitization discourse, which portrayed an increasing number of questions as security-related affairs. The 9/11 attack in 2001 initiated several developments in Finland, where security concerns related to Islam and Muslims were addressed, for example, in the form of an integration policy (Martikainen 2013). These means are not always necessarily anti-Islam or anti-Muslim as such. However, attempts to 'manage Islam' are nonetheless part of the context in which anti-Islam politics is enacted and are thus mentioned here.

In the mid-2000s, voices critical or hostile towards Islam and Muslims became more prominent. Availability and accessibility of new online platforms played a part. In Finland, several blogs and social media sites began to gain traction. Among the most popular was a blog called Scripta, started in 2003 and written by the linguist Jussi Halla-aho, who would become the chair of the Finns Party a decade later, holding the position from 2017 to 2021. Facebook started to gain popularity in Finland in late 2007, with other social media platforms following soon after. Politicians quickly learned new ways to communicate to the potential voters, bypassing the traditional news media.

Anti-Islam and anti-immigration discourses are in many ways imported from the United States and the other European countries. The oldest example is Finnish charismatic Christian literature containing these elements (e.g. Islam as the Antichrist) that emulates similar American works (Steward 2015). A more secular and recent example, Halla-aho, can be viewed as a central translator of the discourse found in blogs such as Gates of Vienna and Jihadwatch into the Finnish language via his blog Scripta.

Concerning the Christian roots of the Finnish anti-Islam discourse, Finnish Christian missionaries to Palestine in the early twentieth century, for example, tended to view Muslims with suspicion or saw them as pagans and considered Islam as an unfortunate phenomenon, whereas Jewish and Zionist perspectives received more sympathy (Steward 2015). Later, the charismatic Christian literature, often originating from or influenced by American Pentecostal or Evangelical writers, circulated by Finnish Christian bookstores like Ilon Polku and Kristillinen kirjakauppa or publishers like Kuva ja Sana, Kristillinen Kirja-ja Musiikkikustannus and Liekki kustannus, has regularly connected Islam with the biblical end times. As an illustrative example, the Liekki kustannus publisher has one of their product categories titled 'Israel, Islam, and end-times' in their online bookstore.[2]

An anti-Islam political stance is not a valid generalization of Finnish charismatic Christianity as a whole, but such contour is nonetheless existent within it. Today, certain Finnish charismatic Christian figures, such as Pekka Sartola, Juha Ahvio and Mika Niikko, have not shied away from connecting such discourse with more general political claims, sometimes landing unambiguously in far-right territory.

For example, Juha Ahvio, a docent of dogmatics at the University of Helsinki and a leading figure of the Patmos Foundation, a Christian relief organization, has written that ethnic, linguistic and cultural differences are part of the order of creation. Thus, immigration, ethnic mixing and overt foreign influences are against creation. He also circulates the far-right conspiracy about the 'globalists', who, through international bodies such as the UN, seek to destroy the nation-states via endless immigration. While he firmly and vocally supports the state of Israel, this does not prevent him from employing the anti-globalist discourse, which is often used in anti-Semitic contexts (see Rensman 2011).[3]

To be clear, I am not suggesting that there is a clear lineage from the early charismatic Christian suspicion or hostility towards Islam to twenty-first-century far-right politics.[4] Most of the politicians or extra-parliamentary activists of the Finnish far right have no particular Christian connection other than their cultural background in Lutheran Finland. The former chair of the Finns Party, Jussi Halla-aho, disaffiliated from the Lutheran Church in his youth[5] and has stated that he is an atheist or agnostic,[6] although he does not bring this up often. The current chair Riikka Purra has also stated that she does not have strong religious convictions herself. Instead, when immigration became a considerable public debate in the mid-2000s, and the Finns Party gained traction because of it, the pre-existing Christian attitudes and the contemporary political aims, to an extent, found each other within the Finns Party, and to a lesser degree, within the Christian Democrats. This is visible in their voter bases, parliamentary speeches and social media posts.

In the following, I will chart the forms of Finnish anti-Islam politics and their relationship to the questions of identity. Special attention is paid to discourse on religion and nationality. Parliamentary and social media examples are explored, and the ways in which Finland is constructed as a 'culturally Christian' nation against the threat of pluralism are illustrated. While Finland has its particularities, I expect many things explored here to be quite familiar to readers from other Nordic and European countries, and also from North America to an extent, as several fundamental trends are found in all of these locations in some form. These include the rise of conservative populism and the far right, the resurgence of the questions of cultural identity, increased mobility of people globally and changing media landscape.

Background: The conventional understanding of religion and politics in Finland

The historical generalization of the religious gap between the political parties in post-independence Finland is that the right has defended the prevailing Lutheran morality and societal order. In contrast, the left has criticized it. In the early twentieth century, the political left in Finland was hostile towards the hegemonic position of the Lutheran Church, visible, for example, in the so-called Forssa programme (1903) – a declaration of the Social Democratic Party. Concerning religion directly, the programme had the following demands:

> 5. Religion must be declared as a private matter. The church must be separated from the state, and ecclesiastical and religious communities must be deemed as private associations that handle their internal matters. Religious education must be removed from schools.[7]

During the Finnish Civil War (1918), occurring shortly after the collapse of the Russian Empire – of which Finland had been a grand dutchy – the Lutheran Church mainly aligned with the right-wing Germany-supported White Guards. The White Guards eventually won the war against the socialist Red Guards. However, unlike in many civil war aftermaths, proponents of the losing side were allowed into the democratic parliament of the newly founded independent state, which turned out to be a stabilizing decision. In the following years, leftist parties continued to mount criticism against the Lutheran power and the special position of the church in a modern state. It is noteworthy, however, that mass disaffiliations from the Lutheran Church did not occur on the scale that was feared by some, although this became legally possible in 1923. This, again, reflected the cultural position of the Lutheran Church: despite the political differences, Finns felt a strong attachment to it.

During the Second World War, Finland fought against the Soviet Union and the threat of losing its independence. It became strategically necessary to bridge the old political gap between the left and the right against the common enemy. This succeeded relatively well through large media campaigns, convincing the Finnish public of a necessary endeavour, partly via Christian and nationalistic holy war rhetoric. The Lutheran Church participated in the war effort via close collaboration with the army (Kivimäki and Tepora 2012, 249–51).

From the 1950s onwards, Finland saw a period of fast population and economic growth, as well as urbanization and modernization, during which people moved from agricultural work into factory and service occupations, such as retail, in significant numbers. Rises in education levels and gender equality also occurred. The 1960s is often considered a decade of generational conflict between the younger, left-leaning liberals and more conservative older folk, who saw their traditional values as threatened. At this point, the societal influence of the Lutheran Church and the morality connected to it also began to decline. However, membership of the Lutheran Church remained above 80 per cent until 2008.

Two of the most prominent right-wing parties, the National Coalition (Kokoomus) and the Center Party (Keskusta), have somewhat Christian backgrounds, although in different ways. The National Coalition was founded in 1918 by supporters of monarchy, who valued Christian ethics and respected the authorities in addition to their core economic policies (right to private property and trade). However, Christian tones have since faded from the party's language. The Center Party, in turn, was initially founded in 1906 as the Agrarian League, which sought to improve the position of the rural areas. Many of its core support areas are, to this day, Lapland and North Ostrobothnia, which is reflected in its policies. As it turns out, these regions, sometimes called 'Finland's Bible belt', are the core areas of Pietistic Lutheran revival movements. Like the National Coalition, however, the Center Party has also developed into a generalist party that rarely relies on religious language today.

The National Coalition Party, a combination of liberal and conservative political traditions, was divided by ideological disagreements. Indeed, certain former supporters founded the Finnish Christian League (today known as the Christian Democrats) in 1958 as a reaction towards 'non-Christian' orientations in other parties and the perceived secularization of society, evident in developments such as more liberal sexual ethics, less restrictive alcohol regulations and abortion rights. The party gained its first MP in the 1970 parliamentary elections and has maintained a steady though small support to this day (Mickelson 2015). The Lutheran Church, however, has never officially supported the party.

The Finns Party (Perussuomalaiset) is much younger, founded in 1995 as a nationalistic and populist party. Christian values were emphasized from the beginning. Timo Soini, who was the party's chair from 1997 to 2017, and famously converted to Catholicism in the 1980s, describes himself as similar to the US Republicans in values. The Finns Party remained a marginal party until 2011, when it grew its parliamentary seats from five to thirty-nine in a landslide victory. The background for this change is the politicization of immigration in Finnish politics and the inclusion of the 'immigration critics', as they were called, within the Finns Party. This proved a risky move for Soini, as the party's hard-line wing on immigration dethroned him in 2017, shifting the party more clearly towards the far right (Äystö 2017). However, the party has retained its nationalistic Christian tones, as I will explore here.

Table 9.1 shows the changes in parliamentary seats between 1999 and 2019, as well as the parties which formed the government during each term. The Centre Party, National Coalition Party and the Social Democratic Party – the big three – have maintained steady support. However, the massive success of the Finns Party in the 2011 elections shook the conventional political divisions and practices, as the Finns claimed seats from others and became the fourth biggest party. Other clear trends include the decline of the Left Alliance and the Christian Democrats, likely losing some of their support to the Finns Party.

Table 9.1 Parliamentary Seats and Government Parties between 1999 and 2019 in Finland. Minor Parties and Mid-term Changes Are Not Included

	1999–2003		2003–7		2007–11		2011–15		2015–19	
	Gov	Seats	Gov	Seats	Gov	Seats	Gov	Seats	Gov	Seats
Centre Party		48	x	55	x	51		35	x	49
National Coalition Party	x	46	x	40	x	50	x	44	x	37
Social Democratic Party	x	51		53		45	x	42		34
Green League	x	11		14	x	15	x	10		15
The Finns Party		1		3		5		39	x	38
Left Alliance	x	20		19		17		14		12
Christian Democrats		10		7		7	x	6		5
Swedish People's Party	x	11	x	8	x	9	x	9		9

Voter studies allow another perspective into the relationship between Finnish politics and religion. While one cannot equate voters' opinions with the parties, they nonetheless offer an essential context for interpreting the various policies and political communication. Religion has often been considered a less significant factor among the Finnish voters than their many European counterparts (Westinen 2015, 117). However, a statistical connection has been found between voting for anti-establishment parties (Left Alliance, Finns and Green League) and not being a member of any official religious community or church, particularly among the youngest voters (Mykkänen 2012, 306). Furthermore, many voters for the Christian Democrats are members of non-majority Christian churches, such as Pentecostal-style groups (Borg et al. 2015, 45).

The Church Research Institute did a national survey in 2017, where they asked, among other things, which party was voted for in the latest municipal election and about opinions on same-sex marriage in the Lutheran Church.[8] Based on this study, one sees pretty clear differences between the voters of different parties, keeping in mind that the survey concerned voting in the municipal and not parliamentary elections and the fact that the marriage law is a national and not a municipal affair. Seventy-two per cent of the voters for the Christian Democrats, 63 per cent of the Finns Party and 47 per cent of the Center Party fully agree that the Lutheran Church should only marry a man and a woman. This is markedly different from the liberal left-wing parties. Only 9 per cent of the voters of the Green League fully agreed with the mentioned statement. The corresponding result was 15 per cent for the Left Alliance and 19 per cent of the Social Democratic Party. In the parliamentary debates, too, value questions such as this one introduce a quite clear liberal versus conservative division (Äystö 2020).

Religion in the Parliament of Finland: General observations

References to religion are not very common in the Finnish parliament. If they occur, the language in question is likely to do with Christianity and Finnish Lutheranism. I counted the references to the most common terms, generally considered 'Christian' in parliamentary speeches, and found that only about 0.3 per cent of plenary session speeches between 1999 and 2019 had them (Äystö 2020).[9] I have since supplemented this with an overview regarding references to other religions and found them even rarer. A general collection of the most

Table 9.2 The Biggest Finnish Parliamentary Discussions with Continuous Religion References between 1999 and 2020

Same-sex marriage and formalized relationship (several years)

Sunday shopping hours (2000, 2008, 2015)

Freedom of religion act (2001–3, 2006)

Secular events during religious holidays without permission (2002)

Ecumenical day of prayer (2003)

Royalties in the case of ecclesiastical music (2004–5)

Assisted reproductive technology (2006)

Maternity law (2018)

Conflicts in the Middle East (several years)

Immigration (several years)

extensive discussions with religion references can be seen in Table 9.2. Even those politicians who are known for their anti-Islam positions mainly voice them outside the parliamentary sessions, favouring social media, blog posts, party media and the traditional news media (Table 9.2).

As can be observed from Table 9.2, the topics are often quite Lutheran specific, or otherwise the type of themes that will be addressed in the cultural context of Finnish Lutheranism. Generally, Finnish politicians talking about 'religion' usually have Lutheranism in mind. Islam is the second most common context. The new Freedom of Religion Act, which came into effect in 2003, is perhaps the most important example in terms of multicultural policy, as it defined the latest model of religious education (in which some non-Lutheran groups may receive school teaching in their 'own religion', see Sakaranaho 2013) and relatedly the category of 'registered religious community', which is a legal personality tailored for non-majority religious groups (Seppo 2003, 190–209).

As previously mentioned, Finnishness, Lutheranism and the Lutheran Church are historically often connected. The Finns Party has, however, begun to challenge this link via their ways of speaking. They often talk of Christianity, but they use cultural or ethnicity-related vocabulary, such as by referring to Finns as Christians or defending 'cultural Christianity'. What they do not usually evoke is the authority of the Lutheran Church. This is a feature unique to them when compared to the other parties. I suspect this is likely due to the political differences between the Finns Party and the Lutheran Church, particularly in immigration policy.

Another general observation about religion and particularly Christianity-related language in the Finnish parliament is that the tone is often positive or neutral. In contrast, negative language towards Christianity is very infrequent. The parties with the most positive ways of speaking about Christianity were the Christian Democrats, Finns Party and Center Party. In turn, most speeches with a negative or critical tone towards Christianity can be found from the MPs of the Green League, Left Alliance and National Coalition. Even in those instances, however, the style does not get much nastier than a slight irony, a remark on secularization as a positive development or a reference to the modern boundary between religion and politics as a positive thing (Äystö 2020).

Lövheim and others (2018, 137–8) have suggested that, on the one hand, traditional religious gaps between parties have lost their meaning in the Nordic countries. On the other, Lutheran Christianity is no longer a consensual non-issue, as one can no longer simply assume that 'everyone' is Lutheran. Religion may come up in political debates relating to immigration, environment and sexuality, but this is not automatic.

An examination of the Finnish case certainly supports these observations, as the historical gap between the pro-Church right and the anti-Church left is no longer a political reality. Looking at parliamentary speeches between 1999 and 2020, no clear left versus right division (in the economic sense) emerges in the speaking tones or contents relating to religion. Instead, the difference is between conservative and liberal parts of the parliament. Christian Democrats and Finns can be viewed as conservative anti-establishment parties that seek to question the liberal consensus and do not neatly fit into either the economic left or right. For example, the Finns are nationalistic and critical of the EU, while the National Coalition – the leading right-wing party – considers EU membership highly important. In political publicity, other issues relating to values and culture outweigh economic policy regarding the Christian Democrats and the Finns.

Islam in recent Finnish political discussion

While the parliamentary materials do not say nearly as much about Islam directly as they do about Christianity, they still address immigration (which, in the Finnish context, very often refers to Muslim immigration specifically), and they are pretty useful sources for investigating the construction of Finnishness and the Finnish society against a perceived cultural other. One example is the initiative by Vesa-Matti Saarakkala of the Finns Party, whose initiative (LA 16/2014) – signed by all MPs of the party – calls for the protection of 'cultural Christianity' via changes to the law on primary education (see Taira 2019). Like most members' initiatives, it did not progress into any legislative changes, but it is a noteworthy example from the political discussion. In the initiative it is stated as follows:

Due to non-Christian immigration, pressure from radical freethinkers, and general secularization of society, the right to foster one's identity has come under considerable threat for the Christian majority of this country. The meaning of the cultural Christian identity for the Finnish form of life should not be underestimated. (LA 16/2014)

Three key things occur in this quotation. First, it connects Finnishness, the 'Finnish form of life', encompassing national and cultural identity, and both the public societal life and private life with Christianity. Second, 'non-Christian immigrants' (primarily Muslims), freethinkers and secularization of society are identified as significant threats to this moral order. Third, these things are done without a reference to the Evangelical Lutheran Church of Finland. Instead, they opt for more ambiguous 'cultural Christianity' – a phrase used eleven times in a two-page initiative text.

The MPs made another initiative of the Finns Party in 2018 (TPA 18/2018) which urged the government to ban the Islamic veils in preschool education and kindergartens. Citing the recent decision of Austria to ban the veils in this manner, the MPs argued that Finland, too, should do this to increase equality between children and prevent the development of an alternative immigrant society. Although unsuccessful, this initiative is a classic example of the politics towards Islam the Finns Party has propagated since 2008.

Jussi Halla-aho, the chair of the Finns Party from 2017 to 2021, is a good example of a politician who has risen from an Islam-bashing online influencer into parliamentary politics. As I've previously argued (Äystö 2017), Halla-aho constructed a solid political following via his blog, Scripta, in which he strongly criticized the Finnish officials and their alleged positions on immigration and Islam, as well as Islam and Muslims themselves. During a critical moment of this political career, when he was progressing from the Helsinki municipal council into the EU parliament and later to the Finnish parliament, he was accused and ultimately convicted of incitement to hatred and religious insult by the Supreme Court in 2012. The events granted him a lot of publicity, which he used to deliver his political message and, in the eyes of his followers, prove a point regarding the 'anti-Finnish' bias of the officials.

Online anti-Islam or anti-Muslim discourse in Finnish is vast. To pick an example from a notable political figure, Jussi Halla-ahos' blog post from 3 January 2008 with the related court proceeding is one that garnered a lot of attention. He attacked Muslims by claiming that Prophet Muhammad is a paedophile and sets a reprehensible example for his followers. In the same text, Halla-aho also attacked Somalis, one of the most prominent minority groups in Finland, by claiming, for instance, that living on the tax funds and robbing people on the street is 'perhaps their genetic trait'. The blog underwent a criminal investigation, and Halla-aho was eventually convicted, and fined, for insult of religion and ethnic agitation, as mentioned earlier (see Äystö 2017).

His text had two primary purposes. First, to criticize the Finnish officials via (successfully) 'baiting' them into the legal process, thus proving, in his view, the double standard of granting Islam special protection while leaving Christianity as a free game. Second, he wanted to advance his anti-Islam and anti-Muslim immigration politics, as he does with the bulk of his writings on Scripta. Although he was eventually convicted, one could argue that the legal process mainly served to advance his political career (see Äystö 2017). As highlighted by the legal scholar Heli Askola (2014), his case illustrates the general problem with hate speech laws, which serve a justifiable societal and moral purpose but often place the defendants in a win-win situation. If they are convicted, they can declare themselves as martyrs of free speech and make use of the publicity. On the other hand, if they are acquitted, their actions gain, in a sense, an official legitimation.

Another politician of the Finns Party known for her frequent criticism of Islam and Muslim immigration is Laura Huhtasaari. She was an MP from 2015 to 2019 and has since served as an MEP. While Halla-aho is non-religious and controlled in style, Huhtasaari strongly and publicly identifies with Christianity (she is a former Adventist with charismatic tones, to be more specific) and often employs emotional language. Further are some examples from her Twitter account, @LauraHuhtasaari.

> This is where we are: Islam chooses our politicians, and Sweden is a multicultural nightmare. I hope the Sweden Democrats take the Folkhemmet back. A death threat to Jimmie Åkersson is circulated online. (7.9.2018)

> In the movie, they told Irwin [a Finnish singer] that one must leave Kekkonen [a former Finnish president] and God alone. Today, one must leave Islam alone. You cannot defame or insult Islam. (27.6.2018)

> If we do not defend Western democracy and Christian values, Islam will sweep over us. (26.5.2018)

> The church of Sweden: 'The plan is to push the Son of God aside and place Muhammad as an equal with Jesus.' (26.11.2017)

> Report: The lives of Muslims who have converted to Christianity in Finland are in danger. (19.2.2016)

Huhtasaari's rhetoric is familiar in many international contexts. She circulates the far-right notion of Sweden as a country ruined by Muslim immigration and presents Islam as a threat to freedom of speech, Western civilization and national Christianity. The importance of Christian vocabulary, attempting to link it with Western and European culture and heritage, and portraying these in stark contrast with Islam, are standard features of the contemporary far right. This has been noted, for example, regarding the Fidesz party of Hungary (Glied & Pap 2016), the National Rally of France (Morieson 2019) and the Alternative for Germany (Althoff 2018).

The Finnish Christian Democrats, on the other hand, have transformed from a party that was pro-religious freedom in a relatively general sense in the early 2000s to a party that has since adopted more voices critical of Islam. For example, Päivi Räsänen, the most well-known MP of the party and its chair from 2004 to 2015, delivered a written question to the government (KK 37/2004) in 2004, where she criticized the recent French decision to ban Islamic veils in schools and inquired on the Finnish government's position on the affair. However, in 2009, reflecting the general change in tone in Finnish discussions regarding Islam, she stated in a newspaper interview (Kaleva 12.12.2009) that she was 'worried about the spread of Islam'. More generally, as pointed out by Johanna Konttori (2020), parliamentary discussion on Islamic veils has been relatively infrequent in Finland compared to many other European countries.

Although the Christian Democrats are still very different from the Finns Party, their transformation in a similar direction has since become more pronounced. For example, in 2019, the party opened a new blog site called konservatiivi .fi (English: conservative.fi). It adopted far-right-style rhetoric (see e.g. Jamin 2014), presenting its new site as an alternative to 'post-Marxist', 'post-feminist' and 'post-modern' viewpoints, which they view as dominant over conservative ones.[10] In 2020, the party proposed that unemployment benefits could be cut for those who do not have sufficient Finnish or Swedish skills (LA 1/2020). While the Christian Democrats cannot, as a whole, be characterized as a far-right party, they have nonetheless begun to show some tendencies associated with such parties.

Conclusion

The Finnish developments are not sui generis; they mirror general European trends. As Nicholas Morieson writes (2019, 2), 'throughout the continent, populist radical right politicians are calling for a return to Christian or Judeo-Christian values, and for the Christian identity of their respective nations to be respected and preserved'. Yet national contexts do have their specific features. In Finland, the rise of the Finns Party needs to be viewed against the backdrop of the challenged Nordic welfare-state model, the demographic fact of having relatively few immigrants and the societally strong position of the Lutheran Church, which has since adopted relatively liberal views on immigrants.

Previously, I have argued how Finnish parliamentary speeches infrequently refer to religion. In the parliamentary context, most references concern Lutheran Christianity, and the tones are generally neutral or positive. However, the extra-parliamentary political discussion contains a large corpus of anti-Islam and anti-Muslim language. Most political movements and parties follow the liberal conventions of polite speech. Still, those who are aligned with the conservative, the Finns Party or the Christian Democrats have begun to challenge this, criticizing the Finnish officials and the alleged liberal value hegemony.

I also suggested that most anti-Islam politics in Finland is associated with the Finns Party. They combine anti-Islam and anti-immigration politics with welfare chauvinism,[11] and with Finnish identity politics in which Whiteness, Finnish culture and 'cultural Christianity' intertwine. While Christian discourse considerably overlaps with Lutheranism in Finnish speech in general, the Finns Party conspicuously produces language that often employs Christian vocabulary or authorities but consistently does this without references to the Lutheran Church. This is likely a conscious strategy due to the political cleavage between them. To the disappointment of the Finns, the Lutheran Church has adopted relatively pro-humanitarian and pro-immigration stances. It has made some liberal changes in its dogmas (most notably, the ordination of women in 1986). The former chair of the Finns, Jussi Halla-aho, wrote in his blog in 2007 that the Lutheran Church is a 'lost cause' and that it is, in its current form, a 'dhimmi church', referring specifically to the multiculturalist policies of the parish union of Helsinki.[12]

Religion is, by no means, the only component of far-right and conservative populist politics in Europe. Still, it is nonetheless a very prominent feature, which has recently been noted by political scientists, who have not traditionally always been very interested in religion. In the field of the study of religion, the new visibility of Islam is often vital when one talks about the 'return of religion', but perhaps the prominent reaction to it – anti-Islam politics employing Christian language and authorities – should be included more frequently by scholars of religion in discussion regarding the notion of secularization. For example, a degree to which religious rhetoric can be successfully employed to advance political aims can be incorporated as an indicator (one of several) of the degree of secularization in politics. The rarity of religious references in the Finnish parliamentary language, as demonstrated earlier, indicates that religious language is likely viewed as b-grade rhetoric in an institution widely considered to be secular, thus guiding even religious MPs to employ other rhetorical means to advance their politics (see Bruce 2011, 171).

Part IV

Comparative perspectives

Misrecognizing Muslim consciousness in Europe[1]

Nasar Meer

Introduction

There is a moderately well-known Greek myth, often traced to the *Iliad*, which is deemed to contain one of the earliest invocations of the *idea* of Europe. It is an account which tells of how *Zeus* became enthralled by the Phoenician princess *Europa* to the extent that he abducted and removed her to Crete where she became queen. This queen and her journey are sometimes appropriated symbolically as 'a true illustration of what we collectively recognise as the origins of European culture' (Holm 1999, xi) and more broadly serves, first, as a literary reminder of how, in contrast to Europe's contemporary northern centres of politics and economics, the very *idea* of Europe has its provenance on the shores of the Mediterranean (Braudel 1995). Second, it is an illustration of how Europe is not simply a political entity in the form of the European Union but is also a dynamic matrix of cultural inheritance whose porous boundaries have been shaped both inside and beyond its present frontiers.

This is at least one view. Competing characterizations of the *idea* of Europe employ a more binary approach in maintaining that 'the birth of Europe took place in an age of Carolingians in a world-historical interaction with the still young but expanding Islamic civilisation' (Tibi 2008, 162). The fuller implication being that from this point onwards 'the foundation of a European identity was basically Christian', something that was 'reshaped at the eve of the Renaissance', and later still became 'more secular' in the development of its 'civilizational identity' (Tibi 2008).

While this broad historical view of the provenance of 'a European identity' may be one among very many debated by historians, it is the *contemporary* implications of Tibi's account that set the scene for our discussion. These emerge in his summation that while 'the world of Islam was located beyond the southern and eastern Mediterranean boundaries. Contemporary Islamic migration to Europe has changed this feature: no Mediterranean boundary exists anymore, because Islam is now within Europe itself' (Tibi 2008).

Tibi's statement offers a valuable contextual account because while it is broadly accepted that the categories of 'Islam' and 'Muslim' in Europe are today patterned by a variety of subjective and objective sociological and political differences, a number of intellectual positions rely on the view that despite internal variation there is something overarching which furnishes Muslims in Europe with a collective sense of *self*. This is something, it is maintained, which is evidenced by empirically observable Muslim identity-related challenges to established social and political configurations at local, national and supranational levels. While the notion of a 'Muslim subject' in Europe is by no means uncontested, for it is open to long-established charges of essentialism and reification, this chapter will focus on the tensions *within* – rather than a refutation of – at least three predominant interpretations. The first of these is theologically grounded but socially iterative. It maintains that Europe's Muslims are redefining Islam in the context of their identities *as European Muslims*, and that the consequence is a 'Euro-Islam': something illustrated by how Muslims view Europe as their home while being guided by a revised Islamic doctrine. Two competing exponents of this view are Tariq Ramadan and the aforementioned Bassam Tibi. A second interpretation of a 'Muslim subject' in Europe can be described as the 'Eurabia' trajectory. This predicts the numerical and cultural domination of Europe by Muslims and Islam. Its chief exponents include (but are by no means limited to) Chris Caldwell and Mark Steyn, who, though differing in several respects, share the view that at a time of alleged demographic, political and cultural weakness in Europe, 'pre-modern Islam will beat post-modern Christianity' (Steyn 2006b). A third interpretation is more formally sociological and employs a methodology of political claims-making and reports that Muslims in Europe are 'exceptional' in not following path-dependent institutional opportunity structures of minority integration. That is to say that, taken as an aggregate, accommodating Muslims will be more difficult because Islam is more publicly confessional than other faiths, refuses to be privatized and instead advances into the public realm of politics in collective and exceptional ways. Exponents of this view can include Ruud Koopmans and Paul Statham, and Christian Joppke.

In what follows this chapter tentatively argues that each of these formulations places the burden of adaptation upon Muslim minorities. As such, each displays a normative 'position' or *weltanschauungen* that misrecognizes dynamic components of what may be termed 'Muslim-consciousness' (Meer 2015). Taking up the opportunity presented by this book to consider seriously the issue of religion in general, the chapter maintains that Muslim consciousness encompasses components that contain compelling evidence that Muslim claims-making in Europe is conventional, despite its emergence from contexts of profound social and political adversity. The fruition of Muslim consciousness that is detailed throughout, therefore, denotes the self-conscious adoption of 'Muslim' among actors and groups seeking substantive recognition to remake common membership. To elaborate this argument, the chapter is set out as follows. The next section tackles some issues of definition by considering a 'religious' characterization of Muslim identity. Following this the chapter briefly outlines what is taken to be at least three salient interpretations of the emergence of Muslim presence in Europe, through an account of the writers understood to be their leading exponents. What is offered may be open to the charge of simplification but hopefully not misrepresentation. This is followed by what is deemed a more accurate 'sociological' characterization of Muslim identity that is able to recognize the dynamic components of Muslim consciousness in contemporary Europe.

'Religious' characterizations of Muslim consciousness

It would be relatively uncontroversial to note that writers use the descriptive terms 'Islam' and 'Muslim' in ways that assume they have been operationalized so that we intuitively understand what they mean and represent. Like many other designation, however, on inspection it becomes clear they host a variety of meanings. To begin to unpack these terms we can ask some obvious questions about what Islam denotes and what *being* Muslim entails. Oliver Roy's (2004) account of *Globalised Islam* begins in this way:

> Who do we call Muslim? A mosque-goer, the child of Muslim parents, somebody with a specific ethnic background (an Arab, a Pakistani), or one who shares with another a specific culture? What is Islam? A set of beliefs based on a revealed book, a culture linked to historical civilisation? A set of norms and values that can be adapted to different cultures? An inherited legacy based on a common origin? (Roy 2004, 21)

Since a robust account of Islamic history, civilization and comparative ethnic relations are beyond the scope of this chapter, and definitive and categorical definitions are neither sought nor – it will be argued – a reflection of how Muslims view themselves and Islam; a more modest and relevant exposition could begin by exploring what we mean when we talk about Islam. Is it a religion whose first prophet was Adam and last prophet was Mohammed; is it a state of peace achieved through surrender to God, or is it a political and cultural movement? What is meant by the phrase that 'Islam is a way of life'? And can we distinguish Islam as a name of a religion, from the adjective 'Islamic', the noun 'Muslim'? To begin to answer these questions abstractly, Karamustafa (2004, 108) encourages us to approach our conception of Islam by viewing it as a civilizational project comprising

> a sprawling civilizational edifice under continuous construction and renovation in accordance with multiple blueprints (these are the numerous Islamic cultures at local, regional, and national levels encompassing innumerable individual, familial, ethnic, racial, and gender identities) all generated from a nucleus of key ideas and practices ultimately linked to the historical legacy of the Prophet Mohammed.

With this enormous stress upon heterogeneity, how *in tangible terms* can we derive an understanding of Muslim identity? Karamustafa's answer is to focus on how this nucleus of ideas represents 'a set of beliefs (a version each of monotheism, prophecy, genesis, and eschatology) that underwrite a set of values (dignity of human life, individual and collective rights and duties, the necessity of ethical human conduct – in short, a comprehensive moral program), in turn reflected in a set of concrete human acts (ranging from the necessity of greeting others to acts of humility like prayer)' (Karamustafa 2004). On a day-to-day basis we can find these ideas articulated in Islamic rituals and practices, where Muslims are reminded through the practice of the pillars of Islam – *Iman* (articles of faith), *salat* (daily prayer), *zakat* (charity), *sawm* (fasting during Ramadan) and *hajj* (pilgrimage) – that actions that are deeply spiritual are not devoid of politics. In this way Islam – comprising the beliefs, values, rights and duties emphasized by Karamustafa – is lived rather than simply practised. As Dilwar Hussain (2005, 39) notes:

> The congregational prayer is often held as an example of a community in harmony with believers standing in rows and functioning with one body. Fasting and charity sensitise the believers to those who lead less fortunate lives and make the war against global poverty a vivid reality. The pilgrimage symbolises equality and the breaking of barriers between nations, classes and tongues.

In this religious characterization of Muslim consciousness, participation is necessitated in some or all of the above practices if one is to consider oneself a Muslim, and to conceive the most appropriate definition of what being a Muslim entails, and it is precisely what informs our first interpretation of a 'Muslim subject' in Europe. As it will become clear, however, to my mind Muslim consciousness need not rest on such underpinnings. It is argued instead that we should adopt an approach that is more flexible and that draws on factual evidence while, at the same time, giving weight to the self-perception of individuals – including their identification with groups – as to their own sources of identity. Such an approach might allow us to explore the social contingencies of a Muslim identity, and its salience and interaction with other sources of identity to the extent, for example, a range of factors other than religion, such as ethnicity, race, gender, sexuality and agnosticism, make shape Muslim identities without invalidating self-designation as 'Muslim'.

Euro-Islam – the promise of theology

This is a view that is theologically grounded but socially iterative. It maintains that Europe's Muslims are redefining Islam in the context of their identities *as European Muslims* and that the outcome is a 'Euro-Islam' illustrated by how Muslims view Europe as their home while being guided by a renewed Islamic doctrine. Two competing exponents of this view are Tariq Ramadan and Bassam Tibi. The origins of the term *Euro-Islam* may be traced to a variety of sources but is forthrightly claimed by Tibi,[2] though it may also be sourced to AlSayyad and Castells (2002) and Ramadan (1999). Its precise provenance, however, is less at issue than what it denotes. For Ramadan (2004, 4), it describes a process already underway in which 'more and more young people and intellectuals are actively looking for a way to live in harmony with their faith while, participating in the societies that are their societies, whether they like it or not'. Ramadan perceives this as the cultivation of a 'Muslim personality', one that is 'faithful to the principles of Islam, dressed in European and American cultures, and definitively rooted in Western societies' (Ramadan 2004). He continues:

> While our fellow-citizens speak of this 'integration' of Muslims 'among us', the question for the Muslims presents itself differently: their universal principles teach them that wherever the law respects their integrity and their freedom of worship, they are at home and must consider the attainments of these societies

as their own and must involve themselves, with their fellow-citizens, in making it good and better. (Ramadan 2004, 5)

Ramadan is thus prioritizing a *scriptural inheritance* that needs to be reconciled with current and future lived practice, in a manner that reflects 'a testimony based on faith, spirituality, values, a sense of where boundaries lie', something that 'reverses the perception based on the old concepts' (Ramadan 2004, 73). A key theological obstacle that Ramadan therefore seeks to overcome is that of the distinction between *Dar Al-Islam* (abode of Islam) and *dar Al-Harb* (abode of war), a concern that is illustrative of his wider thesis.

Muslims can recognize the 'abode of Islam', maintains Ramadan, by the fact that they are able to practise their religion freely and live their lives in a manner that is consistent with Islamic prescription. For Ramadan, this is a question of freedom worship that is *quite different* from a question of the wider institutionalization of Islam and/or non-practise of Islam in any given society. He elaborates this at length to contrast it with its antithesis, 'the abode of war', in which the legal system and the government are anti-Islamic. The important point for Ramadan is to recognize that this distinction does not turn on the distinction between Muslims and non-Muslim contexts since it may well be the case that a majority-Muslim society, where the legal and political system prevents Muslims from living in accordance with their Islamic prescription, constitutes *dar Al-Harb*.

This reasoning leads to an interesting juxtaposition in that 'Muslims may feel safer in the West, as far as the free exercise of their religion is concerned, that in so called Muslim countries' (Ramadan 2004, 65). The implication of this position is that the dichotomy between the two 'abodes' can no longer be sustained. The resolution to this, Ramadan suggests, rests in an exercise of critical interrogation in which European Muslims 'have no choice but to go back to the beginning and study their points of reference in order to delineate and distinguish what, in their religion, is unchangeable (*thabit*) from what is subject to change (*mutaghayyir*), and to measure, from the inside, what they have achieved and what they have lost by being in the West' (Ramadan 2004, 9).

To pursue this, Ramadan proposes that Islam can be appropriated in movements of reform and integration in new environments as long as the idea of the *alamiyyat al-islam* (the universal dimension of the teaching of Islam) is retained. Just as, he argues, the concepts of *dar al-islam* and *dar al-harb* 'constituted a human attempt, at a moment in history, to describe, to describe the world and to provide the Muslim community with a geopolitical scheme that seemed appropriate to the reality of the time' (Ramadan 2004, 69), in the current era what is proposed is the recognition of a third abode *dar al-dawa* ('abode of prayer'). This is consistent with the ethic Islam, he maintains, for 'Mecca was neither *dar al-islam* nor *dar al-harb*, but *dar al-dawa* and in the eyes of the Muslims, the whole of the Arabian Peninsula, was *dar al-dawa*' (Ramadan 2004, 72). He summarizes his position thus:

> I have investigated the tools that can give an impetus, from the inside, to a movement of reform and integration into the new environments. The power and effectiveness of the 'principles of integration', which is the foundation upon which all the juridical instruments for adaptation must depend, lie in the fact that it comes with an entirely opposite perspective; instead of being sensitive, obsessed by self-protection and withdrawal and attempts to integrate *oneself* by the 'little door', on the margin, or 'as a minority', it is on the contrary, a matter of *integrating*, making one's own all that people have produced that is good, just, humane-intellectually, scientifically, socially, politically, economically, culturally, and so on. (Ramadan 2004, 5)

Ramadan's project might then be characterized as *both* classicist and revisionist in that he stakes out an ethical resource in Islamic scriptures to propose a qualitatively novel solution that is calibrated to modern – traditionally non-Muslim majority – environments. Yet it is precisely this project of *reconciliation* between Islamic doctrines and European conventions which is challenged by Bassam Tibi (2008, 177), the other key exponent of 'Euro-Islam'. For if Europe is no longer perceived as *dar al-Harb*, and instead considered to be part of the peaceful house of Islam, he maintains, 'then this is not a sign of moderation, as some wrongly assume: it is the mindset of an Islamization of Europe'. He continues:

> In defence of the open society and of its principles, it needs to be spoken out candidly: Europe is not *dar al-Islam* (or, in the cover language of some, *dar al-shahada*), i.e. it is not an Islamic space but a civilisation of its own, albeit an exclusive one that is open to others, including Muslims. These are, however, expected to become Europeans if they want to be part of Europe as their new home. (Tibi 2008, 159)

In Tibi's view, the burden of adaptation required to cultivate a Euro-Islam must necessarily be greater on the part of Muslims than among the institutions and conventions that constitute European societies. That is to say that a civilizational notion of Europe must be the vessel in which Islam in Europe comes to rest. Tibi's formulation is principally driven by an anxiety over the disproportionate development of sizeable Muslim communities in Europe and the concomitant emergence of a Muslim consciousness (or in Ramadan's terms 'Muslim personality'). This leads Tibi (2008, 180) to insist that without *religious* reforms in Islam, that is, 'without a clear abandoning of concepts such as *da'wa*, *hijra* and shari'a, as well as jihad', there can be no Europeanization of Islam.

One source of Tibi's objection to publically recognizing Islam in Europe centres on the relationship between religious doctrine and migration – that is, proselytization. He thus insists that 'if *da'wa* [prayer] and *hijra* [migration] combined continue to be at work, the envisioned "Islamization of Europe" will be the result on the long run' (2008, 177). This can only be averted in Tibi's view if Muslims acknowledge that the identity of Europe is not Islamic:

> It is perplexing to watch the contradictory reality of Europeans abandoning their faith while the global religionization of politics and conflict enters Europe under the conditions of Islamic immigration [. . .] The substance of the notion of Euro-Islam is aimed at the incorporation of the European values of democracy, laicite, civil society, pluralism, secular tolerance and individual human rights into Islamic thought. (2008, 153, 157)

The direction of travel here is the key distinction between Ramadan and Tibi, which is why the latter has elsewhere promoted the notion of a European *Leitkulture* – a guiding culture or leading culture – characterized by values of 'modernity: democracy, secularism, the Enlightenment, human rights and civil society' (Tibi 1998, 154).

Eurabian nights – demographics and culture

Tibi's concern with a civilizational identity is found in a more exclusionary manner in our second account of an emergence of a large-scale modern Muslim presence in Europe. Unlike the first this provides an indisputably pessimistic interpretation because it associates the Muslim presence with a number of detriments to European culture and social harmony, something deemed to be a consistent feature across the continent. Sometimes sourced to the interventions of the controversial polemicist Bat Ye'or's (2001, 2005), the notion of 'Eurabia' describes a numerical and cultural domination of Europe by Muslims and Islam. It is an idea which features prominently in the accounts of various bestselling authors including the late Italian intellectual Orianna Fallaci (2003), the German economist Thilo Sarrazin (2010), the British historian Niall Ferguson (2004) and the polemicist Melanie Phillips (2005), among many others, and allows our first exponent illustrative of this view, Mark Steyn (2006a), to maintain that 'much of what we loosely call the Western world will not survive this century, and much of it will effectively disappear in our lifetimes, including many, if not most Western European countries'. As such, and in his *America Alone: The End of the World as We Know It*, Steyn (2006b) insists that levels of fertility are so low that

> [N]ative populations are ageing and fading and being supplanted remorselessly by a young Muslim demographic. The EU will need to import so many workers from North Africa and the Middle East that it will be well on its way to majority Muslim by 2035. [. . .] The average European Muslim has 3.5 children, whereas the average native woman has 1.5. Europe's successor population is already in place and the only question is how bloody the transfer of real estate will be. Europe is dying and America isn't.

These statistics have not gone undisputed and indeed have been refuted by Hawkins (2009), Kuper (2007), Laurence and Vaïsse (2006), Carr (2006) and Jones (2005), among others, principally on the grounds that they both radically overestimate base figures and then extrapolate implausible levels of population growth. The demography panic has nonetheless achieved a degree of traction, and the same demographic fatalism is shared by Christopher Caldwell (2010) in his *Reflections on the Revolution in Europe* (subtitled: *Can Europe Be the Same with Different People In It?*). As with Steyn, Caldwell maintains that, with the exception of its Muslim members, all European societies presently fall beneath the 'total fertility rate' required for a society to remain the same size. Muslims are the exception, he insists, because in contrast to a reticent Europe 'Muslim culture is usually full of messages laying out the practical advantages of procreation' (Caldwell 2010, 15).[3] The outcome is that while 'in the middle of the twentieth century, there were virtually no Muslims in Western Europe. At the turn of the twenty-first, there were between 15 and 17 million' (Caldwell 2010, 10).

The important thing to note, however, is that the numbers are not for Caldwell significant in and of themselves but instead for the critical mass they potentially generate in incrementally expanding political challenges to European nation-state conventions. As Caldwell (2010, 19) puts it:

> If you understand how immigration, Islam, and native European culture interact in any Western European country, you can predict roughly how they will interact in any other – no matter what its national character, no matter whether it conquered an empire, no matter what its role WWII, and no matter what the provenance of its Muslim immigrants.

That this bold claim is open to substantial critique from both empirical and theoretical quarters is not the core issue here (Meer 2015). We are instead concerned with Caldwell's characterization of the nature of this interaction between Muslims and European societies. In summary this comprises a combination of Muslim hostility, subversion and ultimately domination because in contrast to Judaism and Catholicism, in his view, 'Islam in Europe is different' for:

> Since its arrival half a century ago, Islam has broken-or required adjustments to-a good many of European customs, received ideas, and state structures with which it has come into contact. Sometimes the adjustments are minor accommodations to Muslim tradition-businesses eliminating the tradition of drinks after work, women-only hours at swimming pools, or prayer rooms in office buildings, factories and department stores . . . occasionally what needs adjusting is the essence of Europe. (Caldwell 2010, 11)

This is, for Caldwell, principally a reflection of the fact that Islam in Europe rests uneasily with European traditions of secularism. Moreover, in a competition between the two – Islam and secularism – the 'arrogant view' that Europeans hold the upper hand will prove the 'biggest liability in preserving its culture' (Caldwell 2010, 22). This emerges as self-evident, maintains Caldwell, in the observation that 'Europeans know more about Arabic calligraphy and kente cloth because they know less about Montaigne and Goethe' (Caldwell 2010, 17). The implication being that 'Europe is not welcoming its newest residents but making way for them' (Caldwell 2010). That is to say that an appreciation of the vibrancy of Islamic cultural forms goes hand in hand with a depreciation of European cultural forms. This zero sum trade-off takes a more sinister turn, however, where cultural diversity is associated with political violence because 'If the spread of Pakistani cuisine is the single greatest improvement in British public life over the past half-century, it is also worth noting that the bombs used for the failed London transport attacks of 21 July 2005 were made from a mix of hydrogen peroxide and chapatti flour' (Caldwell 2010, 17). Steyn (2006b, 84) too stresses the intersections between a critical mass of Muslims and broader political outcomes but goes much further in his assertions by observing that

> Mohammed is (a) the most popular baby boy's name in much of the Western world; (b) the most common name for terrorists and murderers; (c) the name of the revered Prophet of the West's fastest-growing religion. It's at the intersection of these statistics-religion, demographic, terrorist-that a dark future awaits.

There is then a linear relationship between religion and jihadist violence in the current period due to the 'deep the psychoses of jihadism reach within Islam in general and the West's Muslim populations in particular' (Steyn 2006, 81). This is neatly reflected in his question of whether the problem is not that Muslims in the West are unfamiliar with the customs of their new land but rather that they are all too familiar with them – and explicitly reject them. The result being 'a mutated form of Islam' (Steyn 2006, 82) which functions as a new European pan-Islamic identity. Unlike its Euro-Islam counterpart then this second interpretation of a Muslim subject does not envisage space for synthesis. On the contrary, it predicts that the numbers and sheer will of Muslims will subsume the present European landmass into an Islamic enclave characterized by a 'mutated form' of Islam to be known as 'Eurabia'.

Exceptional Muslim claims-making – the limits of integration

The third interpretation employs a methodology of political claims-making to report that Muslims in Europe are exceptional in not following path-dependent institutional opportunity structures of minority integration. That is to say that, taken as an aggregate, accommodating Muslims will be more difficult because Islam is more publicly confessional than other faiths, refuses to be privatized and instead advances into the public realm of politics in collective and exceptional ways. Different exponents of this view can include Joppke (2009a and b), and Koopmans and Statham (2005), as well as O'Leary (2006), and Hansen (2006), among others.

In Joppke's (2009b, 108) account, 'if one considers that explicit Muslim claims did not emerge in earnest before 1989, the year of the Rushdie controversy in Britain and of the first Foulard affair in France, the speed and depth of accommodating Muslims have been breathtaking, up to the point of "laiscist" France is now providing state financed Imam education'. The explanation for this sustained and rapid claims-making may be found in the force with which 'in pious Muslims there reverberates the archaic power of religion, which is not merely subjective belief, but objective truth, which cannot leave room for choice' (2009a, 111). The presence of Muslims in Europe has therefore resurrected religious disputes from an earlier age, yet Joppke does not share with Caldwell the notion that there is little difference between national contexts, for while he does point to a European-wide phenomenon, it is also at least one feature of what he characterizes as the 'paradox' of British integrationist policies. By this he refers to his assessment that 'while the British state has done more than other European states to accommodate the claims of Muslim minorities, recent polls have shown British Muslims to be more disaffected and alienated than other Muslims in Europe' (2009b, 454).

This he interprets as evidence of 'the limits of [British] integration policy' and orients his stiffest critique to how 'the neologism "Islamophobia" has functioned as a symbolic device of the British state to recognise the Muslim minority' (2009b). Indeed, and in a challenging and provocative account, Joppke rejects the analytical value of Islamophobia on the grounds that it has deflected from the 'real' causes of disadvantage and that it fuelled a quest for recognition that stands to be disappointed. He continues:

> Britain is a particularly interesting case in this respect. This is because the British case shows a puzzling disjunction between an apparently ill-adapted and dissatisfied Muslim minority and a rather accommodative state policy, which has rarely been far from what organised Muslims want the state to do. Formulated as a counter-factual, if you look for a place in Europe where you would not expect Muslim integration to pose a particular problem, you would expect this place to be Britain. Of all European societies, Britain has perhaps gone the furthest in accommodating her ethnic minorities by means of explicit state policy, Muslims included. Britain was the first European country to devise remedial 'race relations' policies for her immigrants, whose logic of combating not just personal insult and injury but structural exclusions in key societal sectors became the European mainstream only 40 years later. This first and paradigm-setting anti-discrimination policy in Europe was framed within a consensual view of Britain as a multicultural society, where 'diversity' was extolled as a virtue long before this happened elsewhere. (2009b, 455)

Contrastingly, in a more thorough and dispassionate analysis, Koopman et al. (2005, 21) come to the same task not to prescribe a position in political theory but instead to identify distinct features of citizenship practice and to let them interact in order to create four possibilities. Using the two dimensions of (i) a formal basis of citizenship – civic-territorial versus ethno-cultural; and (ii) cultural obligations tied to citizenship – cultural monism and cultural pluralism, they chart the emergence of four conceptions of citizenship as follows. The first is termed an *Ethnic Assimilationism* (found in Germany and Switzerland); the second is an *Ethnic Segrationism*; the third is a type of *Civic Republicanism* (evidenced in France and, in a qualified manner, in the UK); and finally they chart *Civic Pluralism* (e.g. the Netherlands). In Koopman et al. (2005, 73) they apply this model to the position of five countries (as bracketed earlier) at three moments

(1980, 1990 and 2002) and find that there are two important movements between the periods of 1980 and 2002. The first is a movement towards cultural pluralism in all five countries, though to differing degrees and from quite different starting points, and the second is a movement towards civic conceptions of citizenship. What is most relevant to our discussion is that in related analysis they come to the view that taken as an aggregate Muslims are exceptional in their group demands for accommodation because, unlike other faiths, 'Islam cannot simply be confined to privatized religious faith, but advances into the public realm of politics where the state's authority and civic citizenship obligations reign supreme' (Statham et al. 2005, 455). To elaborate this, they stake out the difference between group demands which seek parity and group demands that are exceptional, and discuss the issue of education to illustrate how these differ:

> The example of separate schooling for Muslim girls in Britain is a parity group demand because other faith groups have state-sponsored single-gender school. One difference between Catholic girl's schools and Islamic ones, however, is that Islamic schools make a religious faith central to education that promotes values that are less commensurable with liberalism than modern Catholicism. Sometimes Muslim parents' arguments for faith schools make little effort to fit within the culturalism of the civic community, for example, when they express feat at the possible 'westernization' of their children. Important here is that some Muslims see Islam as being more 'true' than other faiths, and more authoritative than the state, which is problematic for liberal democracies. (Statham et al. 2005, 431–2)

What makes Muslim claims-making exceptional in this view are the ways in which group identity and cultural demands routinely coalesce in a novel and challenging manner because, to some extent, Muslims are promoting a way of life that is antithetical to liberal–democratic norms and conventions. Through this last account of the writers understood to be their leading exponents, we have now considered what is taken to be at least three salient interpretations of the emergence of Muslim consciousness in Europe. What is offered may be open to the charge of simplification but hopefully not misrepresentation.

Misrecognizing Muslim consciousness

Having summarized these positions, we are now able to critically engage with each. The first account of a Muslim subject is theologically grounded but socially iterative. It maintains that Europe's Muslims are redefining Islam in the context of their identities *as European Muslims* and that the consequence is a 'Euro-Islam' – something illustrated by how Muslims view Europe as their home while being guided by a renewed Islamic doctrine. While differing profoundly in important respects, both Tariq Ramadan and Bassam Tibi *anchor* the development of a Muslim consciousness in Europe to a doctrinal innovation in Islam.

The argument presented here is that the Euro-Islam thesis assumes too linear a relationship between Islamic doctrine and Muslim identity in a way that minimizes the role of the social. A key issue is that when outlining what a doctrine of Islam requires, there emerge a variety of sources in addition to the Qu'ran, including the *Sunnah*, which accounts for 'what the Prophet said, did, and observed others doing but did not comment on' (Bullock 2002, 155). This is believed to be preserved in the *Hadith* and, in particular, in the *Sirah*, which is akin to a biography of the Prophet Mohammed and is found in the Qu'ran. However, because the *Hadith* are subject to a number of interpretative controversies, given that they were written after the life of the Prophet and are variously classified as 'authentic, good, weak, and fabricated' (Bullock 2002), Bullock argues that up until the nineteenth century, Islam recognized

> other sources of law after the Qu'ran and Sunnah, including the actions and opinions of the Companions of the Prophet, the generation after them, juristic consensus, local customs . . . analogical reasoning, considerations of the public good, and so on [. . .] Because the early scholars recognised that there was no way of adjudicating between differing reasonable interpretations of the Qu'ran and Sunnah, the understanding between them developed that no matter what the differences in legal opinion, each was said to be correct. (Bullock 2002)

The implication is that – no less than with any text – Islamic scriptures offer guidance that are interpreted and applied by human agents in social contexts. As Omid Safi (2004, 22) reminds us: 'in all cases, the dissemination of the Divine teachings is achieved through human agency. Religion is always mediated.' One outcome being that competing accounts of religiously informed Muslim identities can simultaneously be held without necessarily invalidating one another.

It is suggested here that the relationship between Islam and a Muslim identity might be better conceived as instructive but not determining, something analogous to the relationship between the categorization of one's sex and one's gendered identity.[4] That is to say, one may be biologically female or male in a narrow sense of the definition, but one may be a woman or man in multiple, overlapping and discontinuous ways – one's sex reflects something that emerges on a continuum that can be either (or both) internally defined or externally ascribed. This allows that in addition to the scriptural conception, we could view Muslim identity as a quasi-ethnic sociological formation – 'Quasi' is used to denote something *similar* but *not the same as* because, on the one hand, ethnic and religious boundaries continue to interact and are rarely wholly demarcated, hence the term 'ethno-religious' (Modood 1997, 337).

Compared to the purely theological variety, this sociological category might be preferred as a less exclusive and more valid way of operationalizing Muslim consciousness because it includes opportunities for self-definition (such as formally on the census or on 'ethnic' monitoring forms (see Aspinall 2000) or informally in public and media discourse). Equally, it can facilitate the description of oneself as 'Muslim' and take the multiple (overlapping or synthesized) and subjective elements into account independently or intertwined with objective behavioural congruence to the religious practices outlined earlier. It is maintained that this space for self-definition is a helpful means of conceptualizing the difference between externally imposed and self-ascribed identities, with both potentially becoming more prominent at some times and less at others. Within this process of categorizations, however, just as on a census form or other prescriptive sources, when a category is operationalized and imposed externally, it need not constitute the making of a group identity. As Cornell and Hartman (1997, 20) argue,

> others may assign us an ethnic identity, but what they establish by doing so is an ethnic category. It is our own claim to that identity that makes us an ethnic group. The ethnic category is externally defined, but the ethnic group is internally defined.

This emphasizes the element of choice in self-definition. For example, one might view Islam as a historical, civilizational edifice that has contributed to modern science and philosophy and take pride in this but, simultaneously, disassociate oneself from the religious teachings. One implication being that non-Muslims might share this association, as described in Hodgson's (1974, 57) adoption of the designation 'Islamicate' to refer to the 'overall society and culture associated historically with the religion'. The historical or civilizational role of Islam may yet be discarded in favour of the elevation and re-imagining of a particular religious doctrine, or way of being a Muslim, based upon an adherence to articles of divine and confessional faith.

The point is to recognize the pragmatic possibilities that emphasis and dis-emphasis confer upon the bearers of such identification, which includes the recognition that the element of choice is not a total one. By this it is meant that although one may imagine a Muslim identity in different ways, when one is born into a Muslim family one becomes a Muslim. This is not to impose an identity or a way of being onto people who may choose to passively deny or actively reject their Muslim identity because, consistent with the right of self-dissociation, this rejection of Muslim identification (or adoption of a different self-definition) should be recognized where a claim upon it is made. What is being argued is that when a Muslim identity is mobilized, it should be understood as a mode of classification according to the particular kinds of claims Muslims make for themselves, albeit in various and potentially contradictory ways.

Rather than moving to the second interpretation of Muslim subject, this last point brings us to the third account which characterizes Muslims in Europe as exceptional in not following path-dependent institutional opportunity structures of minority integration. That is to say that, taken as an aggregate, accommodating Muslims will be more difficult because Islam is more publicly confessional than other faiths, refuses to be privatized and instead advances into the public realm of politics in collective and exceptional ways. Different exponents of this view can include Christian Joppke, Ruud Koopmans and Paul Statham.

It is suggested that these different positions do not offer a fair reflection of the content of mobilizations undertaken by Muslims *qua* Muslims. To consider this, we can reflect on the issue of Muslim schools in Britain, which is raised by each author as illustrative of exceptional group demands. I have elsewhere argued that Muslim identities can inform the movement for Muslim schools in a variety of ways, and that where Muslim constituencies are granted greater participatory space in the shape of provisions for Muslim schooling, it is evident from the testimonies of Muslim educators and school curricula that a synthesis between faith requirements and citizenship commitments is a first-order priority (Meer 2009).

Yet what commentators frequently overlook in the deployment of Muslim identities in the case for Muslim schools in Britain is how the imagining of a Muslim identity goes hand in hand with the imagining of a British identity. This is very evident in the characterization by head teacher Abdullah Trevathan of *Islamia Primary's* 'ethos'; the first Muslim school in Britain to receive state funding maintains:

> [I]f anything – this school is about creating a British Muslim culture, instead of,
> as I've often said in the press, conserving or saving a particular culture, say from
> the subcontinent or from Egypt or from Morocco or from wherever it may be.

Obviously those cultures may feed into this British Muslim cultural identity, but we're not in the business of preserving . . . it's just not feasible and it's not sensible . . . it's dead: I mean I'm not saying *those* cultures are dead but it's a dead duck in the water as far as being *here* is concerned. (Trevathan, Interview with author)

Islamia Primary is not unique in trying to partner the Muslim dimension with the national, so instead of suffocating hybridity or encouraging reification, for example, the outward projection of this internal diversity informs a pursuit of hyphenated identities. The casualty in this 'steering' of Muslim identity is the geographical-origin conception of ethnicity, and the scramble to de-emphasize the 'ethnic culture' in favour of an ecumenical Islamic identity soon gives rise to a key complaint. This includes the lack of provisions within comprehensive schooling to cater for identity articulations that are not premised upon the recognition of minority status per se but which move outward on their own terms in an increasingly confident or assertive manner, based upon the subscription to a common Islamic tradition. Idris Mears, director of the Association of Muslim Schools (AMS), stresses this position:

I think a general point which is very important to get across is that state schools do not handle the meaning of Muslim identity well for the children. In actual fact, the way that general society looks at Muslims is as an immigrant minority-ethnic-racial-group and how young people are made to look at themselves through the teaching in state schools tells them 'you are this marginal group/minority group and have therefore got to integrate with the mainstream'. So there's a process of marginalisation and that often leads to resentment. But in a Muslim school that identity is built upon being a Muslim *not* an ethnic minority. The impact of being Muslim is very different because the role of the Muslims in any situation is to be the middle nation to take the middle ground and be the model as witnesses of humanity. I think it gives young people a greater sense of who they are and how they can interact in society and therefore learn that Islam is not just a thing that is relevant to minority rights. Islam is relevant to economy, to foreign policy, etc which means that we're not getting on to a stationary train but a train that is moving. (Mears, Interview with author)

This 'train' – which moves between different sites of boundary maintenance – is an articulation of Muslim consciousness. Mears expresses a 'clean' version of Muslim consciousness that is free from ethnic and racial markers and therefore does not correspond to the lived reality but is expressed as an aspiration to be realized through Muslim schooling environments. It is a desire reflected in the findings of Kelly (1998, 203), who, in her ethnographic study of schooling choices made by Muslim parents with both secular and Islamic worldviews, concluded that 'as some less-religious families do opt for specifically Muslim education, we can consider this as an example of a decision to selectively emphasise this pan-ethnic (Muslim) group identity, in order to reap whatever benefits – economic, social and psychological as well as spiritual – it offers'.

While this emphasizes that much of the motivation for Muslim schooling reflects the desire of Muslim parents to instil some sense of a Muslim heritage in all its heterogeneity, this is not incommensurable with liberal–democratic norms and conventions. As Soper and Fetzer (2010, 13) insist: 'it is theologically naïve and historically misguided to assume Islam is any more inherently incapable of making peace with liberal–democratic values than are Christian and Jewish traditions.' Thus, Mears is at pains to stress the distinction between a school premised upon an ethnic origin conception of Islam, driven by a desire for 'cultural protection zones', and an Islamically driven environment that moves outward to build upon evaluative criteria already established and in place (Mears, Interview).

This brings us to the Eurabia thesis, which predicts the numerical and cultural domination of Europe by Muslims and Islam. By now it should be apparent that the weight of evidence does not support this determinate outcome. This is because Muslims are either innovating with Islam in Europe – both Ramadan and Tibi are evidence of this – or are pursuing well-established policy traditions within European states. Muslims are not, for example, seeking to establish the right to practise polygamy, Forced Genital Mutilation (FGM) or forced marriages. Moreover, as Soper and Fetzer (2010, 12) have it: 'Muslims are religiously active, but they lack the political power that well established churches have historically enjoyed, thereby threatening their capacity to win state recognition for their religious needs.' Recalling this reverses Caldwell's (2010) question to ask not whether Europe can remain the same with Muslims in it, but instead at what point, if at all, the emergence of a Muslim consciousness be recognized as a legitimate constituent in Europe; at what cost Muslim constituencies will be denied a participatory space in the form of such things as provisions for Muslim schooling, discrimination legislation and non-derogatory representation in mainstream public and media discourses? It is evident that there is a movement for some sort of synthesis by Muslims themselves. Europe boasts a varied public sphere that has historically included and incorporated other religious minorities. The question with which it is currently wrestling concerns the extent to which it can accommodate Muslims in a manner that will allow them to reconcile their faith commitments with their citizenship requirements. The alternative is to leave Muslims experiencing oneself as invisible at the same time that one is marked out as different. The invisibility comes about when dominant groups fail to recognize the perspective embodied in their cultural expressions as a perspective. These dominant cultural expressions often have little place for the experience of other groups, at most only mentioning or referring to them in stereotyped or marginalized ways. (Young 1990, 60)

This kind of civic status will confer upon Muslims a sort of *veil* from behind which they must look out at dominant society, while those in front of it do not see them as full and legitimate co-members of their polity. That is, institutions and social practices attribute minority status to some inherent qualities, as if those qualities were the *reason* that rather than the *rationalization* for neither recognizing their presence nor taking their sensibilities into account. This seems especially true at moments of acute objectification, in that being 'singled out for particular interrogation in the west, Muslims have been asked to commit to patriotism, peace at home, war abroad, modernity, secularism, integration, anti-sexism, anti-homophobia, tolerance and monogamy' (Younge 2005, 31). The point is that Muslims are not being asked to sign up to these because they are intrinsically valuable, but as 'a pre-condition for belonging in the west at all' (Younge 2005).

Conclusions

Taking up the opportunity presented by this book to reconsider seriously the issue of religion in general and concomitantly by drawing upon notions of identity, politics and contemporary debates about Islam, the chapter maintains that three prominent and influential characterizations of Muslim consciousness misrecognize key features in the emergence of a Muslim subject among Muslims in Europe. By taking up a key objective of this special book, it is maintained that, unlike the intellectual tendency permeating some of the early theorizations of recognition, a context-sensitive approach can reveal how Muslim identities are routinely imagined and re-imagined in ways that cannot being reduced to binary categories. Our focus instead must pivot to the very contexts in which they face profound social and political adversity, in the knowledge that Muslim consciousness does not stand apart from social process.

11

Afterword

Grace Davie

It is more than two years since I agreed to write an Afterword to this fascinating volume: the correspondence with the editors began in the fall of 2019. To say that a great deal has happened since then is an understatement. Important for me personally – and for the thinking that I bring to this reflection – has been the completion of *The Oxford Handbook of Religion and Europe*, a volume that I co-edited with Lucian Leustean (Davie and Leustean 2021). Common to us all have been the experiences of Covid-19, including a series of lockdowns which seriously restricted movement both within and between countries. Finally, the chapters arrived for my comment in exactly the same week as Russia invaded Ukraine, an event that has prompted new, urgent and complex questions about the place of religion in modern Europe.

I will start by expanding on each of these points. I will then look at how the chapters in this volume, and the questions that they raise, speak to these issues from the following perspectives: first, the failures of social science to deal well with religion and, second, the marked shifts in political alignment unfolding before our eyes – paying particular attention to the ways in which these relate to recent changes in the religious life of Europe.

Co-editing the 800-plus pages of the *Oxford Handbook* took four years from start to finish. Critical in this process was the moment when the chapters that made up the final part came together. These case studies, thirteen in all, cover the countries or clusters of countries that constitute modern Europe and bring to life the historical and thematic sections that precede them. Two trends and an additional challenge emerged with great clarity. The first trend is continuing, some would say relentless, secularization. The narrative unfolds differently in different parts of Europe and is more advanced in some places than others, but – with the partial exception of selected countries in the East – it shows little sign of reversing. At the same time, there is a steady and equally widespread increase in religious diversity brought about by immigration. This has ebbed and flowed since the mid-twentieth century but currently continues apace, bringing with it controversies that foreground the place of religion in *public* debate. The additional challenge reflects this combination. Developed secularization results – as night follows day – in a decrease in religious literacy. Europeans are, therefore, less and less able to create – never mind sustain – a constructive conversation about faith and faith communities just when they need it most.

The same combination reveals a continent ill at ease with itself and nervous about the associated tensions: author after author came to the same conclusion. Put differently, had we edited the *Handbook* in the 1990s, a far more optimistic picture would have emerged.

Most of our chapters had been submitted by the time that the pandemic hit Europe in January 2020. Its impact, however, has been immense for both Europe as a whole and its constituent nations, never mind the faith communities within these. Almost immediately, borders closed and lockdowns started; the former redefined Schengen, and the latter spared no one: religious organizations of all kinds – alongside their secular equivalents – were obliged to close their doors, raising profound questions about their roles and rights in late modern European societies. Here, in a very literal sense, was a fortress mentality. Rather, more positive have been the responses of the same organizations that, remarkably fast, found new ways to respond to the virus in the form of online liturgies, innovative forms of pastoral care and effective practical support.

The careful – and necessarily comparative – analysis of these many and diverse initiatives has only just begun. Two points, however, are already clear: first, the situation varied considerably from nation state to nation state depending on the options available to religious communities. There was more room for manoeuvre in some parts of Europe than others. Second, the impact on and the reactions of minorities, whether ethnic or religious, were critical. Both are captured with respect to the UK in Ala et al. (2021), which covers not only the disproportionate burden of COVID-associated illness and death among religious minorities but also possible ways to overcome this. Gaining the trust of such communities is central to the endeavour, not least with respect to vaccine hesitancy. The article is all the more valuable given that it is short, focused and very practical. Interestingly, it does indeed pay close attention to faith and faith communities, but it is written by a medical rather than religious or social scientific team and was published in a premier medical journal.

The pandemic is far from over. In late February 2022, however, it more or less vanished from the news as Russia invaded Ukraine. Shocked and bewildered,

European populations tried first to offer such practical help as they could and second to understand what was happening. How could such an invasion take place in twenty-first-century Europe, and how should the latter be defined in the first place? Is Russia part of Europe, and where are the critical fault lines? Most insightful, but often overlooked, are the analyses which take into account the religious – indeed civilizational – fissures that lie across both Russia and Ukraine. These are complex and for the most part concern the Orthodox churches rather than the dominant confessions of Western Europe that feature in this book. That said, they serve to remind us of the critical importance of religious issues if we are to discover solutions to the violence and the seemingly intractable differences that lie beneath this conflict. Equally important, and equally dismaying (though in some ways 'understandable'), is the very different welcome given by Europeans to refugees from Ukraine as opposed to those fleeing conflict in the Middle East some six to seven years earlier.

Turning now to the chapters that precede this Afterword, the narratives are – mercifully – rather less dramatic than those discovered in the current confrontation. But to an extent the same, or very similar, issues are at stake: first, religion matters and discrimination on the grounds of religion is both deeply felt and highly destructive; second, religion confused with culture lays itself open to dangerous misuse; and third, not only those involved but the social scientists who observe them are at a loss to know how to proceed.

Taking the last of these statements first, we are obliged to ask yet again why the disciplines of social science fail to grasp the significance of religion and its continuing salience in Europe in the twenty-first century. This is particularly true in relation to immigration. There are profound ironies in this situation in so far as social scientists interested in race or ethnicity were among the first to appreciate the disadvantages of recent immigrants and to seek ways to address these. The mood changed, however, as bit by bit exactly the same minorities began to define themselves in terms of religion rather than race – Pakistanis and Indians in the UK became Muslims, Hindus and Sikhs; North Africans in France and Turks in Germany became Muslims; and so on. The shift became increasingly apparent from the 1990s onwards, epitomized by the Salman Rushdie controversy in the UK and the *affaire du foulard* in France. These disputes were triggered at more or less the same time (1988–9), and tellingly the underlying questions remain largely unresolved some thirty years later.

But why are the social sciences so discomfited by this situation? First, the claiming of seriously held religious identities disturbs the expectation that modern societies are necessarily secular societies, and – more radically – it unsettles, to say the least, the emphatically secular philosophies of science that underpin the disciplines under review. An additional point follows from this: given these tendencies, the perceived conservatism of religion exposes the minorities in question to unreasonable pressures to conform. Put differently, ethnic or racial differences are possible to accommodate in late modern democracies but not when they are 'translated' into strongly held *group* identities predicated on religion. Precisely, these tensions lie beneath several of the preceding chapters but are particularly clear in John Holmwood's analysis of the multicultural anxieties found in the English school system. Drawing on the work of Adam Seligman and David Montgomery (2020), Holmwood underlines the central question: 'how do we recognize the importance of community (especially, religious community) in a liberal polity?' (p. 33). All too often the 'solution' is found in suppressing the widely acknowledged right to the freedom of belief. Hence the following paradox: actions that claim such a right are perceived as a stance that, in and of itself, is deemed threatening not only to the lifestyles of modern Europeans but also to the notion of (secular) human rights per se.

This thinking must be set alongside the current and largely unexpected politico-religious alignments discovered in many parts of Western Europe. I consider these shifts a dominant finding of this volume and am fascinated by its articulation across societies, which in other ways are very different. The catalyst in almost every case is the presence of Islam in many parts of the continent, a well-documented phenomenon brought about by economically motivated immigration. The reactions to this situation are meticulously described in the relevant case studies which vary from the Netherlands, known for its advanced secularity, to the situation in Ireland, which until very recently was overwhelmingly Catholic. Also covered are Switzerland and Finland. The details, including a series of well-chosen examples, are deftly deployed to illustrate what is happening. Central to all of them, however, is the reclaiming of Christian heritage by both individuals and organizations that – on conventional readings – are very far from 'Christian'. Even more intriguing is the fact that some of these groups locate themselves on the political right (more accurately far right) and others on the left. Conspicuously absent in many cases are the churchgoing constituencies of modern Europe. What emerges, therefore, requires very careful scrutiny by scholars from many disciplines.

Examples of such scholarship can be found in a steadily growing literature, much of it included in the Bibliography. The findings brought together in Hennig and Weiberg-Salzmann (2021) should also be noted. From a personal point of view, I am intrigued by the way in which 'vicarious religion'

(Davie 2000, 2007) has found a place in this debate. Originally devised to rebalance the discussion surrounding 'believing without belonging', vicarious religion has changed in nature. As conceived in 2000, it captured an investment in the historic churches of Europe, understanding these as institutions which operated on behalf of a wider constituency that were appreciative of what the churches were doing but were themselves largely, if not totally, inactive. Both the concept itself and the constituency that I had in mind were entirely benign and would, I thought, be unlikely to outlast the generation born in the aftermath of the Second World War. I was wrong, in so far as the debate has taken an unexpected turn: the essence of vicarious religion has been deployed very differently at least by some. No longer do the Christian churches represent a cherished and somewhat wistful connection to the past; they become instead a bulwark to resist Islam. The link is found in the disconnect between belief and belonging: without a firm base in theology – or, as Max Weber put it, a religious ethic – Christianity, together with the heritage that it represents, is vulnerable to misuse. Its re-modelling as 'culturalized religion' (Astor and Mayrl 2020) or 'Christianism' may be well intentioned in the first instance but brings with it associated risks. As explained in these pages, it is a shift that active churchgoers frequently, and quite rightly, resist.

One further point brings this Afterword to a close. As Mike Salven indicates in his scene-setting chapter, borders and boundaries are not only found on the edge but penetrate the workings of society at every level. It follows that they are experienced differently by religious minorities in comparison with the mainstream. Nasar Meer's insightful overview starts in a different place but comes to a similar conclusion: that binary categories are less than helpful if we are to understand the pressures on Muslims in different parts of Europe. Adversities are not simply abstract forces but take the form of specific encounters between real people who live in very varied politico-legal contexts. It is for this reason that I particularly like the chapters in which religious minorities are able to speak for themselves, explaining to the reader how it feels to be in this position. We hear a variety of voices: younger generations of Shia Pakistani–Scottish, young Alevis in Germany, Muslim schoolboys in Switzerland, as well as Mormons in Ireland. This is a field in which it is unwise to generalize; each of these minorities has its own story to tell. I am also mindful that in more than one case the focus lies on a minority within a minority. Sensing the need to work at several levels, I conclude this Afterword with a revealing sentence from the account of four young Alevis and their struggles to be accepted in German society:

> By showcasing the plurality among young Alevis in Germany, I give voice and visibility to individual strategies to confront and respond to the growing climate of hostility facing those perceived as Muslims. (Loth, in this book: chapter five)

Individual difference and the ambiguity between reality and perception are foregrounded, but there can be no doubt at all about the climate of hostility regarding Muslims in Germany. Social scientists should be at the forefront of these enquiries if we are to understand this situation better and find the right way forwards. It is for this reason that I congratulate both authors and editors and commend this book very warmly.

Notes

Chapter 3

1 In the UK, Prime Minister David Cameron announced the death of multiculturalism at a speech to the Munich Security Conference in February 2011. Available at: https://www.gov.uk/government/speeches/pms-speech-at-munich -security-conference. In this chapter, I deliberately refer to England, rather than Great Britain or the UK, because since the Devolution Acts of the late 1990s, schooling has been a matter for the devolved jurisdictions.

2 Indeed, while religious tolerance among religious groups is not a given, it would be unusual for those who experience themselves as a minority to express intolerance of others since they are dependent upon it. For a detailed account of ethnic minority attitudes to being 'British', see Karlsen and Nazroo (2015). They show the strong identification of British Muslims, while Guveli and Platt (2011) show a positive correlation between British identification and higher religiosity.

3 Significantly, she also argues that the shrinking membership of clubs and declining social capital found by Putnam can be attributed to de-segregation and changing laws of association which meant that many associations closed their doors rather than open them to diverse others (Allen 2019).

4 This section draws on material presented in Holmwood and O'Toole (2018), where full citations are provided.

5 Ofsted is an independent agency of the Department for Education responsible for school performance. Ofsted Reports for the schools have been deleted from their website. See Holmwood and O'Toole (2018).

6 In fact, its chair from 2003 until September 2012 had been Trevor Philips, who was outspoken in his opposition to multiculturalism and propounded the view that Muslim communities were self-segregated.

7 It is described as part of Goal 2, 'to build a more equal and rights-respecting society' in their Strategic Plan for 2019–22, here: https://www.equalityhumanrights.com/en/ what-we-do/our-strategic-plan

8 *The Guardian*, 13 October 2017. 'The Guardian view on school segregation: the origins of inequality'. Available here: https://www.theguardian.com/

commentisfree/2017/oct/13/the-guardian-view-on-school-segregation-the
-origins-of-inequality.

9 See the report by Rocker (2022). The Ofsted Report is available here: https://files
.ofsted.gov.uk/v1/file/50179320.

10 In fact, the enumeration is a little misleading. Schools are required to teach in
the context of 'stable relationships' and so bi-sexuality is precluded as a 'queer'
perspective seeking to de-stabilize 'binaries'. Once again, as this chapter was being
prepared, the Attorney General declared that schools need not accommodate the
needs of transgender pupils because under-18s do not have the right to change sex.
See Badshah (2022).

11 https://www.theguardian.com/education/2019/mar/04/birmingham-school-stops
-lgbt-lessons-after-parent-protests.

12 For example, the *Guardian* columnist Kenan Malik (2019) wrote that 'there is never
a reason for bigotry at the school gate'.

13 As reported in the *Birmingham Mail* on 7 March 2019. Report available here:
https://www.birminghammail.co.uk/news/midlands-news/parkfield-school-lgbt
-row-councillor-15935577.

14 As reported by Sally Weale in the *Guardian*, 21 February 2019, 'Ofsted chief backs
teaching about same-sex couples after parent protests'. Available at: https://www
.theguardian.com/education/2019/feb/21/ofsted-chief-backs-teaching-of-same-sex
-couple No Outsiders: Researching approaches to sexualities equality in primary
schools-after-parent-protests.

15 As reported by Eleanor Busby in the *Independent*, 3 November 2019, 'Primary
schools should not consult parents before teaching LGBT+ relationships, watchdog
chief says'. Available here: https://www.independent.co.uk/news/education/
education-news/lgbt-lessons-school-parents-consultation-equality-human-rights
-commission-a9181326.html.

Chapter 4

1 Effective Altruism is a philosophical school and a social movement which promotes
improving other people's lives through careful, evidence-based reasoning. The idea
is that this approach will revolutionize philanthropy by encouraging responsible
citizens to do as much good as possible (Gabriel 2016).

2 The Big Society is a political ideology introduced and adopted by David Cameron's
government in the UK ('Building the Big Society' 2010). It has been interpreted as
a method of the Conservative Party to distance itself from Thatcherism by adopting
a policy approach which enables and empowers the citizens to look after their own
communities.

Chapter 5

1 'Most of the Muslims in Germany are part of this country. Their attitudes and standpoints are strongly orientated towards Germany's fundamental values like democracy and plurality' (Religionsmonitor 2015, 4f). Regardless, a significant portion of the non-Muslim population is hostile towards Muslims (Religionsmonitor 2017).

2 The estimated number of Alevis in Germany is around 550 thousand (Haug, Müssig and Stichs 2009). However, the leading organization of Alevis in Germany (AABF) cites figures as high as 700 thousand (website AABF) https://alevi.com/ueber-uns/, last accessed 28 March 2022.

3 The survey was operationalized by the opinion research institute TNS Emnid on behalf of the University of Münster's Cluster of Excellence 'Religion and Politics'. The separate calculation of the categorizes 'Muslims' and 'Alevis' was made by Olaf Müller.

4 There is no data on Shiite persons among people of Turkish origin, but estimated numbers are very low. (cf. Schloßmacher 2014).

5 Original question in German: 'Egal wie sehr ich mich anstrenge, ich werde nicht als Teil der deutschen Gesellschaft anerkannt.'

6 Original question in German: 'Die deutsche Gesellschaft sollte stärker auf die Gewohnheiten und Besonderheiten der türkeistämmigen Einwanderer Rücksicht nehmen.'

7 Original wording in German: 'Fanatismus', 'Gewaltbereitschaft', 'Benachteiligung der Frau'.

8 According to Martin Sökefeld, the movement of 'Coming Out of *Takiye*' had its political roots in leftist movements such as those described earlier, from which it cannot be separated. (Sökefeld 2013, 19).

9 The same applies to other European countries, although legal conditions are non-identical and might lead to different options, but also challenges. Handan Aksünger-Kizil compares the case of Germany to the one of Austria, in which the Austrian 'Islamgesetz' (Islam law) from 2015 demanded Alevis organise under one Muslim umbrella organization and defined Alevism within Islam (Aksünger-Kizil 2018) until the organization of the free Alevis Austria, 'Frei-Aleviten Österreich', was recognized as a confessional community on their own and seperate from Islam in April 2022.

10 In contrast to Sephardi youth in France who, 'escaped some forms of French racism by enacting [other types of racism] essentializing and individualizing Jewishness through conspicuous consumption', (Arkin 2009), young Alevis in Germany are forming a religious identity which incorporates Germany's fundamental values like democracy and plurality.

11 'Hurtful relationships'. The concept refers to intergroup relationships which are strongly influenced by past and (sometimes) present physical or/and psychological violations with consequent explicit or implicit effects for present-day members.

12 All names and person-related data are anonymized for personal protection.

13 I have translated all interview quotations in this paper from German to English.

14 Kurdish-Alevi region of Dersim (today Tunceli) (see section: Alevis in Turkey: Oppression then and now).

15 The analyses of the cases Umut and Duygu have been compared to my above-mentioned colleague Dilek Tepeli's cases Lale & Ali and Zeynep in Loth and Tepeli 2019.

16 See Pierre Bourdieu 1977. *Outline of a Theory of Practice.*

Chapter 6

This chapter is a revised version of the working paper 'Who gets excluded from "Christian culture"? On culturalised religion, Islam and Confessional Christianity' written for the Alwaleed Centre for the Study of Islam in the Contemporary World, University of Edinburgh, April 2021. The research conducted for this chapter was made possible by a visiting fellowship at the Alwaleed Centre and a postdoctoral appointment within the research project Religious Matters in an Entangled World at Utrecht University. I am grateful for the helpful comments I received on earlier versions from Christopher Cotter, Morteza Hashemi, Birgit Meyer, an anonymous reviewer and the members of the Alwaleed Centre's work-in-progress seminar: İdil Akıncı, Yahya Barry, Alexis Blouët, Elvire Corboz, Tom Lea and Giulia Liberatore.

1 De Tafel van Tijs [The Table of Tijs], EO, 14 February 2017. https://www.npostart .nl/de-tafel-van-tijs/14-02-2017/VPWON_1267321 (accessed on 30 May 2022). All translations from Dutch are mine.

2 My use of the terms identitarian and heritage Christianity builds on Rogers Brubaker's (2017) concept of 'identitarian Christianism' and Marian Burchardt's (2020, chap. 5) notion of 'heritage religion', respectively.

3 The composite term 'Judeo-Christian' is often used in narratives that posit the 'Western' religious tradition over and against that of Islam. This term has had a long and varied history, in which its use to describe the cultural background of a secular present emerged only quite recently. The inclusion, for different reasons, of Judaism in this Western cultural framework has provoked critique, among other things for obscuring long histories of prosecution of Jews in Europe (for a discussion of the term's genealogy, see Wallet 2012; Van den Hemel 2014).

4 'Bolkestein: moslims geen recht op eigen scholen', *Nederlands Dagblad*, 22 May, 2009.

5 Gert-Jan Segers, 'Straatvoetbal kip zonder kop', *Nederlands Dagblad*, 21 April 2009.

6 Algemene Politieke Beschouwingen naar aanleiding van de Miljoenennota voor het jaar 2016, the House of Representatives, 16 September 2015. https://zoek.officielebe kendmakingen.nl/h-tk-20152016-2-7.html (accessed on 16 June 2020). Translation mine.

7 Next to largely positive narratives about Christian heritage, Dutch popular culture also exposes a recurrent concern with the perceived oppressive nature of – particularly strictly Calvinist – Christian culture. A recent example of this trend is Marieke Lucas Rijneveld's book *De avond is ongemak*. Its English translation, *The Discomfort of Evening*, was awarded the International Booker Prize in 2020.

8 Writing on Quebec, Marian Burchardt (2020, chap. 5) has identified a similar group of actors who strongly reject religious doctrines while embracing Christian culture or heritage. Morteza Hashemi similarly writes about 'tourist atheism', spearheaded by intellectuals such as Alain de Botton, in which religion (especially Christianity) is approached not in terms of faith but as a 'repository of cultural heritage' (Hashemi 2017, 40).

9 'Er wordt niets meer geweten; interview Nicolaas Matsier, schrijver', *De Volkskrant*, 11 April, 2009.

10 Ibid.

11 Ibid.

12 Ibid.

13 See Wesselink (2018) and research conducted by the Dutch daily newspaper *Trouw*: 'Een op de vijf Nederlandse kerken is geen kerk meer', *Trouw*, 25 June, 2019.

14 *Vertrouwen in de toekomst: regeerakkoord 2017–2021. VVD, CDA, D66 en ChristenUnie.* 10 October 2017, p. 19.

15 'Extra cultuurgeld naar talent, educatie en kerkgebouwen', *NRC*, 12 March, 2018.

16 'De kerk die een moskee werd: dat gebeurt nu niet meer', *Trouw*, 2 July, 2019.

17 'De kerk die een moskee werd,' *Trouw*. See also Van der Linde (2013).

18 I conducted fieldwork on the abandonment and conversion of – especially Roman Catholic – church buildings in the Netherlands between 2014 and 2018, focusing on both religious and secular forms of repurposing in Amsterdam and on the process of closing down church buildings in Utrecht.

19 For similar analyses of the implicit, yet significant, place of Islam in debates about Christian heritage in Europe, see Oliphant (2015) and Meyer (2019).

20 In contrast to Protestant churches (Kuyk 2017), the multiple use of church buildings for both religious services and non-religious activities (beyond talks and musical performances that can be connected to Christianity) is unusual for Roman Catholic churches in the Netherlands, due to the consecrated nature of these buildings.

21 Website of the Society of Saint Pius X, see especially 'Confusion in the Church and World: The Society's Stance'. https://sspx.org/en/about/major-concern (accessed on 1 June 2022).

22 RTV Utrecht, 'Commotie rond verkoop Sint-Willibrordkerk', 11 April, 2017.

23 'Prominenten: verkoop Utrechtse kerk niet aan conservatieve broederschap', *Trouw*, 17 May, 2017.

Chapter 7

1 Whereby the striking difference marking 'but also' between humanistic and secular is no longer present, while secular becomes secularized.

2 For applications of the concept in the study of religions see Bürgin on the *Revue Internationale de Théologie* as medium of multiple alliances (Bürgin 2019, 322–6) and Eichenberger on the historical reception of Mazdak (Eichenberger 2020, 247–9).

3 In the context of the culture war in the 1870s, the Catholic-conservatives would hardly have used a transnational concept such as a Christian-occidental Europe. Rather, they defended themselves against the liberals' accusation of being unpatriotic elements, agents controlled from abroad, and *ultramontanes* in obedience to papal power politics. They strove to be perceived as Catholic but patriotic citizens of Switzerland. In terms of spatial reference, Catholic-conservative discourses of affiliation were based on the borders of the Swiss federal state.

4 The syllabus rejected philosophical movements and modes of thought such as naturalism and rationalism, religious tolerance towards other Christian churches or towards an Enlightenment pantheism, the possibility of a free choice of religious affiliation, political ideologies that have emerged from modernity such as socialism, communism and liberalism, the establishment of secular states, and the mandatory attendance at secular public schools (Sancta Sedes 1864; Wolf 1998).

5 In this connection, Birgit Meyer accurately wrote of a 'heritagization of Christianity' and a 'taken-for-granted Christian heritage in Europe' (Meyer 2012, 38; cf. Meyer 2020).

Chapter 8

1 This chapter refers specifically to the Republic of Ireland and not Northern Ireland. For ease, the Republic of Ireland will be referred to as 'Ireland' hereafter.

2 Teachta Dála (TD), an elected representative to the lower house of the national parliament, Dáil Eireann. Equivalent to Member of Parliament or Member of Congress.

3 Ireland's national parliament.

4 It should be noted that these figures represent the official church statistics, and therefore will not be reflected in the numbers as calculated from other sources such as the Central Statistics Office. Recent census figures estimate the Mormon population to be 0.03 per cent of the general population about half of what is reported in church figures (Central Statistics Office 2017).

Chapter 9

1 Latest data on the Lutheran Church membership: https://www.kirkontilastot.fi

2 See: www.liekkikustannus.fi

3 Ahvio (2016, 2018).

4 For the purposes of this chapter, the far right is defined following Cas Mudde (2019) as right-wingers, who are anti-system and hostile against liberal democracy.

5 Seurakuntalainen.fi 'Perusuomalaisen uusi puheenjohtaja on agnostikko'. 10 June 2017. https://www.seurakuntalainen.fi/uutiset/perussuomalaisten-uusi -puheenjohtaja-kristillisia-arvoja-puolustava-agnostikko/

6 Helsingin Sanomat 17 May 2015.

7 This and other quotes in this chapter are my translations.

8 https://www.kirkontilastot.fi

9 The search terms were jeesu*, raamat*, jumal*, kristin* (English: Jesus, Bible, God and Christian).

10 Kristiina Kunnas, 'Konservatiivi-blogisivusto avautunut' – 'Rinteen vasemmistolainen hallitus ajaa Suomea koti punaisen hämärän maata'. KD-lehti, 4 Ocober 2019. https://www.kdlehti.fi/2019/10/04/konservatiivi-blogisivusto -avautunut-rinteen-vasemmistolainen-hallitus-ajaa-suomea-koti-punaisen -hamaran-maata/

11 The view that social and economic benefits in Finland should primarily help native Finns instead of, for example, immigrants (see Keskinen 2016).

12 Halla-aho (2007).

Chapter 10

1 This chapter is an updated version of Meer, N. (2012). Misrecognizing Muslim consciousness in Europe. Ethnicities, 12(2), 178–196. https://doi.org/10.1177/ 1468796811431295. Reproduced with permission.

2   He states: 'I claim the concept of Euro-Islam, first presented in Paris and published in French and German in 1992–5. [. . .] Others use the notion "Euro-Islam" without a reference to its origins and often in a different, clearly distorted meaning. I prefer not to mention names, but nevertheless it is imperative to dissociate my reasoning on Euro-Islam from that of Tariq Ramadan, whom I consider a rival within Islam in Europe' (Tibi 2008, 156).

3   Or as Steyn (2006b) puts it: 'Islam has youth and will, Europe has age and welfare.'

4   It should be stressed that this distinction is problematic but is adopted as a heuristic device to develop this particular point. For example, in her landmark *Gender Trouble*, Butler (1990) argues that any coherence achieved within categories of sex, gender and sexuality does in fact reflect a culturally constructed mirage of coherence that is achieved through the repetition of what she calls 'stylized acts'. She argues that, in their repetition, these acts establish the appearance of what she describes as an essential or ontological 'core' gender. This leads Butler to consider one's 'sex' – along with one's 'gender' and 'sexuality' – as being 'performative', and since this challenges biological accounts of sexual binaries, it is recognized that Butler would both support *and* problematize the above analogy. That is, while she may support it by agreeing with the contested nature of 'gender', she might also problematize it by rejecting 'sex' as something given – rather than produced.

References

Chapter 1

Ambasciano, Leonardo (2018). *An Unnatural History of Religions: Academia, Post-Truth, and the Quest for Scientific Knowledge*. London: Bloomsbury.

Berger, Peter L. (1999). 'The Desecularization of the World'. In P. L. Berger (ed.), *The Desecularization of the World: Resurgent Religion and World Politics*, 1–18, 1st edn. Michigan: Wm. B. Eerdmans Publishing Co.

Bullivant, Stephen (2017). 'The "No Religion" Population of Britain: Recent Data from the British Social Attitudes Survey (2015) and the European Social Survey (2014)'. 3. Catholic Research Forum Reports. London: St Mary's University, Twickenham. https://www.stmarys.ac.uk/research/centres/benedict-xvi/no-religion-population.aspx.

Bullivant, Stephen and Lois Lee (2012). 'Interdisciplinary Studies of Non-Religion and Secularity: The State of the Union'. *Journal of Contemporary Religion*, 27 (1): 19–27.

Carr, Matthew (2012). *Fortress Europe: Inside the War Against Immigration*. London: C. Hurst & Co.

Cotter, Christopher R. (2020). *The Critical Study of Non-Religion: Discourse, Identification and Locality*. London: Bloomsbury.

Davie, Grace (2002). *Europe: The Exceptional Case. Parameters of Faith in the Modern World*. London: Darton, Longman & Todd.

Fitzgerald, Timothy (2000). *The Ideology of Religious Studies*. New York and Oxford: Oxford University Press.

Hashemi, Morteza (2016). 'A New Typology of Modern Atheisms: Pilgrim Atheism Versus Tourist Atheism'. *Culture and Religion*, 17 (1): 56–72.

Lee, Lois (2013). 'Western Europe'. In S. Bullivant and M. Ruse (eds), *The Oxford Handbook of Atheism*, 587–600. New York: Oxford University Press.

Nielsen, Jørgen (2002). *Towards a European Islam*. Basingstoke: Palgrave Macmillan.

Pew Research Center (2015). 'The Future of World Religions: Population Growth Projections, 2010–2050'. 2 April. https://www.pewforum.org/2015/04/02/religiousprojections-2010-2050/.

Van den Bos, Matthijs (2012). 'European Shiism? Counterpoints from Shiites' Organization in Britain and the Netherlands'. *Ethnicities*, 12 (5): 556–80. doi:10.1177/1468796811432687

Zuckerman, Phil, Luke W. Galen and Frank L. Pasquale (2016). *The Nonreligious: Understanding Secular People & Societies*. Oxford: Oxford University Press.

Chapter 2

Adler, Emanuel (1997). 'Seizing the Middle Ground: Constructivism in World Politics'. *European Journal of International Relations*, 3 (3): 319–63.

Agnelli, Giovanni (1988). 'The Europe of 1992'. *Foreign Affairs*, 68: 61.

Alink, Fleur, Arjen Boin and Paul T'Hart (2001). 'Institutional Crises and Reforms in Policy Sectors: The Case of Asylum Policy in Europe'. *Journal of European Public Policy*, 8 (2): 286–306. https://doi.org/10.1080/13501760151146487.

Aradau, Claudia (2004). 'Security and the Democratic Scene: Desecuritization and Emancipation'. *Journal of International Relations and Development*, 7 (4): 388–413.

Balibar, Étienne (2002). *Politics and the Other Scene*. London: Verso Books.

Barker, Martin (1981). *The New Racism: Conservatives and the Ideology of the Tribe*. Junction Books.

Barutciski, Michael (1994). 'EU States and the Refugee Crisis in the Former Yugoslavia'. *Refuge*, 14 (3): 32–5.

Basaran, Tugba (2015). 'The Saved and the Drowned: Governing Indifference in the Name of Security'. *Security Dialogue*, 46 (3): 205–20. https://doi.org/10.1177/0967010614557512.

Behnke, Andreas (2008). '"Eternal Peace" as the Graveyard of the Political: A Critique of Kant's Zum Ewigen Frieden'. *Millennium - Journal of International Studies*, 36 (3): 513–31. https://doi.org/10.1177/03058298080360030701.

Berger, Mark T. (2008). 'The Real Cold War Was Hot: The Global Struggle for the Third World'. *Intelligence and National Security*, 23 (1): 112–26. https://doi.org/10.1080/02684520701798171.

Bergsten, C. Fred (1990). 'The World Economy after the Cold War'. *Foreign Affairs*, 69 (3): 96–112. https://doi.org/10.2307/20044403.

Bhambra, Gurminder K. (2016). 'Whither Europe?' *Interventions*, 18 (2): 187–202. https://doi.org/10.1080/1369801X.2015.1106964.

Bhambra, Gurminder K. (2017). 'The Current Crisis of Europe: Refugees, Colonialism, and the Limits of Cosmopolitanism'. *European Law Journal*, 23 (5): 395–405. https://doi.org/10.1111/eulj.12234.

Bialasiewicz, Luiza (2012). 'Off-Shoring and Out-Sourcing the Borders of EUrope: Libya and EU Border Work in the Mediterranean'. *Geopolitics*, 17 (4): 843–66. https://doi.org/10.1080/14650045.2012.660579.

Bigo, Didier (2002). 'Security and Immigration: Toward a Critique of the Governmentality of Unease'. *Alternatives*, 27 (Special Issue): 63–92.

Bommes, Michael and Andrew Geddes (2000). 'Introduction: Immigration and the Welfare State'. In Michael Bommes and Andrew Geddes (eds), *Immigration and Welfare: Challenging the Borders of the Welfare State*, 1–12. Routledge/EUI Studies in the Political Economy of Welfare. London: Routledge.

Bommes, Michael and Giuseppe Sciortino, eds (2011). *Foggy Social Structures : Irregular Migration, European Labour Markets and the Welfare State*. Amsterdam University Press. https://doi.org/10.26530/OAPEN_401761.

Boswell, Christina (2000). 'European Values and the Asylum Crisis'. *International Affairs*, 76 (3): 537–57. https://doi.org/10.1111/1468-2346.00150.

Boswell, Christina (2007). 'Migration Control in Europe After 9/11: Explaining the Absence of Securitization'. *Journal of Common Market Studies*, 45 (3): 589–610.

Brambilla, Chiara (2015). 'Exploring the Critical Potential of the Borderscapes Concept'. *Geopolitics*, 20 (1): 14–34. https://doi.org/10.1080/14650045.2014 .884561.

Brochmann, Grete (1991). '"Fortress Europe" and the Moral Debt Burden: Immigration from the "South" to the European Economic Community'. *Cooperation and Conflict*, 26 (4): 185–95. https://doi.org/10.1177 /001083679102600402.

Bulmer, Simon and William E. Paterson (1996). 'Germany in the European Union: Gentle Giant or Emergent Leader?' *International Affairs*, 72 (1): 9–32. https://doi.org /10.2307/2624746.

Buzan, Barry, Ole Wæver and Jaap de Wilde (1998). *Security: A New Framework for Analysis*. London: Lynne Rienner.

Callovi, Giuseppe (1992). 'Regulation of Immigration in 1993: Pieces of the European Community Jig-Saw Puzzle'. *The International Migration Review*, 26 (2): 353–72. https://doi.org/10.2307/2547062.

Casella Colombeau, Sara (2020). 'Crisis of Schengen? The Effect of Two "Migrant Crises" (2011 and 2015) on the Free Movement of People at an Internal Schengen Border'. *Journal of Ethnic and Migration Studies*, 46 (11): 2258–74. https://doi.org/10 .1080/1369183X.2019.1596787.

Cruz, António (1995). *Shifting Responsibility: Carriers' Liability in the Member States of the European Union and North America*. Gems 4. Stoke-on-Trent: Trentham Books.

De Genova, Nicholas (2018). 'The "Migrant Crisis" as Racial Crisis: Do Black Lives Matter in Europe?' *Ethnic and Racial Studies*, 41 (10): 1765–82. https://doi.org/10 .1080/01419870.2017.1361543.

Dennison, James and Andrew Geddes (2018). 'Brexit and the Perils of "Europeanised" Migration'. *Journal of European Public Policy*, 25 (8): 1137–53. https://doi.org/10 .1080/13501763.2018.1467953.

Du Bois, W. E. Burghardt (1917). 'Of the Culture of White Folk'. *The Journal of Race Development*, 7 (4): 434–47. https://doi.org/10.2307/29738213.

Düvell, Franck (2006). 'Irregular Migration: A Global, Historical and Economic Perspective'. In Franck Düvell (ed.), *Illegal Immigration in Europe: Beyond Control?*, 14–39. London: Palgrave Macmillan UK. https://doi.org/10.1057/9780230555020_2.

Ebenroth, Carsten Thomas (1990). 'Gaining Access to Fortress Europe— Recognition of U. S. Corporations in Germany and the Revision of the Seat Rule'. *The International Lawyer*, 24 (2): 459–85.

Ellermann, Antje (2015). 'Do Policy Legacies Matter? Past and Present Guest Worker Recruitment in Germany'. *Journal of Ethnic and Migration Studies*, 41 (8): 1235–53. https://doi.org/10.1080/1369183X.2014.984667.

Engbersen, Godfried and Dennis Broeders (2011). 'Fortress Europe and the Dutch Donjon: Securitization, Internal Migration Policy and Irregular Migrants' Counter Moves'. In Thanh-Dam Truong and Des Gasper (eds), *Transnational Migration and Human Security: The Migration-Development-Security Nexus*, 81–9. Hexagon Series on Human and Environmental Security and Peace. Berlin: Springer. https://doi.org /10.1007/978-3-642-12757-1_6.

Evans, Geoffrey and Jonathan Mellon (2019). 'Immigration, Euroscepticism, and the Rise and Fall of UKIP'. *Party Politics*, 25 (1): 76–87. https://doi.org/10.1177 /1354068818816969.

Faist, Thomas (1994a). 'Immigration, Integration and the Ethnicization of Politics'. *European Journal of Political Research*, 25 (4): 439–59. https://doi.org/10.1111/j.1475 -6765.1994.tb00430.x.

Faist, Thomas (1994b). 'How to Define a Foreigner? The Symbolic Politics of Immigration in German Partisan Discourse, 1978–1992'. *West European Politics*, 17 (2): 50–71. https://doi.org/10.1080/01402389408425014.

Ferrera, Maurizio (2005). *The Boundaries of Welfare: European Integration and the New Spatial Politics of Social Protection*. Oxford: Oxford University Press.

Finnemore, Martha and Kathryn Sikkink (1998). 'International Norm Dynamics and Political Change'. *International Organization*, 52 (4): 887–917.

Fox, Jonathan and Yasemin Akbaba (2015). 'Securitization of Islam and Religious Discrimination: Religious Minorities in Western Democracies, 1990–2008'. *Comparative European Politics*, 13 (2): 175–97. https://doi.org/10.1057/cep.2013.8.

Freeman, Gary P. (1994). 'Can Liberal States Control Unwanted Migration?' *Annals of the American Academy of Political and Social Science*, 534: 17–30.

Freyberg-Inan, Annette (2004). *What Moves Man: The Realist Theory of International Relations and Its Judgment of Human Nature*. New York: SUNY Press.

Gani, J. K. (2017). 'The Erasure of Race: Cosmopolitanism and the Illusion of Kantian Hospitality'. *Millennium*, 45 (3): 425–46. https://doi.org/10.1177/0305829817714064.

Geddes, Andrew (2001). 'International Migration and State Sovereignty in an Integrating Europe'. *International Migration*, 39 (6): 21–42. https://doi.org/10.1111 /1468-2435.00177.

Geddes, Andrew (2018). 'The Politics of European Union Migration Governance'. *JCMS: Journal of Common Market Studies*, 56 (Annual Review): 120–30. https://doi .org/10.1111/jcms.12763.

Goldgeier, James M. and Michael McFaul (1992). 'A Tale of Two Worlds: Core and Periphery in the Post-Cold War Era'. *International Organization*, 46 (2): 467–91. https://doi.org/10.1017/S0020818300027788.

Guild, Elspeth (2006). 'The Europeanisation of Europe's Asylum Policy'. *International Journal of Refugee Law*, 18 (3–4): 630–51. https://doi.org/10.1093/ijrl/eel018.

Guiraudon, Virginie (2000). 'European Integration and Migration Policy: Vertical Policy-Making as Venue Shopping'. *JCMS: Journal of Common Market Studies*, 38 (2): 251–71. https://doi.org/10.1111/1468-5965.00219.

Guiraudon, Virginie and Christian Joppke (2001). 'Controlling a New Migration World'. In Virginie Guiraudon and Christian Joppke (eds), *Controlling a New Migration World*, 1–27. London: Routledge.

Hansen, Bent (1993). 'Immigration Policies in Fortress Europe'. In Lloyd Ulman, William T. Dickens and Barry Eichengreen (eds), *Labor and an Integrated Europe*, 224. Washington: Brookings Institution Press.

Hansen, Randall (2000). *Citizenship and Immigration in Post-War Britain: The Institutional Origins of a Multicultural Nation*. Oxford: Oxford University Press.

Hatton, Timothy J. (2004). 'Seeking Asylum in Europe'. *Economic Policy*, 19 (38): 6–62. https://doi.org/10.1111/j.1468-0327.2004.00118.x.

Henson, Penny and Nisha Malhan (1995). 'Endeavours to Export a Migration Crisis: Policy Making and Europeanisation in the German Migration Dilemma'. *German Politics*, 4 (3): 128–44. https://doi.org/10.1080/09644009508404417.

Hobolt, Sara B., Wouter Van der Brug, Claes H. De Vreese, Hajo G. Boomgaarden and Malte C. Hinrichsen (2011). 'Religious Intolerance and Euroscepticism'. *European Union Politics*, 12 (3): 359–79. https://doi.org/10.1177/1465116511404620.

Holmwood, John (2020). 'Claiming Whiteness'. *Ethnicities*, 20 (1): 234–39. https://doi.org/10.1177/1468796819838710.

Hurd, Elizabeth Shakman (2006). 'Negotiating Europe: The Politics of Religion and the Prospects for Turkish Accession'. *Review of International Studies*, 32 (3): 401–18.

Huysmans, Jef (1995). 'Migrants as a Security Problem: The Dangers of "Securitizing" Societal Issues'. In Robert Miles and Dietrich Thranhardt (eds), *Migration and European Integration: The Dynamics of Inclusion and Exclusion*, 53–72. London: Pinter Publishers.

Huysmans, Jef (2006). *The Politics of Insecurity: Fear, Migration and Asylum in the EU*. Abingdon: Routledge.

Huysmans, Jef (2014). *Security Unbound: Enacting Democratic Limits*. Abingdon: Routledge.

Ireland, Patrick R. (1991). 'Facing the True "Fortress Europe": Immigrant and Politics in the EC*'. *JCMS: Journal of Common Market Studies*, 29 (5): 457–80. https://doi.org/10.1111/j.1468-5965.1991.tb00403.x.

Jabko, Nicolas (1999). 'In the Name of the Market: How the European Commission Paved the Way for Monetary Union'. *Journal of European Public Policy*, 6 (3): 475–95. https://doi.org/10.1080/135017699343630.

Joppke, Christian (1998). 'Why Liberal States Accept Unwanted Immigration'. *World Politics*, 50 (2): 266–93.

Kant, Immanuel (1795). *Perpetual Peace: A Philosophical Essay*. Trans. M. Campbell Smith. 3rd edn, 1917. London: George Allen & Unwin.

Kaya, Ayhan (2009). *Islam, Migration and Integration: The Age of Securitization*. Berlin: Springer.

Kinnvall, Catarina (2016). 'The Postcolonial Has Moved into Europe: Bordering, Security and Ethno-Cultural Belonging'. *JCMS: Journal of Common Market Studies*, 54 (1): 152–68. https://doi.org/10.1111/jcms.12326.

Kinnvall, Catarina (2018). 'Ontological Insecurities and Postcolonial Imaginaries: The Emotional Appeal of Populism'. *Humanity & Society*, 42 (4): 523–43. https://doi.org/10.1177/0160597618802646.

Kofman, Eleonore and Rosemary Sales (1992). 'Towards Fortress Europe?' *Women's Studies International Forum*, Special Issue A Continent in Transition: Issues for Women in Europe in the 1990s, 15 (1): 29–39. https://doi.org/10.1016/0277-5395(92)90031-P.

Kratochwil, Friedrich (1993). 'The Embarrassment of Changes: Neo-Realism as the Science of Realpolitik without Politics'. *Review of International Studies*, 19 (1): 63–80.

Lavenex, Sandra (2006). 'Shifting Up and Out: The Foreign Policy of European Immigration Control'. *West European Politics*, 29 (2): 329–50. https://doi.org/10.1080/01402380500512684.

Ludlow, N. Piers (2013). 'European Integration in the 1980s: On the Way to Maastricht?' *Journal of European Integration History*, 19 (1): 11–22. https://doi.org/10.5771/0947-9511-2013-1-11.

Meer, Nasar (2019). 'The Wreckage of White Supremacy'. *Identities*, 26 (5): 501–9. https://doi.org/10.1080/1070289X.2019.1654662.

Morokvasic, Mirjana (1991). 'Fortress Europe and Migrant Women'. *Feminist Review*, 39 (1): 69–84. https://doi.org/10.1057/fr.1991.41.

Mudde, Cas (2004). 'The Populist Zeitgeist'. *Government and Opposition*, 39 (4): 541–63. https://doi.org/10.1111/j.1477-7053.2004.00135.x.

Neal, Andrew W. (2009). 'Securitization and Risk at the EU Border: The Origins of FRONTEX'. *Journal of Common Market Studies*, 47 (2): 333–56.

Neal, Andrew W. (2012). 'Normalization and Legislative Exceptionalism: Counterterrorist Lawmaking and the Changing Times of Security Emergencies'. *International Political Sociology*, 6 (3): 260–76.

Niemann, Arne, and Johanna Speyer (2018). 'A Neofunctionalist Perspective on the "European Refugee Crisis": The Case of the European Border and Coast Guard'. *JCMS: Journal of Common Market Studies*, 56 (1): 23–43.

Noronha, Luke de (2019). 'Deportation, Racism and Multi-Status Britain: Immigration Control and the Production of Race in the Present'. *Ethnic and Racial Studies*, 42 (14): 2413–30. https://doi.org/10.1080/01419870.2019.1585559.

Pallister-Wilkins, Polly (2015). 'The Humanitarian Politics of European Border Policing: Frontex and Border Police in Evros'. *International Political Sociology*, 9 (1): 53–69. https://doi.org/10.1111/ips.12076.

Pastore, Feruccio (2001). 'Reconciling the Prince's Two "Arms". Internal-External Security Policy Coordination in the European Union'. 30. Occasional Papers.

European Union Institute for Security Studies. https://www.iss.europa.eu/content
/reconciling-princes-two-arms-internal-external-security-policy-coordination
-european-union.

Perkowski, Nina (2018). 'Frontex and the Convergence of Humanitarianism, Human
Rights and Security'. *Security Dialogue*, 49 (6): 457–75. https://doi.org/10.1177
/0967010618796670.

Phuong, Catherine (2003). 'Enlarging "Fortress Europe": EU Accession, Asylum, and
Immigration in Candidate Countries'. *The International and Comparative Law
Quarterly*, 52 (3): 641–63.

Sales, Rosemary (2002). 'The Deserving and the Undeserving? Refugees, Asylum
Seekers and Welfare in Britain , The Deserving and the Undeserving? Refugees,
Asylum Seekers and Welfare in Britain'. *Critical Social Policy*, 22 (3): 456–78. https://
doi.org/10.1177/026101830202200305.

Sassen, Saskia (1996). 'Beyond Sovereignty: Immigration Policy Making Today'. *Social
Justice*, 23 (3(65)): 9–20.

Selm, Joanne van (2016). 'Are Asylum and Immigration Really a Euroepan Issue?'
Forced Migration Review, 51 (January): 60–2.

Selm-Thorburn, Joanne van (1998). *Refugee Protection in Europe: Lessons of the Yugoslav
Crisis*. The Hague: Martinus Nijhoff Publishers.

Semati, Mehdi (2010). 'Islamophobia, Culture and Race in the Age of Empire'. *Cultural
Studies*, 24 (2): 256–75. https://doi.org/10.1080/09502380903541696.

Shearmur, Yasmin (2021). *British Immigration Policymaking and European Integration,
1973–1990*. Cambridge: University of Cambridge.

Slaven, Mike (2021). 'The "Pull Factor" Problematization in the Emergence of Everyday
Bordering in the UK Welfare State'. *Genealogy*, 5 (4): 93. https://doi.org/10.3390/
genealogy5040093.

Slaven, Mike, Sara Casella Colombeau and Elisabeth Badenhoop (2021). 'What Drives
the Immigration-Welfare Policy Link? Comparing Germany, France and the United
Kingdom'. *Comparative Political Studies*, 54 (5): 855–88. https://doi.org/10.1177
/0010414020957674.

Solomos, John (1993). *Race and Racism in Britain*. New York: Macmillan International
Higher Education.

Sperling, James (1992). 'The Atlantic Economy after German Unification: Cooperation
or the Rise of "Fortress Europe"'. *German Politics*, 1 (2): 200–22. https://doi.org/10
.1080/09644009208404289.

Squire, Vicki (2009). *The Exclusionary Politics of Asylum. Migration, Minorities and
Citizenship*. London: Palgrave Macmillan. https://doi.org/10.1057/9780230233614_6.

Steele, Brent J. (2007). 'Liberal-Idealism: A Constructivist Critique'. *International Studies
Review*, 9 (1): 23–52. https://doi.org/10.1111/j.1468-2486.2007.00644.x.

Thielemann, Eiko (2018). 'Why Refugee Burden-Sharing Initiatives Fail: Public Goods,
Free-Riding and Symbolic Solidarity in the EU'. *JCMS: Journal of Common Market
Studies*, 56 (1): 63–82.

Vaughan-Williams, Nick (2008). 'Borderwork beyond Inside/Outside? Frontex, the Citizen–Detective and the War on Terror'. *Space and Polity*, 12 (1): 63–79. https://doi .org/10.1080/13562570801969457.

Vreese, Claes H. de and Hajo G. Boomgaarden (2005). 'Projecting EU Referendums: Fear of Immigration and Support for European Integration'. *European Union Politics*, 6 (1): 59–82. https://doi.org/10.1177/1465116505049608.

Wæver, Ole (1995). 'Securitization and Desecuritization'. In Ronnie D. Lipschutz (ed.), *On Security*, 46–86. New York: Columbia University Press.

Wæver, Ole (2000). 'The EU as a Security Actor: Reflections from a Pessimistic Constructivist on Post-Sovereign Security Orders'. In Morten Kelstrup and Michael C. Williams (eds), *International Relations Theory and the Politics of European Integration: Power, Security and Community*, 250–94. London: Routledge.

Wæver, Ole, Barry Buzan, Morten Kelstrup and Pierre Lemaitre, eds (1993). *Identity, Migration, and the New Security Agenda in Europe*. London: Pinter Publishers.

Waltz, Kenneth N. (1993). 'The Emerging Structure of International Politics'. *International Security*, 18 (2): 44–79. https://doi.org/10.2307/2539097.

Welsh, Jennifer M. (1993). 'A Peoples' Europe? European Citizenship and European Identity'. *Politics*, 13 (2): 25–31. https://doi.org/10.1111/j.1467-9256.1993.tb00225.x.

White, Jonathan (2015). 'Emergency Europe'. *Political Studies*, 63 (2): 300–18. https:// doi.org/10.1111/1467-9248.12072.

Wodak, Ruth and Salomi Boukala (2015). 'European Identities and the Revival of Nationalism in the European Union: A Discourse Historical Approach'. *Journal of Language and Politics*, 14 (1): 87–109. https://doi.org/10.1075/jlp.14.1.05wod.

Yuval-Davis, Nira, Georgie Wemyss and Kathryn Cassidy (2018). 'Everyday Bordering, Belonging and the Reorientation of British Immigration Legislation'. *Sociology*, 52 (2): 228–44. https://doi.org/10.1177/0038038517702599.

Yuval-Davis, Nira, Georgie Wemyss and Kathryn Cassidy (2019). *Bordering*. Cambridge: Polity.

Chapter 3

Allen, Danielle S. (2004). *Talking to Strangers: Anxieties of Citizenship since Brown v, Board of Education*. Chicago: University of Chicago Press.

Allen, Danielle S. (2019). 'The Road from Serfdom: How Americans can Become Citizens Again'. *The Atlantic*, December. https://www.theatlantic.com/magazine/ archive/2019/12/danielle-allen-american-citizens-serfdom/600778/

Avramenko, Richard (2012). 'Tocqueville and the Religion of Democracy'. *Perspectives on Political Science*, 41: 125–37.

Badshah, Nadeem (2022). 'Attorney General Says Schools do not have to Accommodate Children's Gender Wishes'. *Guardian*, May 27. Available here: https://www

.theguardian.com/society/2022/may/27/attorney-general-says-schools-do-not-have
-to-accommodate-childrens-gender-wishes.

Bellah Robert, N. (2002). 'The Protestant Structure of American Culture'. *Hedgehog Review*, 4 (2). https://hedgehogreview.com/issues/individualism/articles/the
-protestant-structure-of-american-culture

Bhambra, Gurminder K. (2019). 'On European "Civilization": Colonialism, Land, Lebensraum'. In Nick Aikens, Jyoti Mistry, Corina Oprea (eds), *Living with Ghosts: Legacies of Colonialism and Fascism*, L'Internationale Online. https://www.interna
tionaleonline.org/bookshelves/living_with_ghosts_legacies_of_colonialism_and
_fascism.

Bruce, Steve (2011). *Secularization: In Defense of an Unfashionable Theory*. Oxford: Oxford University Press.

Clarke Report (2014). *Report into Allegations Concerning Birmingham Schools Arising from the 'Trojan Horse' letter*. Department for Education. HC 576. https://www
.gov.uk/government/publications/birmingham-schools-education-commissioners
-report.

Clayton, Mathew, Andrew Mason, Adam Swift and Ruth Wareham (2018). *How to Regulate Faith Schools*. Impact Pamphlet Issue 25. https://onlinelibrary.wiley.com/
doi/full/10.1111/2048-416X.2018.12005.x.

Conservative Party (2017). *Election Manifesto - Forward Together: Our Plan for a Stronger Britain and a Prosperous Future*. http://ucrel.lancs.ac.uk/wmatrix/
ukmanifestos2017/localpdf/Conservatives.pdf.

Davie, Grace (1994). *Religion in Britain since 1945: Believing without Belonging*. Oxford: Blackwell.

Department for Education (2019). *Relationships Education, Relationships and Sex Education (RSE) and Health Education: Statutory Guidance for Governing Bodies, Proprietors, Head Teachers, Principals, Senior Leadership Teams, Teachers*. https://
www.gov.uk/government/publications/relationships-education-relationships-and
-sex-education-rse-and-health-education.

Farris, Sara R. (2017). *In the Name of Women's Rights. The Rise of Femonationalism*. Durham: Duke University.

Guveli, Ayse and Lucinda Platt (2011). 'Understanding the Religious Behaviour of Muslims in the Netherlands and the UK'. *Sociology*, 45 (6): 1008–27.

Holmwood, John and Therese O'Toole (2018). *Countering Extremism in Birmingham Schools? The Truth about the Birmingham Trojan Horse Affair*. Bristol: Policy Press.

Johnston, Phillip (2000). 'Straw Wants to Rewrite Our History'. *Daily Telegraph*, 10 October. https://www.telegraph.co.uk/news/uknews/1369663/Straw-wants-to
-rewrite-our-history.html.

Karlsen, Saffron and James Y. Nazroo (2015). 'Ethnic and Religious Differences in the Attitudes of People Towards Being "British"'. *Sociological Review*, 63 (4): 759–81.

Kershaw Report (2014). Investigation Report: Trojan Horse Letter. Prepared for Birmingham City Council and published by Eversheds LIP. Available at:

https://www.birmingham.gov.uk/downloads/file/1579/investigation_report_trojan
_horse_letter_the_kershaw_report.

Malik, Kenan (2019). 'There Is Never a Reason for Bigotry at the School Gate'. *Guardian*, March 10. Available here: https://www.theguardian.com/commentisfree/2019/mar/10/there-is-never-a-reason-for-bigotry-at-the-school-gates.

McLaughlin, Eugene and Sarah Neal (2004). 'Misrepresenting the Multicultural Nation: The Policy-Making Process, News Media Management and the Parekh Report'. *Journal of Policy Studies*, 25 (3): 155–74.

McLoughlin, Sean (1998). 'An Underclass in Purdah? Discrepant Representations of Identity and the Experiences of Young-British-Asian-Muslim-Women'. *Bulletin of the John Rylands Library*, 80 (3):89–106.

Ofsted v Al Hijrah (2017). https://www.judiciary.uk/wp-content/uploads/2017/10/interim-executive-board-of-al-hijrah-school-20171013a.pdf

Payne, Charles M. (2004). '"The Whole United States is Southern!": Brown v. Board and the Mystification of Race'. *The Journal of American History*, 91 (1): 83–91.

Puar, Jasbir K. (2007). *Terrorist Assemblages: Homonationalism in Queer Times*, Durham: Duke University Press.

Report of the Commission on Religion and Belief in British Public Life (2015). *Living with Difference: Community, Diversity and the Common Good*. Cambridge: Woolf Institute. https://www.woolf.cam.ac.uk/research/publications/reports/report-of-the-commission-on-religion-and-belief-in-british-public-life

Rivers, Julian (2020). 'Is Religious Freedom under Threat from British Equality Laws?' *Studies in Christian Ethics*, 33 (2): 179–93.

Rocker, Simon (2022). 'Shock Ofsted Downgrade for King David High School in Manchester'. *The Jewish Chronicle*, March 15. Available here: https://www.thejc.com/family-and-education/all/shock-ofsted-downgrade-for-king-david-high-school-in-manchester-4c8uqNRj1t3G5Ag0DlnPNZ.

Runnymede Trust (2000). *Parekh Report*. Commission on the Future of Multi-Ethnic Britain. London: Runnymede Trust. https://www.runnymedetrust.org/projects/meb.html

Seligman, Adam and David W. Montgomery (2020). 'The Tragedy of Human Rights: Liberalism and the Loss of Belonging'. *Society*, 56 (2): 203–9.

Sen, Amartya (2006). *Identity and Violence: The Illusion of Destiny*, London: Penguin Books.

Spielman, Amanda (2017). 'Speech at the Church of England Foundation for Educational Leadership'. 1 February. https://www.gov.uk/government/speeches/amanda-spielmans-speech-at-the-birmingham-school-partnership-conference.

Tatchell, Peter (2009). 'Multiculturalism vs Human Rights?' *New Politics*, 13 August. https://newpol.org/multiculturalism-vs-human-rights/#:~:text=It%20involves%20respecting%20and%20celebrating,rights%20are%20universal%20and%20indivisible.

Tocqueville, Alexis (2000 [1835]). *Democracy in America*. Ed. J. P. Mayer. Trans. George Lawrence. New York: Perennial Classics.

Chapter 4

Anheier, Helmut K. and Regina A. List (2006). *A Dictionary of Civil Society, Philanthropy and the Third Sector*. London: Routledge.

Brown, Nadia and Sarah Gershon (2019). *Body Politics*. 1st edn. Abingdon: Routledge.

Bourdieu, Pierre and Richard Nice (1992). *The Logic of Practice*. Cambridge: Polity Press.

Building the Big Society (2010). *GOV.UK*. https://www.gov.uk/government/publications/building-the-big-society.

Carsten, Janet (2013). '"Searching for the Truth": Tracing the Moral Properties of Blood in Malaysian Clinical Pathology Labs'. *Journal of The Royal Anthropological Institute*, 19: S130–48. doi:10.1111/1467-9655.12020.

Copeman, Jacob and Alice Street (2014). 'The Image After Strathern: Art and Persuasive Relationality in India's Sanguinary Politics'. *Theory, Culture & Society*, 31 (2–3): 185–220. doi:10.1177/0263276413500321.

Emerson, Ralph Waldo and Brooks Atkinson (1950). *The Complete Essays and Other Writings of Ralph Waldo Emerson*. New York: The Modern Library.

First Minister of Scotland (2018). *Firstminister.Gov.Scot*. https://firstminister.gov.scot/encouraging-blood-donation/.

Gabriel, Iason (2016). 'Effective Altruism and Its Critics'. *Journal of Applied Philosophy*, 34 (4): 457–73. doi:10.1111/japp.12176.

Hashemi, Morteza (2020a). 'Could We Use Blood Donation Campaigns as Social Policy Tools?: British Shi'i Ritual of Giving Blood'. *Identities: Global Studies in Culture and Power*. DOI: 10.1080/1070289X.2020.1856538

Hashemi, Morteza (2020b). 'Andrew's White Cross, Hussain's Red Blood: Being Scottish Shia in Brexit's No-Man's-Land'. *HAU: Journal of Ethnographic Theory*. DOI: 10.1086/709781.

MacLean, Mairi. and Charles Harvey (2020). 'Crafting Philanthropic Identities' In Andrew Brown (ed.), *The Oxford Handbook of Identities in Organizations*, 637–53. Oxford: Oxford University Press.

Mauss, Marcel (1966). *The Gift: Forms and Functions of Exchange in Archaic Societies*. London: Cohen and West Ltd.

Mayblin, Lucy (2019). *Impoverishment and Asylum: Social Policy as Slow Violence*. Abingdon: Routledge.

McGoey, Linsey (2012). 'Philanthrocapitalism and Its Critics'. *Poetics*, 40 (2): 185–99. doi:10.1016/j.poetic.2012.02.006.

McGoey, Linsey (2015). *No Such Thing as a Free Gift: The Gates Foundation and The Price of Philanthropy*. London: Verso.

Nasr, Seyyed Hossein (2007). *The Essential Seyyed Hossein Nasr*. Bloomington: World Wisdom.

Netton, Ian Richard (2017). *Islam, Christianity and the Realms of the Miraculous*. Edinburgh: Edinburgh University Press.

Nietzsche, Friedrich and Thomas Common (1986). *Thus Spoke Zarathustra*. New York: Modern Library.

Points of Light (2019). 'Imam Hussain Blood Donation Campaign'. *Points of Light*. https://www.pointsoflight.gov.uk/imam-hussain-blood-donation-campaign/.

Schrift, Alan (1997). 'Introduction: Why Gift?'. In Alan D. Schrift (ed.), *The Logic Of The Gift: Toward An Ethic Of Generosity*, 1–23. London: Routledge.

Scott, John (2014). 'Official Report: Scottish Parliament'. *Parliament.Scot*. http://www .parliament.scot/parliamentarybusiness/report.aspx?r=9605&mode=html#iob _87268.

Snow, Mathew (2015). 'Against Charity'. *Jacobinmag.Com*. https://www.jacobinmag.com /2015/08/peter-singer-charity-effective-altruism.

Spellman-Poots, Kathryn (2012). Manifestations of Ashura among Young British Shi'is. In: B. Dupret, T. Pierret, K. Spellman-Poots and P. Pinto (eds), *Ethnographies of Islam: Ritual Performances and Everyday Practices*, 1st edn. Edinburgh: Edinburgh University Press.

Titmuss, Richard (2018 [1970]). *The Gift Relationship: From Human Blood to Social Policy*. Bristol: Policy Press.

Chapter 5

Aksünger-Kizil, Handan (2018). 'Zur Situation der anatolischen Aleviten in Deutschland und Österreich'. In Thomas Schirrmacher, Max Klingberg and Martin Warnecke (eds), *Jahrbuch Religionsfreiheit 2018*, 126–46. Bonn: Verlag für Kultur u. Wissenschaft.

Arkin, Kimberly A. (2009). 'Rhinestone Aesthetics and Religious Essence: Looking Jewish in Paris'. *American Ethnologist*, 36 (4): 722–34.

Bourdieu, Pierre (1977). *Outline of a Theory of Practice* (Vol. 16). Cambridge: Cambridge University Press.

Dreßler, Markus (1999). *Die civil religion der Türkei. Kemalistische und alevitische Atatürk-Rezeptionen im Vergleich*. Würzburg: ERGON Verlag.

Dreßler, Markus (2002). *Die alevitische Religion - Traditionslinien und Neubestimmungen. (Abhandlungen zur Kunde des Morgenlandes LIII,4)*. Würzburg: ERGON Verlag.

Dreßler, Markus (2008). 'Religio-Secular Metamorphoses: The Re-Making of Turkish Alevism'. *Journal of the American Academy of Religion*, 76 (2): 280–311.

Dreßler, Markus (2013). 'Was ist das Alevitentum? Die aktuelle Diskussion und historische Traditionslinien'. In *Ocak und Dedelik. Institutionen religiösen Spezialistentums bei den Aleviten, Heidelberger Studien zur Geschichte und Kultur des modernen Vorderen Orients*, edited by Robert Langer, Hüseyin Ağuiçenoğlu, Janina Karolewski and Raoul Motika, 13–35. PL Academic Research.

Gärtner, Christel (2013). 'Religiöse Identität und Wertbindungen von Jugendlichen in Deutschland'. *Kölner Zeitschrift für Soziologie und Sozialpsychologie*, 65 (1): 211–33.

Gorzewski, Andreas (2010). 'Das Alevitentum in seinen divergierenden Verhältnisbestimmungen zum Islam'. In Stephan Conermann (ed.), *Bonner Islamstudien B.17*. Berlin: EB-Verlag.

Haug, Sonja, Stephanie Müssig and Anja Stichs (2009). 'Muslimisches Leben in Deutschland. Im Auftrag der Deutschen Islam Konferenz'. BAMF, Bundesamt für Migration und Flüchtlinge.

Hummrich, Merle (2011). 'Was die jüngere Generation mit der älteren will'. In Birgit Allenbach, Urmila Goel, Merle Hummrich and Cordula Weissköppel (eds), *Jugend, Migration und Religion. Interdisziplinäre Perspektiven*, 67–93. Baden-Baden: Nomos.

Kalbarczyk, Nora and Martina Loth (2017). 'Alevitentum im Gespräch mit Wissenschaft und Christentum – Symposium an der Akademie der Weltreligionen, 8. April 2017, Universität Hamburg'. *CIBEDO-Beiträge*, 2017 (2) (Zum Gespräch zwischen Christen und Muslimen), 89–91. Münster: Aschendorff Verlag.

Kaya, Asiye (2009). *Mutter-Tochter-Beziehungen in der Migration. Biographische Erfahrungen im alevitischen und sunnitischen Kontext*. Wiesbaden: VS Verlag für Sozialwissenschaften.

Kaya, Asiye (2011). 'Geschlecht und soziale Vererbung'. In Birgit Allenbach, et al. (eds), *Jugend, Migration und Religion. Interdisziplinäre Perspektiven*, 137–58. Zürich und Baden-Baden: Nomos.

King, Vera (2013). *Die Entstehung des Neuen in der Adoleszenz. Individuation, Generativität und Geschlecht in modernisierten Gesellschaften*. Wiesbaden: VS Verlag für Sozialwissenschaften.

King, Vera and Hans-Christoph Koller (2006). *Adoleszenz – Migration – Bildung*. Wiesbaden: VS Verlag für Sozialwissenschaften.

Kehl-Bodrogi, Krisztina (2006). 'Von der Kultur zur Religion – Alevitische Identitätspolitik in Deutschland'. In *Max Planck-Institute for Social Anthropology* (Ed.), Working Paper No. 84. Halle/ Saale.

Loth, Martina (2016). 'Reform durch die Diaspora? - Jugendliche Aleviten aus Deutschland auf der "Sivas-Gedenktour 2013"'. In Burcu Doğramacı, Yavuz Köse, Kerem Öktem and Tobias Völker (eds), *Junge Perspektiven der Türkeiforschung in Deutschland Bd. 2*, 179–202. Wiesbaden: VS Verlag für Sozialwissenschaften.

Loth, Martina and Dilek Tepeli (2019). 'Vater, woran glaubst du? " – "An Stock Stein, Natur'. Ein Beitrag über Identitätsfragen junger Alevitinnen und Aleviten. In K. Limacher, A. Mattes-Zippenfenig, C. Novak (eds), *Prayer, Pop and Politics: Researching Religious Youth in Migration Society*, RaT Book Series Vol. 14, 249–74. Wien: V&R Unipress.

Mahçupyan, Etyen (2017). 'European Citizens with Origins in Turkey: A Close Look at Alevi and Sunni Groups'. In *Public Policy and Democracy Studies*.Istanbul: Podem Publications.

Massicard, Elise (2003). 'Alevism as a Productive Misunderstanding: the Hacıbektaş festival'. In Paul J. White and Joost Jongerden (eds), *Turkey's Alevi Enigma*, 125–40. Leiden: Brill.

Özyürek, Esra (2009). '"The Light of the Alevi Fire Was Lit in Germany and then Spread to Turkey": A Transnational Debate on the Boundaries of Islam'. *Turkish Studies*, 10 (2): 233–53.

Pollack, Detlef, Olaf Müller, Gergely Rosta and Anna Dieler (2016). *Integration und Religion aus der Sicht von Türkeistämmigen in Deutschland (IRST)*. Münster: Westfälische Wilhelms-Universität, Exzellenzcluster "Religion und Politik"/Institut für Soziologie, Lehrstuhl für Religionssoziologie.

Sökefeld, Martin (2008). 'Einleitung: Aleviten in Deutschland – von takiye zur alevitischen Bewegung'. In Martin Sökefeld (ed.), *Aleviten in Deutschland – Identitätsprozesse einer Religionsgemeinschaft in der Diaspora*, 7–36. Bielefeld: transcript.

Sökefeld, Martin (2013). 'Die Geschichte der alevitischen Bewegung in Deutschland'. In Friedmann Eißler (ed.), *Aleviten in Deutschland. Grundlagen, Veränderungsprozesse, Perspektiven*, EZW-Texte 211. Evangelische Zentralstelle für Weltanschauungsfragen. Berlin.

Straub, Jürgen (2000). 'Identität als psychologisches Deutungskonzept'. In Werner Greve (ed.), *Psychologie des Selbst*, 279–301. Weinheim: Psychologie Verlags Union.

Straub, Jürgen (2014). 'Verletzungsverhältnisse, Erlebnisgründe, unbewusste Tradierungen und Gewalt in der sozialen Praxis'. *Zeitschrift für Pädagogik*, 60: 74–95.

Taşcı, Hülya (2006). *Identität und Ethnizität in der Bundesrepublik Deutschland am Beispiel der zweiten Generation der Aleviten aus der Republik Türkei*. Berlin: LIT-Verlag.

Tepeli, Dilek (in preparation). Junge Alevit_innen und Sunniten_innen in der post-migrantischen Gesellschaft. Affektive Bindungen in Verletzungsverhältnissen.

Yildiz, Ali A. and Maykel Verkuyten (2011). 'Inclusive Victimhood: Social Identity and the Politicization of Collective Trauma Among Turkey's Alevis in Western Europe'. *Peace and Conflict: Journal of Peace Psychology*, 17 (3): 243–69.

Web Sources

Pew Research Center (2016). 'The Growth of Germany's Muslim Population'. 29 November. https://www.pewforum.org/essay/the-growth-of-germanys-muslim-population/ (accessed 30 March 2022).

Procházka-Eisl, Gisela (2016). 'The Alevis'. 1–20. University of Vienna. https://oxfordre.com/religion/view/10.1093/acrefore/9780199340378.001.0001/acrefore-9780199340378-e-101?print=pdf (accessed 30 March 2022).

Schloßmacher Geron (2014). 'Religionszugehörigkeit in der Türkei'. Bundeszentrale für politische Bildung (bpb). https://www.bpb.de/internationales/europa/tuerkei/187253 /religionszugehoerigkeit (accessed 25 August 2020).

Spuler-Stegemann, Ursula (2003). 'Ist die Alevitische Gemeinde Deutschland e.V. eine Religionsgemeinschaft? Religionswissenschaftliches Gutachten'. *Reported to the Ministerium für Schule, Jugend und Kinder des Landes Nordrhein-Westfalen*. http:// www.inforel.ch/fileadmin/user_upload/dateien/215.AlevSpuler.pdf (accessed 25 August 2020).

'Mikrozensus 2018'. Qualitätsbericht by Statistisches Bundesamt. https://www.destatis .de/DE/Methoden/Qualitaet/Qualitaetsberichte/Bevoelkerung/mikrozensus-2018 .pdf?__blob=publicationFile (accessed 25 August 2020).

Strothmann, Rudolf and Moktar Djebli (2012). 'Taḳiyya'. In Pieri J. Bearman, Thierry Bianquis, Clifford E. Bosworth, Emeri J. van Donzel, Wolfhart P. Heinrichs (eds), *Encyclopaedia of Islam*, 2nd edn. Leiden: Brill. https://referenceworks.brillonline .com/entries/encyclopaedia-of-islam-2/takiyya-SIM_7341 (accessed 30 March 2022).

Vorhoff, Karin (1998). 'Let's Reclaim Our History and Culture! — Imagining Alevi Community in Contemporary Turkey, In Die Welt des Islam'. *International Journal for the Study of Modern Islam*, 220–52, Leiden. Brill. http://www.jstor.org/stable /1570745 (accessed 21 August 2022).

Chapter 6

Asad, Talal (2003). *Formations of the Secular: Christianity, Islam, Modernity*. Stanford: Stanford University Press.

Astor, Avi, Marian Burchardt and Mar Griera (2017). 'The Politics of Religious Heritage: Framing Claims to Religion as Culture in Spain'. *Journal for the Scientific Study of Religion*, 56 (1): 126–42.

Astor, Avi and Damon Mayrl (2020). 'Culturalized Religion: A Synthetic Review and Agenda for Research'. *Journal for the Scientific Study of Religion*, 59 (2): 209–26.

Badone, Ellen (2015). 'Religious Heritage and the Re-Enchantment of the World in Brittany'. *Material Religion*, 11 (1): 4–24.

Balkenhol, Markus and Ernst Van den Hemel (2019). 'Odd Bedfellows, New Alliances: The Politics of Religion, Cultural Heritage and Identity in the Netherlands'. *Trajecta*, 28 (1): 117–41.

Baumgartner, Christoph (2020). 'Kulturell-mehrheitsorientierte Identitätspolitik als Problem für Religionsfreiheit?' *Ethik und Gesellschaft*, 1: 1–34.

Beekers, Daan (2017). 'De waarde van verlaten kerken'. In Oskar Verkaaik (with Daan Beekers and Pooyan Tamimi Arab) (eds), *Gods huis in de steigers: religieuze gebouwen in ontwikkeling*, 161–92. Amsterdam: AUP.

Beekers, Daan (2021). *Young Muslims and Christians in a Secular Europe: Pursuing Religious Commitment in the Netherlands.* London [etc.]: Bloomsbury.

Beekers, Daan and Pooyan Tamimi Arab (2016). 'Dreams of an Iconic Mosque: Spatial and Temporal Entanglements of a Converted Church in Amsterdam'. *Material Religion*, 12 (2): 137–64.

Brubaker, Rogers (2017). 'Between Nationalism and Civilizationism: The European Populist Moment in Comparative Perspective'. *Ethnic and Racial Studies*, 40 (8): 1191–226.

Burchardt, Marian (2020). *Regulating Difference: Religious Diversity and Nationhood in the Secular West.* New Brunswick: Rutgers University Press.

Coleman, Simon (2019). 'On Praying in an Old Country: Ritual, Replication, Heritage, and Powers of Adjacency in English Cathedrals'. *Religion*, 49 (1): 120–41.

Cotter, Christopher R. (2020). *The Critical Study of Non-Religion: Discourse, Identification and Locality.* London and New York: Bloomsbury Academic.

De Koning, Martijn (2016). '"You Need to Present a Counter-Message": The Racialisation of Dutch Muslims and Anti-Islamophobia Initiatives'. *Journal of Muslims in Europe*, 5 (2): 170–89.

DeHanas, Daniel Nilsson and Marat Shterin (2018). 'Religion and the Rise of Populism'. *Religion, State and Society*, 46 (3): 177–85.

Duyvendak, Jan Willem (2011). *The Politics of Home: Belonging and Nostalgia in Europe and the United States.* Houndmills and New York: Palgrave Macmillan.

Duyvendak, Jan Willem, Peter Geschiere and Evelien Tonkens, eds (2016). *The Culturalization of Citizenship: Belonging and Polarization in a Globalizing World.* London: Palgrave Macmillan.

Garner, Steve and Saher Selod (2015). 'The Racialization of Muslims: Empirical Studies of Islamophobia'. *Critical Sociology*, 41 (1): 9–19.

Gauchet, Marcel (1997). *The Disenchantment of the World: A Political History of Religion.* Trans. Oscar Burge. Princeton: Princeton University Press.

Geschiere, Peter (2009). *The Perils of Belonging: Autochthony, Citizenship, and Exclusion in Africa and Europe.* Chicago: University Of Chicago Press.

Hashemi, Morteza (2017). *Theism and Atheism in a Post-Secular Age.* Cham: Palgrave Macmillan.

Hervieu-Léger, Danièle (2000). *Religion as a Chain of Memory.* Trans. Simon Lee. Oxford: Polity Press.

Hirschkind, Charles (2016). 'Granadan Reflections'. *Material Religion*, 12 (2): 209–32.

Isnart, Cyril and Nathalie Cerezales, eds (2020). *The Religious Heritage Complex: Legacy, Conservation, and Christianity.* London and New York: Bloomsbury Academic.

Joppke, Christian (2013). 'A Christian Identity for the Liberal State?' *The British Journal of Sociology*, 64 (4): 597–616.

Kennedy, James C. (1995). *Nieuw Babylon in aanbouw: Nederland in de jaren zestig.* Amsterdam: Boom.

Knibbe, Kim (2018). 'Secularist Understandings of Pentecostal Healing Practices in Amsterdam: Developing an Intersectional and Post-Secularist Sociology of Religion'. *Social Compass*, 65 (5): 650–66.

Knott, Kim, Volkhard Krech and Birgit Meyer (2016). 'Iconic Religion in Urban Space'. *Material Religion*, 12 (2): 123–36.

Kuyk, Elza (2017). 'Multiple Used Church Buildings and Religious Communities'. *Religious Matters in an Entangled World*. 6 September 2017. http://religiousmatters .hum.uu.nl/buildings-images-and-objects/article/multiple-used-church-buildings -and-religious-communities/.

Kuyk, Elza (2018). 'Living in an Exhibition in a Church'. *Religious Matters in an Entangled World*. Refresj | www.refresj.nl. 23 March 2018. http://religiousmatters .hum.uu.nl/buildings-images-and-objects/article/living-in-an-exhibition-in-a -church/.

Marzouki, Nadia and Duncan McDonnell (2016). 'Populism and Religion'. In Nadia Marzouki, Duncan McDonnell and Olivier Roy (eds), *Saving the People: How Populists Hijack Religion*, 1–11. London: Hurst.

Marzouki, Nadia, Duncan McDonnell and Olivier Roy, eds (2016). *Saving the People: How Populists Hijack Religion*. London: Hurst.

Meer, Nasar (2013). 'Racialization and Religion: Race, Culture and Difference in the Study of Antisemitism and Islamophobia'. *Ethnic and Racial Studies*, 36 (3): 385–98.

Mepschen, Paul (2018). 'A Post-Progressive Nation: Homophobia, Islam, and the New Social Question in the Netherlands'. In Achim Rohde, Christina von Braun, and Stefanie Schüler-Springorum (eds), *National Politics and Sexuality in Transregional Perspective: The Homophobic Argument*, 19–38. Abingdon and New York: Routledge.

Mepschen, Paul, Jan Willem Duyvendak and Evelien H. Tonkens (2010). 'Sexual Politics, Orientalism and Multicultural Citizenship in the Netherlands'. *Sociology*, 44 (5): 962–79.

Meyer, Birgit (2019). 'Recycling the Christian Past: The Heritagization of Christianity and National Identity in the Netherlands'. In Rosemarie Buikema, Antoine Buyse and Antonius C. G. M. Robben (eds), *Cultures, Citizenship and Human Rights*, 64–88. Abingdon and New York: Routledge.

Moffitt, Benjamin (2016). *The Global Rise of Populism: Performance, Political Style, and Representation*. Stanford: Stanford University Press.

Oliphant, Elayne (2012). 'The Crucifix as a Symbol of Secular Europe: The Surprising Semiotics of the European Court of Human Rights'. *Anthropology Today*, 28 (2): 10–12.

Oliphant, Elayne (2015). 'Beyond Blasphemy or Devotion: Art, the Secular, and Catholicism in Paris'. *Journal of the Royal Anthropological Institute*, 21 (2): 352–73.

Prins, Baukje (2007). 'Beyond Innocence. The Genre of New Realism and Its Contenders'. In Rosi Braidotti, Charles Esche and Maria Hlavajova (eds), *Citizens and Subjects: The Netherlands, for Example*, 253–64. Utrecht and Zürich: BAK & JRPIRingier.

Righart, Hans (2004). *De wereldwijde jaren zestig: Groot-Britannië, Nederland, de Verenigde Staten.* Hilversum: Uitgeverij Verloren.

Roy, Olivier (2016). 'Beyond Populism: The Conservative Right, the Courts, the Churches and the Concept of a Christian Europe'. In Nadia Marzouki, Duncan McDonnell and Olivier Roy (eds), *Saving the People: How Populists Hijack Religion*, 185–201. London: Hurst.

Schinkel, Willem (2008). 'The Moralization of Citizenship in Dutch Integration Discourse'. *Amsterdam Law Forum*, 1 (1): 15–26.

Strømmen, Hannah and Ulrich Schmiedel (2020). *The Claim to Christianity: Responding to the Far Right.* London: SCM Press.

Sunier, Thijl (2010). 'Islam in the Netherlands: A Nation despite Religious Communities?' In Erik Sengers and Thijl Sunier (eds), *Religious Newcomers and the Nation State: Political Culture and Organized Religion in France and the Netherlands*, 115–30. Delft: Eburon.

Taylor, Charles (2007). *A Secular Age.* Cambridge, MA and London: Harvard University Press.

Van den Hemel, Ernst (2014). '(Pro)Claiming Tradition: The "Judeo-Christian" Roots of Dutch Society and the Rise of Conservative Nationalism'. In Rosi Braidotti, Bolette Blaagaard, Tobijn de Graauw and Eva Midden (eds), *Transformations of Religion and the Public Sphere: Postsecular Publics*, 53–76. New York: Palgrave Macmillan.

Van den Hemel, Ernst (2017). 'The Dutch War on Easter: Secular Passion for Religious Culture & National Rituals'. *Yearbook of Ritual and Liturgical Studies*, 33: 1–19.

Van den Hemel, Ernst (2020). 'The Boomarang-Effect of Culturalized Religion: The Impact of the Populist Radical Right on Confessional Politics in the Netherlands'. In Markus Balkenhol, Ernst Van den Hemel and Irene Stengs (eds), *The Secular Sacred: Emotions of Belonging and the Perils of Nation and Religion*, 21–41. New York: Palgrave Macmillan.

Van der Linde, Irene (2013). 'We verkopen onze kerk niet aan moslims'. *De Groene Amsterdammer*, 137 (35). https://www.groene.nl/artikel/we-verkopen-onze-kerk-niet-aan-moslims.

Van der Veer, Peter (2006). 'Pim Fortuyn, Theo van Gogh, and the Politics of Tolerance in the Netherlands'. *Public Culture*, 18 (1): 111–24.

Van Kessel, Stijn (2016). 'Using Faith to Exclude: The Role of Religion in Dutch Populism'. In Nadia Marzouki, Duncan McDonnell and Olivier Roy (eds), *Saving the People: How Populists Hijack Religion*, 61–77. London: Hurst.

Van Rooden, Peter (2010). 'The Strange Death of Dutch Christendom'. In Callum G. Brown and Michael Snape (eds), *Secularisation in the Christian World*, 175–95. Farnham and Burlington, VT: Ashgate Publishing.

Verkaaik, Oskar (2010). 'The Cachet Dilemma: Ritual and Agency in New Dutch Nationalism'. *American Ethnologist*, 37 (1): 69–82.

Vossen, Koen (2011). 'Classifying Wilders: The Ideological Development of Geert Wilders and His Party for Freedom'. *Politics*, 31 (3): 179–89.

Wallet, Bart (2012). 'Zin en onzin van de "joods-christelijke traditie"'. *Christen Democratische Verkenningen*, 3: 100–8.

Wesselink, Herman E. (2018). 'Een sterke toren in het midden der stad: Verleden, heden en toekomst van bedreigde Nederlandse kerkgebouwen'. PhD Dissertation, Vrije Universiteit Amsterdam.

Zúquete, José Pedro (2018). *The Identitarians: The Movement against Globalism and Islam in Europe*. Notre Dame, IN: University of Notre Dame Press.

Chapter 7

Aeschbach, Mirjam (2021). 'Politisierung von Kultur, Religion, und Geschlecht: Die Kulturalisierungen eines verweigerten Handschlags in Deutschschweizer Medien'. *Zeitschrift für Religionswissenschaft*, 29 (1): 60–82.

Assmann, Aleida (1999). *Erinnerungsräume: Formen und Wandlungen des kulturellen Gedächtnisses*. München: C.H. Beck.

Baumgartner, Christoph (2019). '(Not) Shaking Hands with People of the Opposite Sex: Civility, National Identity, and Accommodation'. In Jonathan Seglow and Andrew Shorten (eds), *Religion and Political Theory: Secularism, Accommodation and the New Challenges of Religious Diversity*, 119–36. London: Rowman and Littlefield International.

Blaschke, Olaf (2000). 'Das Zweite Konfessionelle Zeitalter?' *Geschichte und Gesellschaft*, 26 (1): 38–75.

Bleisch, Petra (2016). 'Der "Fall Therwil": (Nicht-)Händeschütteln in der Schule als Frage berufsethischen Handelns'. *Zeitschrift für Religionskunde / Revue de didactique des sciences des religions*, 3: 102–7.

Bretscher, Fabienne (2017). 'Between Law and Politics: Muslim Religious Practices in Swiss Public Schools'. *Studia z Prawa Wyznaniowego*, 20: 35–52.

Bürgin, Martin (2019). 'Theologische Tribes and Territories: Die Revue Internationale de Théologie als Medium multipler Allianzbildungen'. *Internationale Kirchliche Zeitschrift*, 109: 309–39.

Bürgin, Martin (2021). 'Kulturkampfnarrative im Gesetzgebungsprozess: Gebrauchsgeschichtliche Topoi im Kommentar zur geplanten Änderung der basellandschaftlichen Verfassung im Nachgang zum Fall Therwil'. *Zeitschrift für Religionswissenschaft*, 29 (1): 106–27.

Clark, Christopher and Wolfram Kaiser, eds (2003). *Culture Wars: Secular-Catholic Conflict in Nineteenth-Century Europe*. Cambridge: University Press.

de Reynold, Frédéric Gonzague (1934). *L'Europe tragique*. Paris: Spes.

de Reynold, Frédéric Gonzague (1936). *Portugal*. Paris: Spes.

de Reynold, Frédéric Gonzague (1944). *La formation de l'Europe*. Vol. 1. Fribourg: Egloff.

Eichenberger, Linda (2020). 'Kommunist, Häretiker, Rebell: Mazdak und die Religionsgeschichtsschreibung'. *Zeitschrift für Religionswissenschaft*, 28 (2): 237–58.

Faber, Richard (2002). *Abendland: Ein politischer Kampfbegriff*. Berlin: Philo.

FDP (2017a). 'Bildungsanspruch durchsetzen! (Motion 2016–102)'. In Regierungsrat 2017a, 12–13.

FDP (2017b). 'Staatliches Recht vor Religiösen Vorschriften (Motion 2016–103)'. In Regierungsrat 2017a, 13–14.

Forlenza, Rosario and Bryan Turner (2019). '"Das Abendland": The Politics of Europe's Religious Borders'. *Critical Research on Religion*, 7 (1): 6–23.

Halbwachs, Maurice (1985). *Das Gedächtnis und seine sozialen Bedingungen*. Berlin: Suhrkamp.

Hersi, Laila (2018). *The Refusal to Shake Hands with the Opposite Sex for Religious Reasons: A Comparative Analysis*. Master thesis, University of Oslo.

Hetmanczyk, Philipp (2021). 'Religion als Grenzkategorie von "Diversität": Zur politischen Verhandlung einer Handschlagverweigerung'. *Zeitschrift für Religionswissenschaft*, 29 (1): 128–45.

Hettling, Manfred (2006). *Eine kleine Geschichte der Schweiz: Der Bundesstaat und seine Traditionen*. Frankfurt: Suhrkamp.

Holenstein, André (2014). *Mitten in Europa: Verflechtungen und Abgrenzung in der Schweizer Geschichte*. Baden: Hier und Jetzt.

Jensen, Sune Qvotrup (2011). 'Othering, Identity Formation and Agency'. *Qualitative Studies*, 2 (2): 63–78.

Kühler, Anne (2018a). 'Religionsfreiheit als Herausforderung: die "Handschlag-Affäre"'. In Julia Hänni, Sebastian Heselhaus and Adrian Loretan (eds), *Religionsfreiheit im säkularen Staat. Aktuelle Auslegungsfragen in der Schweiz, in Deutschland und weltweit*, 55–96. Zürich: Dike.

Kühler, Anne (2018b). 'Religionsfreiheit und die Handschlag-Verweigerung: Irritationen und Herausforderungen'. *Jusletter*, 26 February 2018.

Kühler, Anne (2021). 'Symbolische Verfassungsgebung in Aushandlungsprozessen von Religion: Die Verfassungsdynamiken einer Handschlagverweigerung'. *Zeitschrift für Religionswissenschaft*, 29 (1): 83–105.

Lévi-Strauss, Claude (2013). *Das wilde Denken*. Frankfurt: Suhrkamp.

Marchal, Guy (1992). 'Das "Schweizeralpenland": Eine imagologische Bastelei'. In Guy Marchal and Aram Mattioli (eds), *Erfundene Schweiz: Konstruktionen nationaler Identität - La Suisse imaginée: Bricolages d'une identité nationale*. Zürich: Chronos.

Marchal, Guy (2007). *Schweizer Gebrauchsgeschichte: Geschichtsbilder, Mythenbildung und nationale Identität*. Basel: Schwabe.

Mattioli, Aram (1994a). *Zwischen Demokratie und totalitärer Diktatur: Gonzague de Reynold und die Tradition der autoritären Rechten in der Schweiz*. Zürich: Orell Füssli.

Mattioli, Aram (1994b). 'Gonzague de Reynold und die Entzauberung der Welt'. In Urs Altermatt (ed.), *Schweizer Katholizismus zwischen den Weltkriegen 1920–1940*, 81–101. Freiburg: Universitätsverlag.

Mattioli, Aram (2007). 'Gonzague de Reynold (1880–1970)'. In Heinz Duchhardt, Małgorzata Morawiec, Wolfgang Schmale and Winfried Schulze (eds), *Europa-Historiker: Ein biographisches Handbuch*, vol. 2, 189–210. Göttingen: Vandenhoek Ruprecht.

Mesmer, Beatrix, ed. (2006). *Geschichte der Schweiz und der Schweizer*. Basel: Schwabe.

Metzger, Franziska (2019). 'Religion der Geschichte - Geschichte der Religion: Zur Selbstreflexion und Institutionalisierung der römisch-katholischen Geschichtsschreibung und zur Rolle von Zeitschriften in der Schweiz der zweiten Hälfte des 19. und der ersten Hälfte des 20. Jahrhunderts'. *Internationale Kirchliche Zeitschrift*, 109: 240–61.

Meyer, Birgit (2012). *Mediation and the Genesis of Presence: Towards a Material Approach to Religion*. Utrecht: Universiteit Utrecht Faculteit Geesteswetenschappen.

Meyer, Birgit (2020). 'Recycling the Christian Past: The Heritagization of Christianity and National Identity in the Netherlands'. In Rosemarie Buikema, Antoine Buyse and Antonius Robben (eds), *Cultures, Citizenship and Human Rights*, 64–88. London: Routledge.

Mohn, Jügen (2013). 'Mythische Narrationen und ‚Politische Religion'. In Gabriela Brahier and Dirk Johannsen (eds), *Konstruktionsgeschichten: Narrationsbezogene Ansätze in der Religionsforschung*, 55–82. Würzburg: Ergon.

Noll, Peter (1981). 'Symbolische Gesetzgebung'. *Zeitschrift für Schweizerisches Recht*, 1 (4): 347–64.

Pöpping, Dagmar (2002). *Abendland: Christliche Akademiker und die Utopie der Antimoderne 1900–1945*. Berlin: Metropol.

Regierungsrat des Kantons Basel-Landschaft (2017a). *Vorlage an den Landrat "Änderung der Kantonsverfassung betreffend Vorbehalt der bürgerlichen Pflichten und Änderung des Bildungsgesetzes betreffend Aufnahme einer Meldepflicht bei Integrationsproblemen" vom 27. Juni 2017, no. 2017–251 (LRV 2017/251)*. Liestal: Staatskanzlei.

Regierungsrat des Kantons Basel-Landschaft (2017b). *Vernehmlassungsversion der Vorlage an den Landrat (LRV 20XX/XXX)*. Liestal: Staatskanzlei.

Sedes, Sancta (1864). *Litterae apostolicae quanta cura et syllabus compectens praecipuos nostrae aetatis errores*. Rome: Libreria Editrice Vaticana.

Spivak, Gayatri Chakravorty (1985). 'The Rani of Sirmur: An Essay in Reading the Archives'. *History and Theory*, 24 (3): 247–72.

Stadler, Peter (1996). *Der Kulturkampf in der Schweiz: Eidgenossenschaft und Katholische Kirche im europäischen Umkreise 1848–1888*. Zürich: Chronos.

Stahel, Lea (2018). 'Refusing a Handshake Shakes the World: How Collapsing Contexts Complicate Legitimacy Construction in Networked Publics'. In *Proceedings of the 9th International Conference on Social Media and Society*, The Association for Computing Machinery, 385–9. New York: ACM.

Stahel, Lea (2021). 'Ein lokales Ereignis im globalen Fokus: Das Zusammenfallen geografischer, zeitlicher und sozialer Räume in der medialen Verbreitung einer Handschlagverweigerung'. *Zeitschrift für Religionswissenschaft*, 29 (1): 39–59.

von Stuckrad, Kocku (2006). 'Die Rede vom "Christlichen Abendland": Hintergründe und Einfluss einer Meistererzählung'. In Christian Augustin, Johannes Wienand and Christiane Winkler (eds), *Religiöser Pluralismus und Toleranz in Europa*, 235–47. Wiesbaden: VS Verlag für Sozialwissenschaften.

Walthert, Rafael, Katharina Frank, Daniela Stauffacher and Urs Weber (2021). 'Zum Verhältnis von Interaktion, Organisation und Gesellschaft in der Therwiler Handschlag-Affäre: Eine systemtheoretische Analyse'. *Zeitschrift für Religionswissenschaft*, 29 (1): 16–38.

Wolf, Hubert (1998). 'Der "Syllabus errorum" (1864) oder: Sind katholische Kirche und Moderne vereinbar?' In Manfred Weitlauff (ed.), *Kirche im 19. Jahrhundert*, 115–39. Regensburg: Pustet.

Chapter 8

Berger, Peter (2011). '[1963] Invitation to Sociology: A Humanistic Approach'. in J. K. Olick, V. Vinitzky-Seroussi and D. Levy (eds), *The Collective Memory Reader*, 216–21. Oxford and New York: Oxford University Press.

Brannigan, John (2008). '"Ireland, and Black!": Minstrelsy, Racism, and Black Cultural Production in 1970s Ireland'. *Textual Practice*, 22 (2): 229–48. doi: 10.1080/09502360802044943.

Brantlinger, Patrick (2004). 'The Famine'. *Victorian Literature and Culture*, 32 (1): 193–207. http://www.jstor.org/stable/25058660.

Breen, Claire (2008). 'The Policy of Direct Provision in Ireland: A Violation of Asylum Seekers' Right to an Adequate Standard of Housing'. *International Journal of Refugee Law*, 20 (4): 611–36. https://doi.org/10.1093/ijrl/een037.

Brubaker, Rogers (2017). *Why Populism?*, *Theory and Society*. doi: 10.1007/s11186-017-9301-7.

Card, Orson S. (1978). 'The Saints in Ireland'. *Ensign*. https://www.lds.org/ensign/1978/02/the-saints-in-ireland?lang=eng.

Carr, James (2011). 'Regulating Islamophobia: The Need for Collecting Disaggregated Data on Racism in Ireland'. *Journal of Muslim Minority Affairs*, 31 (4): 574–93. doi: 10.1080/13602004.2011.630863.

Carr, James (2016). *Islamophobia in Dublin: Experiences and How to Respond*. Dublin: Immigrant Council of Ireland

Central Statistics Office (2017). 'Details of Census'. Cork: Government of Ireland. http://www.cso.ie/px/pxeirestat/Database/eirestat/Profile 8 - Irish Travellers, Ethnicity and

Religion/Profile 8 - Irish Travellers, Ethnicity and Religion_statbank.asp?SP=Profile 8 - Irish Travellers, Ethnicity and Religion=0.

Clarke, Vivienne, Patrick Logue, Harry McGee and Fiach Kelly (2019). 'Varadkar Calls for Grealish Statement Over "African Sponger" Comments'. *The Irish Times*, September.

Cohen, Robin (1996). 'Diasporas and the Nation-State: From Victims to Challengers'. *International Affairs*, 72 (3): 507–20.

Cosgrove, Olivia, Laurence Cox, Carmen Kuhling and Peter Mulholland (2011). 'Understanding Ireland's New Religious Movements'. In Olivia Cosgrave, Laurence Cox, Carmen Kuhling and Peter Mulholland (eds), *Ireland's New Religious Movements*, 1–27. Newcastle upon Tyne: Cambridge Scholars Publishing.

Cosgrove, Olivia (2013). *The Experience of Religious Stigma and Discrimination Among Religious Minorities in Ireland: A Multi-Faith Approach*. PhD. University of Limerick. http://rian.ie/en/item/view/73067.html.

Crawford, Heather K. (2010). *Outside the Glow*. Dublin: UCD Press.

Davie, Grace (2000). *Religion in Europe: A Memory Mutates*. Oxford: Oxford University Press.

Fanning, Bryan (2012). *Racism and Social Change in the Republic of Ireland*. 2nd edn. Manchester: Manchester University Press.

Fanning, Bryan (2014a). 'A Catholic Vision of Ireland'. In T. Inglis (ed.), *Are The Irish Different?*, 44–54. Manchester: Manchester University Press.

Fanning, Bryan (2014b). 'The New Irish and the Irish Nation'. In T. Inglis (ed.), *Are The Irish Different?*, 155–66 Manchester: Manchester University Press.

Fanning, Bryan (2016). *Irish Adventures in Nation Building*. Manchester: Manchester University Press.

Fanning, Bryan, K. Howard and N. O'Boyle (2010). 'Immigrant Candidates and Politics in the Republic of Ireland: Racialization, Ethnic Nepotism, or Localism?'. *Nationalism and Ethnic Politics*, 16 (3–4): 420–42. doi: 10.1080/13537113.2010.527233.

Ferriter, Diarmaid (2004). *The Transformation of Ireland: 1900–2000*. London: Profile Books.

Gallaher, Conor and Sorcha Pollack (2019). 'How the Far-Right is Exploiting Immigration Concerns in Oughterard'. *The Irish Times*, September.

Ganiel, Gladys (2016). *Transforming Post-Catholic Ireland: Religious Practice in Late Modernity*. Oxford and New York: Oxford University Press. http://0-www.oxfordscholarship.com.lib.exeter.ac.uk/view/10.1093/acprof:oso/9780198745785.001.0001/acprof-9780198745785-miscMatter-1.

Garner, Steve (2007). 'Ireland and Immigration: Explaining the Absence of the Far Right'. *Patterns of Prejudice*, 41 (2): 109–30. doi: 10.1080/00313220701265486.

Garner, Steve (2009). 'Ireland: From Racism without "Race" to Racism without Racists'. *Radical History Review*, 2009 (104): 41–56. doi: 10.1215/01636545-2008-067.

Garner, Steve (2016). 'Making "Race" an Issue in the 2004 Irish Citizenship Referendum'. In Rosie Meade and Fiona Dukelow (eds), *Defining Events: Power, resistance and identity in twenty-first-century Ireland*, 70–88. Manchester: Manchester University Press. https://doi.org/10.7765/9781847799913.00012.

Goldberg, David T. (2002). *The Racial State*. Oxford: Blackwell.

Harris, Claudia W. (1990). 'Mormons on the Warfront: The Protestant Mormons and Catholic Mormons of Northern Ireland'. *BYU Studies Quarterly*, 30 (4): 7–19. http://scholarsarchive.byu.edu/byusq/vol30/iss4/2.

Ignatiev, Noel (1995). *How the Irish Became White*. London: Routledge.

Inglis, Tom (1998). *Moral Monopoly: The Rise and Fall of the Catholic Church in Modern Ireland*. Dublin: UCD Press.

Inglis, Tom (2007). 'Catholic Identity in Contemporary Ireland: Belief and Belonging to Tradition'. *Journal of Contemporary Religion*, 22 (2): 205–20. doi: 10.1080/13537900701331064.

Inglis, Tom (2014). *Are the Irish Different?* United Kingdom: Manchester University Press.

Joseph, Ebun (2018). 'Whiteness and Racism: Examining the Racial Order in Ireland'. *Irish Journal of Sociology*, 26 (1): 46–70. doi: 10.1177/0791603517737282.

Kearney, Richard (1997). *Postnationalist Ireland: Politics, Culture, Philospohy*. London and New York: Routledge.

Kenny, Mary (2000). *Goodbye to Catholic Ireland*. Dublin: New Island Books.

Kirby, Peadar, Luke Gibbons and Michael Cronin (2002). 'Conclusions and Transformations'. In Peadar Kirby, Luke Gibbons and Michael Cronin (eds), *Reinventing Ireland: Culture, Society, and the Global Economy*, 196–209. London: Pluto Press.

Kmec, Vladimir (2017). 'Transnational and Local: Multiple Functions of Religious Communities of EU Migrants in Dublin'. *Journal of the Irish Society for the Academic Study of Religions*, 5: 20–39. https://jisasr.org/current-issue-volume-5-2017.

Kuhling, Carmen and Kieran Keohane (2007). *Cosmopolitan Ireland: Globalisation and Quality of Life*. United Kingdom: Pluto Press.

Lentin, Ronit (2001). 'Responding to the Racialisation of Irishness: Disavowed Multiculturalism and its Discontents'. *Sociological Research Online*, 5 (4). http://www.socresonline.org.uk/5/4/lentin.html (accessed 29 April 2015).

Lentin, Ronit (2007). 'Ireland: Racial State and Crisis Racism'. *Ethnic and Racial Studies*, 30 (4): 610–27. doi: 10.1080/01419870701356023.

Lentin, Ronit (2012). 'Turbans, Hijabs and Other Differences: "Integration From Below" and Irish Interculturalism'. *European Journal of Cultural Studies*, 15 (2): 226–42. doi: 10.1177/1367549411432028.

Loyal, Steve (2003). 'Welcome to the Celtic Tiger: Racism, Immigration and the State'. In C. Coulter (ed.), *The End of Irish History? Reflections on the Celtic Tiger*, 112–36. Manchester: Manchester University Press.

Loyal, Steven and Stephen Quilley (2016). 'Categories of State Control: Asylum Seekers and the Direct Provision and Dispersal System in Ireland'. *Social Justice*, 43 (4): 69–97. https://www.jstor.org/stable/26380314.

Maguire, Mark and Fiona Murphy (2012). *Integration in Ireland: The Everyday Lives of African Migrants*. Manchester: Manchester University Press.

Maguire, Mark and Fiona Murphy (2015). 'Ontological (in)Security and African Pentecostalism in Ireland'. *Ethnos*, (August 2015): 1–23. doi: 10.1080/00141844.2014.1003315.

Maher, Eamon (2009). *Cultural Perspectives and Globalisation in Ireland*. Oxford: Oxford University Press.

Malesecic, Sinisa (2014). 'Irishness and Nationalisms'. *Irish Journal of Sociology*, 22 (1): 130–42.

McCarthy, Justin (2019). 'Fine Gael by-Election Candidate Apologises over Asylum Seeker Comments' [Online]. *RTE*. Available at: https://www.rte.ie/news/politics /2019/1117/1092465-by-election/ (accessed 12 August 2022).

McDermott, Stephen (2020). 'Far-Right Parties Barely Register after Polling Less Than 1% in Most Constituencies'. *The Journal*. https://www.thejournal.ie/far-right-parties -ireland-election-2020-5001966-Feb2020/.

McGee, Harry (2019). 'TD Criticised for Allegedly Saying African Asylum Seekers "Sponge Off System"'. *The Irish Times*.

McGinnity, Frances, et al. (2018). *Monitoring Report on Integration 2018*. http://emn.ie/ files/p_201811071011402018_MonitoringReportonIntegration.pdf.

Moane, Geraldine (2002). 'Colonialism and the Celtic Tiger'. In P. Kirby, L. Gibbons andM. Cronin (eds), *Reinventing Ireland: Cutlure, Society ,and the Global Economy*, 109–24. London: Pluto Press.

Moane, Geraldine (2014). 'Postcolonial Legacies and the Irish Psyche'. In T. Inglis (ed.), *Are The Irish Different?*, 121–33. Manchester: Manchester University Press.

Mokyr, Joel (1985). *Why Ireland Starved: A Quantitative and Analyitical History of the Irish Economy 1800–1850*. 2nd edn. London: George Allen and Unwin.

Mondon, Aurelien and Aaron Winter (2020). *Reactionary Democracy: How Racism and the Populist Far Right Became Mainstream*. London: Verso Books.

Morrison, Angeline D. (2004). 'Irish and White-ish: Mixed "Race" Identity and the Scopic Regime of Whiteness'. *Women's Studies International Forum*, 27 (4): 385–96. doi: 10.1016/j.wsif.2004.10.007.

Mudde, Cas and C. Rovira Kalwasser (2014). 'Populism and Political Leadership'. in R. A. Rhodes and Paul Hart (eds), *The Oxford Handbook of Political Leadership*. Oxford and New York: Oxford University Press.

Nuttall, Deirdre (2015). 'Keeping Their Heads Down: Shame and Pride in the Stories of Protestants in the Irish Republic'. *Journal of the Irish Society for the Academic Study of Religions*, 2 (1): 47–72. https://jkapalo.files.wordpress.com/2015/04/keeping-their -heads-down-shame-and-pride-in-the-stories-of-protestants-in-the-irish-republic -pdf1.pdf.

O'Brien, Hazel (2019). 'The Marginality of "Irish Mormonism": Confronting Irish Boundaries of Belonging'. *Journal of the British Association for the Study of Religions*, 21: 52–75. http://www.jbasr.com/ojs/index.php/jbasr/article/view /40/43.

O'Brien, John (2017). *States of Intoxication: The Place of Alcohol in Civilisation*. London and New York: Routledge.

Poole, Ross (2008). 'Memory, History and the Claims of the Past'. *Memory Studies*, 1 (2): 149–66. doi: 10.1177/1750698007088383.

Ritter, Christian S. and Vladimir Kmec (2017). 'Religious Practices and Networks of Belonging in an Immigrant Congregation: The German-Speaking Lutheran Congregation in Dublin'. *Journal of Contemporary Religion*, 32 (2): 269–81. doi: 10.1080/13537903.2017.1298907.

Röder, Antje (2017). 'Old and New Religious Minorities: Examining the Changing Religious Profile of the Republic of Ireland'. *Irish Journal of Sociology*, 25 (3): 324–33. doi: 10.1177/0791603516660562.

Ruane, Joseph and Jennifer Todd (2009). 'Protestant Minorities in European States and Nations'. *National Identities*, 11 (1): 1–8. doi: 10.1080/14608940802680953.

Scharbrodt, Oliver (2015). 'Being Irish, Being Muslim'. in Oliver Scharbrodt, et al. (eds), *Muslims in Ireland: Past and Present*, 216–29. Edinburgh: Edinburgh University Press. http://www.jstor.org/stable/10.3366/j.ctt14brwn5.13%0AJSTOR.

Smyth, Jim (1995). 'Manning the Ramparts: Ireland and the Agenda of the Roman Catholic Church'. *History of European Ideas*, 20 (4–6): 681–7. https://0-doi-org.lib .exeter.ac.uk/10.1016/0191-6599(95)95798-L.

Stivers, Richard (1991). *Hair of the Dog: Irish Drinking and its American Stereotype*. Pennsylvania: Penn State University Press.

Tanner, Marcus (2001). *Ireland's Holy Wars: The Struggle for a Nation's Soul, 1500–2000*. New Haven: Yale University Press.

The Church of Jesus Christ of Latter-day Saints (no date). *Facts and Statistics: Ireland, The Mormon Newsroom*. http://www.mormonnewsroom.org/facts-and-statistics/ country/ireland/ (accessed 12 November 2014).

Ugba, Abel (2008). 'A Part of and Apart From Society? Pentecostal Africans in the "New Ireland"'. *Translocations: Migration and Social Change*, 4 (1): 86–101. http://www .translocations.ie/docs/v04i01/Vol_4_Issue_1_Abel_Ugba.doc.

Ugba, Abel (2009). *Shades of Belonging: African Pentecostals in Twenty-First Century Ireland*. Trenton; Asmara, Eritrea: Africa World Press.

Walsh, Tony (2015). 'Learning from Minority: Exploring Irish Protestant Experience'. *Journal of the Irish Society for the Academic Study of Religions*, 2 (1): 73–93. https:// jkapalo.files.wordpress.com/2015/04/learning-from-minority-exploring-irish -protestant-experience-pdf.pdf.

Whyte, John Henry (1976). *Church and State in Modern Ireland 1923–1979*. 2nd edn. Dublin: Gill and Macmillan.

Wilde, Melissa and Lindsay Glassman (2016). 'How Complex Religion Can Improve Our Understanding of American Politics'. *Annual Review of Sociology*, 42 (1): 407–25. doi: 10.1146/annurev-soc-081715-074420.

Zerubavel, Eviatar (2011). '[1996] Social Memories: Steps Towards a Sociology of the Past'. In J. K. Olick, V. Vinitzky-Seroussi and D. Levy (eds), *The Collective Memory Reader*, 221–25. Oxford and New York: Oxford University Press.

Chapter 9

Ahvio, Juha (2016). *Avoimet rajat ja maahanmuutto. Euroopan ja Suomen itsemurha?*, 107–24. Helsinki: Kuva ja Sana.

Ahvio, Juha (2018). *Sananvapaus uhattuna Suomessa – Vihapuhe, ihmisoikeudet ja media*. Helsinki: Kuva ja Sana.

Althoff, Andrea (2018). 'Right-Wing Populism and Religion in Germany: Conservative Christians and the Alternative for Germany (AfD)'. *Zeitschrift für Religion, Gesellschaft und Politik*, 2: 335–63.

Askola, Heli (2014). 'Taking the Bait? Lessons from a Hate Speech Prosecution'. *Canadian Journal of Law and Society*, 30 (1): 51–71.

Borg, Sami, Elina Kestilä-Kekkonen and Jussi Westinen (2015). *Demokratiaindikaattorit*. Helsinki: Oikeusministeriö.

Bruce, Steve (2011). *Secularization: In Defence of an Unfashionable Theory*. Oxford: Oxford University Press.

Furseth, Inger, Lars Ahlin, Kimmo Ketola, Annette Leis-Peters and Randver Sigurvinsson Bjarni (2018). 'Changing Religious Landscapes in the Nordic Countries'. In Inger Furseth (ed.), *Religious Complexity in the Public Sphere Comparing Nordic Countries*, 31–80. Cham: Palgrave Macmillan.

Glied, Viktor and Norbert Pap (2016). 'The "Christian Fortress of Hungary" – The Anatomy of the Migration Crisis in Hungary'. *Yearbook of Polish European Studies*, 19: 133–49.

Halla-aho, Jussi (2007). 'Allah rantautuu, Simola antautuu'. www.halla-aho.com/scripta (19 April 2007).

Hjelm, Titus (2014). 'National Piety: Religious Equality, Freedom of Religion and National Identity in Finnish Political Discourse'. *Religion*, 44 (1): 28–45.

ISSP (2018). International Social Survey Programme.

Jamin, Jérôme (2014). 'Cultural Marxism and the Radical Right'. In Paul Jackson and Anton Shekhovtsov (eds), *The Post-War Anglo-American Far Right: A Special Relationship of Hate*, 84–103. New York: Palgrave Macmillan.

Keskinen, Suvi (2016). 'From Welfare Nationalism to Welfare Chauvinism. Economic Rhetoric, Welfare State and the Changing Policies of Asylum in Finland'. *Critical Social Policy*, 36 (3): 1–19.

Kivimäki, Ville and Tuomas Tepora (2012). 'Meaningless Death or Regenerating Sacrifice? Violence and Social Cohesion in Wartime Finland'. In Tiina Kinnunen and Ville Kivimäki (eds), *Finland in World War II: History, Memory, Interpretations*, 233–76. Leiden & Boston: Brill.

Konttori, Johanna (2020). 'Huivista burkiniin. Katsaus eduskunnan dokumentteihin 2000-luvulla'. *Teologinen Aikakausikirja*, 3: 266–73.

Lövheim, Mia, Jonas Lindberg, Pål Ketil Botvar, Henrik Reintoft Christensen, Kati Niemelä and Anders Bäckström (2018). 'Religion on the Political Agenda'. In Inger Furseth (ed.), *Religious Complexity in the Public Sphere: Comparing the Nordic Countries*. Cham: Palgrave Macmillan.

Martikainen, Tuomas (2008). 'Muslimit suomalaisessa yhteiskunnassa'. In Tuomas Martikainen, Tuula Sakaranaho ja Marko Juntunen (eds), *Islam Suomessa: Muslimit arjessa, mediassa ja yhteiskunnassa*, 62–84. Helsinki: SKS.

Martikainen, Tuomas (2013). 'Uskonnon hallinta ja turvallistaminen valtiollisena toimintana'. In Tuomas Martikainen and Marja Tiilikainen (eds), *Islam, hallinta ja turvallisuus*, 255–77. Turku: Eetos.

Mickelson, Rauli (2015). *Suomen puolueet — Vapauden ajasta maailmantuskaan.* Tampere: Vastapaino.

Morieson, Nicholas George (2019). *Religion and the Populist Radical Right in Western Europe.* Doctoral thesis. Institute of Religion, Politics, and Society Faculty of Education and Arts, Australian Catholic University

Mudde, Cas (2019). *Far Right Today.* Cambridge: Polity Press.

Mykkänen, Juri (2012). *Uskonto ja äänestäminen. Sami Borg (toim.), Muutosvaalit 2011.* Helsinki: Oikeusministeriö, 292–309.

Rensman, Lars (2011). '"Against Globalism": Counter-Cosmopolitan Discontent and Antisemitism in Mobilizations of European Extreme Right Parties'. In Lars Rensmann and Julius H. Schoeps (eds), *Politics and Resentment. Antisemitism and Counter-Cosmopolitanism in the European Union*, 117–46. Leiden: Brill.

Sakaranaho, Tuula (2013). 'Religious Education in Finland'. *Temenos*, 49 (2): 225–54.

Seppo, Juha (2003). *Uskonnonvapaus 2000-luvun Suomessa.* Helsinki: Edita.

Stewart, Timo R. (2015). *Ja sana tuli valtioksi. Suomalaisen kristillisen sionismin aatehistoria.* Helsinki: University of Helsinki.

Taira, Teemu (2019). 'Suvivirsi ja kristinuskon "kulttuuristuminen" katsomuksellisen monimuotoisuuden aikana'. *Uskonnontutkija*, 8 (1). Online only. https://doi.org/10 .24291/uskonnontutkija.v8i1.83000

Tervonen, Miika (2014). 'Historiankirjoitus ja myytti yhden kulttuurin Suomesta'. In Pirjo Markkola, Hanna Snellman and Ann-Catrin Östman (eds), *Kotiseutu ja kansakunta: miten suomalaista historiaa on rakennettu*, 137–62. Helsinki: SKS.

Westinen, Jussi (2015). *Cleavages in Contemporary Finland. A Study on Party-Voter Ties.* Turku: Åbo Akademi.

Chapter 10

Äystö, Tuomas (2017). 'Insulting the Sacred in a Multicultural Society: The Conviction of Jussi Halla-aho Under the Finnish Religious Insult Section'. *Culture and Religion*, 18 (3): 191–211.

Äystö, Tuomas (2020). 'Kristinuskoon viittaaminen eduskunnan täysistuntopuheenvuoroissa 1999–2019'. *Teologinen Aikakausikirja*, 3: 217–32.

Al Sayyad, Nezar and Manuel Castells, eds (2002). *Muslim Europe or Euroislam: Politics, Culture and Citizenship in the Age of Globalization*. Lanham, MD: Lexington Books.

Aspinall, Peter (2000). 'Should a Question on "Religion" be Asked on the 2001 British Census? A Public Policy Case in Favour'. *Social Policy & Administration*, 34 (5): 584–600.

Braudel, F. (1995). *A History of Civilisations*. New York: Penguin.

Bullock, Katherine (2002). *Rethinking Muslim Women and the Veil: Challenging Historical and Modern Stereotypes*. London: The International Institute of Islamic Thought.

Caldwell, Christopher (2010). *Reflections of a Revolution in Europe: Can Europe be the same with different people in it?* St. Ives: Penguin.

Carr, Matt (2006). 'You are Now Entering Eurabia'. *Race & Class*, 48: 1–22.

Cornell, Stephen E. and Douglas Hartman (1997). *Ethnicity and Race: Making Identities in a Changing World*. New York: Pine Forge Press.

Fallaci, O. (2003). *The Rage and the Pride*. New York: Rizzoli International Publications.

Ferguson, Niall (2004). 'The End of Europe?'. *American Enterprise Institute Bradley Lecture*, 1 March 2004.

Hansen, Randall (2006). 'The Danish Cartoon Controversy: A Defence of Liberal Freedom'. *International Migration*, 44 (5): 7–16.

Hawkins, Oliver (2009). *Disproving the Muslim Demographics Sums*. http://www.bbc.co .uk/programmes/b00xw21x (accessed 25 January 2011).

Hodgson, Marshall (1974). *The Venture of Islam: Conscience and History in a World Civilisation*, Vol. 3. Chicago: University of Chicago Press.

Holm, E. (1999). 'Forward'. In Gema M. Munoz (ed.), *Islam, Modernism, and the West*. London: I. B. Taurus.

Hussein, Dilwar (2005). 'Can Islam make us British'. in Madeleine Bunting (ed.), *Islam, Race and Being British*. London: The Guardian Books.

Joppke, Christian (2009a). *Veil: Mirror of Identity*. Cornwall: Polity.

Joppke, Christian (2009b). 'Limits of Integration Policy: Britain and her Muslims'. *Journal of Ethnic and Migration Studies*, 35 (3): 453–72.

Jones, Thomas (2005). *Short Cuts: How to Concoct a Conspiracy Theory*, London Review of Books, July 2005.

Karamustafa, Ahmet (2004). *Progressive Muslims on Justice, Gender and Pluralism*. Ed. Omid Safi. Oxford: Oneworld.

Kelly, P. (1999). 'Integration and Identity in Muslim Schools: Britain. United States and Montreal'. *Islam and Christian–Muslim Relations*, 10: 197–21.

Kuper, Simon (2007). 'The Crescent and the Cross'. *Financial Times*, 11 October, 2007.

Laurence, Jonathan and Justin Vaïsse (2006). *Integrating Islam Political and Religious Challenges in Contemporary France*. Washington, DC: Brookings Institution Press.

Meer, Nasar (2009). 'Identity Articulations, Mobilisation and Autonomy in the Movement for Muslim Schools in Britain'. *Race, Ethnicity and Education*, 12 (3): 379–98.

Meer, Nasar (2015). *Citizenship, Identity, and the Politics of Multiculturalism: The Rise of Muslim Consciousness*. 2nd edn. New York: Palgrave.

Modood, Tariq (1997). '"Difference": Cultural Racism and Anti-Racism'. In P. Werbner and T. Modood (eds), *Debating Cultural Hybridity: Multi-Cultural Identities and the Politics of Anti-Racism*. London: Zed Books.

O'Leary, Brendan (2006). 'Liberalism, Multiculturalism, Danish Cartoons: Islamist Fraud and the Right of the Ungodly'. *International Migration*, 44 (5): 427–47.

Ramadan, Tariq (1999). *To Be A European Muslim*. Leicester: Islamic Foundation.

Ramadan, Tariq (2004). *Western Muslims and the Future of Islam*. New York: Oxford University Press.

Roy, Oliver (2004). *Globalised Islam*. London: Hurst & Company.

Safi, Omid (2004). 'Introduction: "The Times They Are A-Changing"'. In Omid Safi (ed.), *Progressive Muslims on Justice, Gender and Pluralism*, 1–32. Oxford: Oneworld.

Soper, J. C. and J. S. Fetzer (2010). 'The Not So Naked Public Sphere: Islam and the State in Western Europe'. *German Journal for Politics, Economics and Culture of the Middle East*, 11 (2): 6–14.

Statham, P., R. Koopmans, M. Giugni and F. Passy (2005). 'Resilient or Adaptable Islam?'. *Ethnicities*, 5 (4): 427–59.

Steyn, Mark (2006a). 'European Population Will be "40 Percent Muslim" by 2025'. *Wall Street Journal*, 4 January 2006.

Steyn, Mark (2006b). *America Alone: The End of the World as We Know It*. New York: Regerny Publishing.

Tibi, Bassam (1998). *Europa ohne Identität, Die Krise der multikulturellen Gesellschaft*. Berlin: Verlag.

Tibi, Bassam (2008). *Political Islam, World Politics and Europe: Democratic Peace and Euro-Islam versus Global Jihad*. Chippenham: Routledge.

Ye'or, Bat (2001). *Islam and Dhimmitude: Where Civilizations Collide*. Madison: Fairleigh Dickinson University Press.

Ye'or, Bat (2005). *Eurabia: The Euro-Arab Axis*. Fairleigh: Dickinson University Press.

Young, I. M. (1990). *Justice and the Politics of Difference*. Princeton: Princeton University Press.

Younge, Gary (2005). 'We Can Choose Our Identity, But Sometimes It Also Chooses Us'. In M. Bunting (ed.), *Islam, Race & Being British*. London: The Guardian Books.

Chapter 11

Ala, Aftab, Chantal Edge, Alimuddin Zumlac and Shuja Shafi (2021). 'Specific COVID-19 Messaging Targeting Ethnic Minority Communities'. *EclinicalMedicine*, 35 (100862): 1–2. https://doi.org/10.1016/j.eclinm.2021.100862

Astor, Avi and D. Damon Mayrl (2020). 'Culturalized Religion: A Synthetic Review and Agenda for Research'. *Journal for the Scientific Study of Religion*, 59 (2): 209–26. https://doi.org/10.1111/jssr.12661

Davie, Grace (2000). *Religion in Modern Europe: A Memory Mutates*. Oxford: Oxford University Press.

Davie, Grace (2007). 'Vicarious Religion: A Methodological Challenge'. In Nancy Ammerman (ed.), *Everyday Religion: Observing Modern Religious Lives*, 21–36. New York: Oxford University Press.

Davie, Grace and Lucian Leustean, eds (2021). *The Oxford Handbook of Religion and Europe*. Oxford: Oxford University Press.

Hennig, Anja. and Mirjam Weiberg-Salzmann (2021). *Illiberal Politics and Religion in Europe and Beyond: Concepts, Actors and Identity Narratives*. Frankfurt and New York: Campus Verlag.

Seligman, Adam and David W. Montgomery (2020). 'The Tragedy of Human Rights: Liberalism and the Loss of Belonging'. *Society*, 56 (2): 203–9.

Index